Kenyon College In 1925

KENYON COLLEGE
Its Third Half Century

by

THOMAS BOARDMAN GREENSLADE

KENYON COLLEGE
Gambier, Ohio

Cover Photography by Yale Greenfield (K1968).

For my wife,

MARY

IN MEMORIAM

Thomas Boardman Greenslade
1910-1990

A 1931 cum laude graduate of Kenyon College, Thomas Boardman Greenslade went on to a graduate degree at Columbia
University and a distinguished career as a science educator in
the New York City Public Schools before returning to Gambier
in 1967. For the next twenty-three years, until his death on
September 25, 1990, he served with distinction as Kenyon's
archivist and historian. His many services to the College
community, including the publication of this history, were
recognized in 1976 with an honorary doctor of letters degree,
awarded for "giving unstintingly to Kenyon of your time,
energy, and wisdom." In 1989, the College's alumni presented
Greenslade with the Gregg Cup, Kenyon's highest alumni
honor, citing him as an "indispensable resource for those who
seek to learn more about people and events that have shaped
the College's history." The archives and other special collections in Kenyon's libraries now bear the name "The Thomas
Boardman Greenslade Special Collections" as a remembrance
and as a signal to future generations of his crucial role in
collecting, preserving, and publicizing the materials that tell
the College's unique story.

PREFACE

It will become apparent that this is not the work of a trained historiographer, but it is my hope that it will also become apparent that it has been written by one who has a love for and devotion to Kenyon College.

In April 1973 Kenyon President William G. Caples asked me if I would "write a book to update Smythe." I approached the task with humility, since I had known Dr. George F. Smythe during my student days at Kenyon, had admired him as a man, and over the years have enjoyed his history, *Kenyon College — Its First Century*. Dr. Smythe's task was quite different from mine. He dealt with a period which was sparsely documented, and was forced to carry on his narrative with surmises which he was not always able to authenticate. In the preparation of this book I faced mountains of material to be digested and summarized. The result is perhaps too factual an account, but it is my hope that the facts are accurately set forth. I have tried to let the characters speak for themselves whenever possible, and I have left to the reader the opportunity to catch the essence of that which is Kenyon College.

Except for a few minor items, all of the materials used in the preparation of this book are in the Kenyoniana Room, the Kenyon College Archives, located in Chalmers Memorial Library. I have chosen not to burden the pages of this book with cumbersome footnotes, but have, in most cases, included the references directly in the text. As did Dr. Smythe, I intend to make additional notes and references on the margins of several copies of this book, and leave them in Chalmers Library, where those who need more information may examine them.

I am indebted to many Kenyon-connected people who have assisted me in the preparation of this book. Dr. Caples initiated and gave his valuable backing to the project. Other members of the administration who have given generously of their time in providing information include Bruce Haywood, Samuel S. Lord, Lewis F. Treleaven, Thomas J. Edwards, William H. Thomas, Jr., D. Gertrude Fesler, Louis Szalontai, Donald J. Omahan, and Douglas L. Givens. Valuable suggestions have come from members of the faculty, among them Stuart R. McGowan, Paul M. Titus, H. Landon Warner, James E. Michael, Paul Schwartz, Joseph F. Slate, Ronald E. McLaren, and Perry C. Lentz. William R. Chadeayne provided me with background material from his undergraduate days. The members of the Athletic Department and their secretary, Kathleen King (Mrs. Garth E.) Keller, opened their files for reference material. William Long and Samuel Barone of the Department of Public Relations assisted me with suggestions for getting the book into print. Help and encouragement came from my colleagues at Chalmers Library, especially William T. Dameron, Librarian, and Col. Owen T. McCloskey, Reference Librarian. Student assistants in the Archives who helped in this work were Kim Stapleton, Susan C. Lucke, and especially James G. Carson, who did some of the research. Gambier residents who gave me information on village history included Louise G. Adams, historiographer of Gambier and Harcourt Parish, and Harold Parker, a long-time faithful employee of the College. My son, Thomas B. Greenslade, Jr., was of great assistance during the entire preparation of the book in reading the manuscript and helping to select the pictures. Finally, I wish to express my heart-felt thanks to my wife, Mary MacWilliam Greenslade, for her help and encouragement throughout the writing of this book.

Thomas Boardman Greenslade

Gambier, Ohio
September 1, 1974

CONTENTS

Preface

Chapter

Presidents for Kenyon's Third Half Century

William Foster Peirce
1896 - 1937

Gordon Keith Chalmers
1937 - 1956

Franze Edward Lund
1957 - 1968

William Goff Caples
1968 -

CHAPTER I

Smythe's Kenyon College

In the closing pages of *Kenyon College — Its First Century*, George Franklin Smythe wrote:

> The fact that (Kenyon) offers only a simple college course, with no adjuncts of musical, or commercial, or advanced scientific training, will not bring her into favor with the multitude in these days. Her character as a college of the Protestant Episcopal Church gives her no added attraction to those whose denominational views differ from hers. But she accepts these limitations and believes in them; and to discard them would be to break with her entire history. In a time when nearly every college in the Middle West is coeducational, Kenyon remains a college for men only, and will not change. Again, Kenyon is wedded to the dormitory system. Only under stress of the recent very rapid growth in numbers did she, as a temporary measure, permit students to room in the village; and that necessity passes away with the building of Leonard Hall.

Smythe's predictions were based soundly on facts which he had painstakingly and lovingly gathered over a long period of time in the preparation of his book, and perhaps his projections into the future were somewhat clouded by a nostalgic hope that the College would remain just as it had been during the years he had labored in Gambier as priest, teacher, and historiographer. In an almost exponential manner, change has exploded at Kenyon since he made these statements; the severance of all connection between the Protestant Episcopal Church and the College, the acceptance of and by Kenyon of students of all religious and ethnic groups, the presence of women students on the campus, and apartment living arrangements all negate Smythe's forecast of the future, and are but a few of the tremendous changes which have taken place.

1

Philander Chase

The beginnings of Kenyon College are told accurately, succinctly, and delightfully in the words of Smythe's song, "Philander Chase":

> The first of Kenyon's goodly race
> Was that great man, Philander Chase;
> He climbed the Hill and said a prayer,
> And founded Kenyon College there.
>
> He dug up stones, he chopped down trees,
> He sailed across the stormy seas,
> And begged at every noble's door,
> And also that of Hannah More.
>
> The king, the queen, the lords, the earls,
> They gave their crowns, they gave their pearls,
> Until Philander had enough,
> And hurried homeward with the stuff.
>
> He built the College, built the dam,
> He milked the cow, he smoked the ham,
> He taught the classes, rang the bell,
> And spanked the naughty freshmen well.
>
> And thus he worked with all his might,
> For Kenyon College day and night;
> And Kenyon's heart still holds a place
> Of love for old Philander Chase.

Chase, a native of New Hampshire, a graduate of Dartmouth, and an Episcopal clergyman, migrated to Ohio in 1817, settling in Worthington. A year later he was elected the first Bishop of the newly organized Protestant Episcopal Diocese of Ohio. It was to meet the sore need of ministers for the Episcopal Church of Ohio that Kenyon College came into being. Chase's successful efforts in raising money for his educational venture during a trip to England in 1823 and 1824 made possible the official incorporation of the College on December 29, 1824, the purchase of land in Gambier, and the moving of the College from Worthington in 1828. Local names memorialized many of the British donors: Lord Kenyon, Lord Gambier, Lord Bexley, Lady Rosse, Bishop Ward, Sir Thomas Acland, George Gaskin, George Marriott, and Timothy Wiggin. The school was first quartered in crude, temporary buildings just north of the present Chapel. By the fall of 1829 Old Kenyon was sufficiently completed to allow partial occupancy.

Bishop Chase was a strong-willed autocrat who labored mightily and demanded absolute authority over all aspects of college life. Inevitably a head-on collision came up between him and the combined forces of the faculty and trustees which resulted in his resignation on September 8, 1831, less than seven years after the founding of the College. In 1835, he was elected the first Bishop of the Diocese of Illinois, where he repeated his early missionary labors in Ohio, founding a college, Jubilee College (now defunct), and visiting England to solicit funds.

Nineteenth Century Kenyon

His successor, Charles Petitt McIlvaine, was elected Bishop of Ohio and, as such, President of Kenyon College, within two hours after the acceptance of Bishop Chase's resignation. Under his regime Bexley Hall, the theological seminary, was established as a separate part of the College, and a new constitution was drawn up under which David Bates Douglass became president. Douglass, an engineer, army officer, and former teacher at West Point, designed the College Park south of the gates as we know it today, laid out the Middle Path, and constructed the stone gate pillars at the entrance to the Park.

Although during the 1830's and 40's Kenyon educated some of the nation's leading men: David Davis, Stanley Matthews, Edwin Stanton, and Rutherford B. Hayes, financial insolvency made the continuation of the College a year-to-year crisis, which usually had to be solved by selling college land.

During the 1850's Kenyon achieved a period of relative affluence and growth under the leadership of the highly popular and respected President Lorin Andrews. This era brought to Kenyon such teachers as Hamilton Smith who invented the tin-type photograph while a professor at Kenyon, and Francis Wharton who would later become legal adviser to the Department of State.

The years during and following the Civil War were disastrous for the College. The theological strifes during the regime of President James Kent Stone in 1868 alienated many of the

Bexley alumni who were foremost in sponsoring students for admission to the College, and the effect of the War on Fundraising activities brought the affairs of the College to a new low. In 1873 and again in 1875 there were no Bexley students at all, and by 1890 enrollment at the College had declined to 33, not all of whom were in attendance at any one time.

Bishop Chase and President Peirce. Drawing by John Carr Duff for the Centennial *Reveille* of 1924.

William Foster Peirce

The election of William Foster Peirce as President of Kenyon College in 1896 went a long way toward solving the problems. He may be credited with saving the College financially and putting it on the map scholastically. When he retired in 1937 after 41 years, he was the only president remembered by most of the alumni. "Fat," as he was nicknamed early in his career because of his slim build, was an excellent fund raiser. In this he was assisted greatly by the Bishops and clergy of the Dioceses of Ohio and Southern Ohio. An ordained Episcopal minister, he made it a custom to preach in many of the large churches all over the country, and in this way brought Kenyon to the attention of many who became supporters. Enrollment dipped sharply during World War I, but recovered soon after and rose to 250-275, a figure which was thought to be a desirable limit for that time.

In submitting his Twenty-fifth Annual Report in 1921, President Peirce was able to state that the value of the college buildings and equipment had doubled during his administration, and that endowment funds had grown from $265,000 to $1,340,000. The college balance sheet had shown a slender but constant surplus for several years.

The Centennial Celebration

It was against this promising background that the stage was now set for the great Centennial Celebration of 1924. Set in motion by the report of a committee headed by Dr. Smythe, Dr. Reeves, and Professor Watson, the formal announcement of the plans was made in the President's Report for 1923-24:

> The work of the special committee is before the Board in the announced program and the existing arrangements for the celebration June 14-17. Because of certain guaranties as to attendance it is impossible to determine the exact cost in advance but if conditions are favorable the expense will be kept well within the appropriation of $15,000.00 made last year. Two of the best and finest features of the programme have been provided by outside subscription, namely, the Centennial Pageant staged under the direction of Joseph Lindon Smith, and the music furnished by fifty members of the Cleveland Symphony Orchestra under the direction of Walter Logan. A fund of about $9,000.00 has been raised for these purposes by the Finance Committee of which Charles B. Raymond is the Chairman. The Pageant and the Orchestra will put the Kenyon Centennial celebration on a higher plane and will add much to its dignity and excellence.

Meticulously planned and forcefully executed, the Celebration was the most elaborate affair ever given in Gambier. Drawn from the trustees, faculty, alumni, and students, committees covering every phase of the production were assembled: Executive, Programme, Finance, Housing, Registration, Commissary, Exhibits, Pageant, Alumni Rally, Music, Transportation, Parking, College Tea, Decoration, and Publications.

In order to attract alumni from the East to the Celebration, special railroad Pullman cars were provided, with three cars starting from New York at 6 p.m. on June 13th. A car from Philadelphia and one from Washington were added on at Harrisburg, and the five cars proceeded from Orville, Ohio to Gambier as a special train. A typical fare was $22.14 one-way from New York, plus $6.38 for a Pullman lower berth.

Kenyon Students waiting at the railroad station to greet Lord Kenyon and his party.

Directed by Joseph Lindon Smith, who had achieved considerable success with similar projects at Amherst and St. Louis, the Centennial Pageant was a most ambitious undertaking and turned out to be the highlight of the Celebration. There were performances on Saturday evening and Tuesday evening on a stage set up in the natural amphitheater east of Ascension Hall. Professor Reeves described Smith's painting of the backgrounds in the *Bulletin*:

> No commercial scene-painter could have so transformed plaster-board into the oaks and sandstones of the Hill. Students who watched "Joe" Smith spatter his paint into mosses and lichens and vines had revealed to them the seeing eye and the eloquent hand of the born artist.

In the elaborate pageant style of the day, the production traced Kenyon's hundred year history in a series of nine episodes: "The Coming of the White Man;" "Inspiration;" "The Benefactors;" "On Gambier Hill;" "The Corner Stone;" "The

6

Second Builder;" "The Leaders;" "The Tablets of Honor;" and "The Torch Bearers." This last episode is described in the synopsis as follows:

> President, Faculty, Trustees, Presidents of the classes, and of the Kenyon College Assembly now come upon the stage, and standing before Alma Mater and the hallowed names of those who served during the hundred years, will sing "The Thrill" and bring the Pageant to a close.

The cast of more than thirty principal characters plus scores of bit players was headed by The Rev. E. G. Mapes as Bishop Chase, F. A. Wade (K1925) as Lord Kenyon, and M. O. Terry II (K1924) as Admiral Lord Gambier.

Sunday's program started with the Ordination Service, and the Centennial Sermon was given by The Right Reverend Thomas F. Gailor, Bishop of Tennessee and President of the National Council of the Episcopal Church. In the afternoon there was a Symphony Concert in Rosse Hall, and in the evening President Peirce preached the Baccalaureate Sermon. At the Baccalaureate Service Mrs. Warren G. Harding, widow of the President of the United States, accepted a diploma for the degree of Doctor of Laws for the late President. Just before his death President Harding had agreed to be honored at the Centennial.

The Centennial Pageant. F.A. Wade as Lord Kenyon, M.O. Terry as Admiral Lord Gambier.

7

Almost dwarfed by the other events of the Centennial was the Ninety-sixth Commencement, which took place on Monday in Rosse Hall. Thirty-one men were graduated from Kenyon, nine from Bexley, and seven received the degree of Master of Arts. The first honor man, Alexander M. Duff, Jr., was the speaker for the class. Other events of the day were the President's Reception and another Orchestra Recital.

At the Centennial exercises on Tuesday morning in Rosse Hall the audience crowded the building to its utmost capacity. This was the day for honoring Lord Kenyon, who had come for the Celebration accompanied by his cousins, Col. and Mrs. W. S. Kenyon-Slaney. At the conclusion of his speech, Lord Kenyon presented the College with a book containing about 60 letters from Bishop Chase which had been preserved by his family. This volume is now one of the prize exhibits in the Kenyon College Archives. Lord Kenyon must have been an engaging person, because the Kenyon *Collegian* in its next issue gave this impression:

> Tallest man in the College Park, smoking cigars of a length proportional to his height but wearing a Panama hat that would have been more becoming to a man of much shorter stature.
> The habit of speaking with arms akimbo, revealing a nickle plated chain upon which hung a six-inch jack-knife.
> Fraternizing with undergraduates and with men who count their fortunes in millions. Accommodating, affable — and completely dispelling the illusion that our British cousins are without a sense of humor.
> That is the impression of the Rt. Hon. Lord Lloyd Tyrrel-Kenyon at the Kenyon College Centennial. He is the pro-chancellor of the University of Wales, the grandson of the Lord Kenyon whose friendship for Bishop Philander Chase, founder of Kenyon College in 1824, caused the Bishop to name his frontier Ohio institution Kenyon.

The second performance of the Pageant, with its climactic finale, brought the Centennial Celebration to its close on Tuesday night. Interspersed among the main events were the dedication of Leonard Hall, the President's Reception, meetings of the trustees and alumni, a baseball game, an alumni parade, the illumination of Old Kenyon, historical tours of the college grounds, fraternity and non-fraternity banquets, an illustrated historical lecture, a college tea, the initiation and supper of Phi Beta Kappa, and the Junior Reception to the graduating class.

It is reported that although the previous week had been chilly and rainy, the four days of the Centennial were blessed with some of the most ideal June weather Gambier has ever known.

Some of the official guests at the Centennial Celebration. Front row, from left: President Peirce; Bishop Leonard; Lord Kenyon; William P. Elliott (K1870), grand marshal of the Alumni Parade; James N. Gamble (K1854), oldest living alumnus; Samuel Mather; Colonel Kenyon-Slaney; and Bishop Gailor.

In order to obtain the widest possible publicity for the celebration, President Peirce felt justified in hiring Donald C. Dougherty of Cleveland, a publicity and organization counsellor, to handle the public relations work at a fee of about $3500. This was probably the first full-scale professional attempt on the part of Kenyon to gain the national spotlight.

Kenyon and Gambier in 1924

In 1924 the geographical outline of the College remained pretty much the same as it was when President Douglass laid out the Middle Path and set up the College Gates in 1842. Except for Bexley Hall, the old Commons building, and faculty homes, there were no college buildings north of the gates. Old Kenyon was flanked by the two other dormitories, Hanna Hall on the west, and the just-completed Leonard Hall on the east. North of Hanna a location had been reserved for a science building, but Samuel Mather Hall was still a year or two in the future. North of Rosse Hall stood three houses used as dwellings by members of the faculty. The first was moved from this spot when Chalmers Library was built in 1962 and is at present the Music Building. Park Cottage, the middle building, was demolished in the middle 1930's, and Cromwell Cottage, then and now the home of the President, stands on the same location as it did in 1924. Turning to the east side of the Middle Path, Ascension Hall was in dire need of repairs and about to be completely reconstructed internally. Separating Ascension and the Alumni Library (now renamed Ransom Hall) was the pleasant expanse of lawn where the freshmen of the Twenties were lined up once a week and made to atone for their sins. The present Stephens Hall was then called Stephens Stack Room and functioned as an annex to the Library. The Church of the Holy Spirit, the Chapel, completed the roster of college buildings.

During this period almost all of the members of the faculty were housed in college-owned and college-maintained residences, some in the College Park, and others scattered all over the Village of Gambier. The use of a house was considered part of the faculty member's salary. In the Report of the President, 1924-25, there is the statement:

> For many years the (yearly) charge for the rental of college houses has been carried on the books at the absurdly low figure of $200.00. As houses are assigned to faculty members in order of seniority this simply means that the older professors get a larger compensation but even the poorest of our houses are worth $300.00 a year. I have mentioned this matter to the Chairman of the Finance Committee who approved of this change and I therefore recommend that in the future the rental value of college houses be carried on our books at the figure of $300.00.

Even though the student population has increased over sixfold since 1924 while the Village has remained about the same size in area, Gambier still manages to retain the uncrowded appearance it had 50 years ago. Part of this is because in 1924 virtually all the faculty and other college employees resided within the village limits or in the immediate vicinity, whereas today many of them come from considerable distance. Some of the building of the past half century has been done on the sites of buildings which have been demolished, but most of the new construction has been on vacant lots, or in allotments opened up on college land for faculty housing.

With the coming of the automobile, the shopping habits of the Gambier residents changed radically, so that by 1924 the dozens of small local businesses and shops of the 19th century had dwindled considerably, and shopping was done principally in Mount Vernon, where the selection was greater and the prospect of a trip exciting.

The one-block-long Gambier "business district" between Wiggin and Brooklyn Streets has undergone considerable change since 1924, but many landmark buildings are still standing, although changed greatly in usage. The structure on the northeast corner of Gaskin and Wiggin Streets was the Post Office then. The house just north of it (now the Student Affairs Center) was owned and occupied by William A. Adams and his family. Then going north on Gaskin came Doolittle's General Store, Heagreen's Meat Market, and Miss Mary Doolittle's residence (now owned and occupied by James Hayes). Just north of the alley, on the site where Farr Hall now stands, were Vernon's Restaurant, the "Gothic style" Vernon home, Jacobs Shoe Store and Repair Shop, a barber shop, a tailor shop, and Benedict's General Store. On the northwest corner of Chase Avenue and Wiggin Street, directly opposite the old Post Office, stood Scott's General Store. North along Chase Avenue, the next two houses which are now joined and occupied by the College Development Center, were at that time faculty houses. Just before the alley still stands the large building which was the College Commons. Where the present Post Office is now situated there was a double dwelling and Stoyle's Bakery, which was a restaurant and poolroom. The southwest corner of Chase Avenue and Brooklyn Street was and still is the site of the Peoples Bank.

Nothing reveals the tremendous shift in direction and emphasis which has taken place in American colleges over the past fifty years more than a comparison of the number of students and employees of Kenyon College in 1923-24 and 1973-74:

	1923-24	1973-74
Students	250	1392
Administration	2	34
Faculty	21	98
Athletics	1	8
Health	0	6
Guidance	0	3
Security	1	7
Maintenance	15	90
Secretarial and Clerical	1	53

The tabulation reflects the myriad services which are provided today's students: health services; counseling, including psychological help; vastly increased library services; off campus studies; graduate school activities, including assistance in obtaining scholarship grants; job placement arrangements; the great number of extra curricular cultural activities which have made necessary complex scheduling arrangements; equitable housing arrangements; and a host of other services including even the parking and traffic control regulations brought on by the proliferation of the automobile.

The competition for educational funds has made necessary the establishment of developmental and public relations programs to bring the attention of foundations and individuals to Kenyon.

Probably the most significant observation indicated by these data is that the faculty members are now able to play more truly professional roles as teachers, scholars, and researchers.

CHAPTER II

The Stable Twenties

This was the time of the flapper, the *College Humor* cartoons of John Held, Jr., Fitzgerald's novels of decadent youth, and bootleg booze. It was a time when college students felt called upon to moon over their fate as The Lost Generation. Although the flippancy and disenchantment of the 1920's was mirrored at Kenyon as well as at other American colleges, this must be regarded as the most stable period of Kenyon's history. That this was the heyday of President William Foster Peirce is certainly one of the compelling factors in this stability. With his wit, scholarship, administrative ability, speaking talents, and personal charm tempered and sharpened by twenty-five years of presidential labor and frustrations with fires, financial worries, personnel problems, and two major wars, Dr. Peirce was during this period finally able to accomplish his dreams of the past quarter century.

When he became President of Kenyon in 1896 at the age of twenty-eight, Peirce was probably the youngest college president in the United States. The son of L.M. Peirce of Springfield, Mass., who was a dealer in pianos and organs, he traced his lineage back to John "Purs," who came from England to Massachusetts in 1636. After preparing for college at Springfield High School, he entered Amherst at sixteen. In college his field of interest until his senior year was natural science, particularly chemistry. However, in his last year he was attracted to the study of philosophy with Professor Garman, and determined to become a teacher of philosophy. His all-around scholarship was recognized by his election to the Senior Scientific Society and to the Phi Beta Kappa Society. After a year in business with his father, he took a year of graduate work in philosophy and economics at Cornell, but his thesis for the degree of M.A. was presented to Amherst. He taught for a year at Mount Hermon School, then came west to teach psychology

13

and pedagogy at Ohio University, leaving there after a year to come to Kenyon as the Spencer and Wolfe Professor of Mental and Moral Philosophy.

In 1894 he was ordained to the Diaconate, and a few years later became a Priest, thus cementing his relationship with the Episcopal Church and enabling him to conduct services and preach throughout the country.

His election to the Presidency of Kenyon College in 1896 met with enthusiastic approval. The students admired him for his youth, his vigor, his athletic ability, his sense of humor, his scholarship, and his fairness; while the alumni, trustees, and faculty saw in him a far-sighted man of great ability and unlimited energy who would lead Kenyon out of the depths to which it had sunk in the 1890's.

By the middle of the 1920's Dr. Peirce was in his late fifties, yet his activities were enough to exhaust a man twenty years younger. In the school year 1921-22, which is selected at random as a typical year, he made 84 appearances connected with Kenyon *outside of Gambier*: 25 official appointments, 11 alumni meetings, 21 special addresses, 9 school addresses, and 14 sermons. When we remember that travel for these engagements was by train, with a little help from the automobile, and that he carried on a teaching program as well, he emerges as a man of immense vitality.

Although he had a remarkably good memory for names and faces, Dr. Peirce left nothing to chance, and usually carried with him a current alumni directory which he studied on the train while traveling to a speaking engagement. It was said that he changed the format of the directory in order to include a geographical listing of alumni, so that he could easily concentrate on the men living in the city to which he was going and be able to greet them enthusiastically by their first names.

He had a supreme mastery of words. His writing was clear and descriptive, albeit somewhat flowery as was the custom of the day, but it was in speaking that he really excelled, whether he was giving a prepared address or an informal talk. His sermons were apparently very moving; for example, his address from the Chapel pulpit at the opening of College in September 1926 was printed and distributed, with dozens of approving letters coming back. One of these from the mother of several Kenyon men began, "I think that I have never read anything more beautiful than your sermon on College Friendship. How can boys ever go wrong who have the opportunity of hearing such sermons?"

There were few alumni who did not look back on some personal experience with President Peirce with great fondness. John McClain (K1927), a well-known New York newspaper columnist for over thirty years until his death in 1967, wrote, "In all my travels among American colleges I have never come upon a president (or anyone else, for that matter) who combines a forceful, scholarly and yet pious nature with a sense of humor as well as Dr. Peirce." These words were written by a man whom "Fat" Peirce had thrown out of college near the end of his senior year for overcutting Chapel. Many years later McClain wrote in his column in the *New York Journal-American:*

> On the very eve of graduation (I had refused to leave the premises) I requested an interview alone with Dr. William F. Peirce, the then president. It was granted, and during the period of an hour, through sheer histrionic impact, I was able to convince him that I should be permitted to be graduated with my class. He admitted later that my acting was "superb."

Dr. Peirce was especially attentive to the educational needs of the local Knox County boys, and there are many cases of his helping to further their schooling. Perhaps in his wise way the president was trying to get a better educational "mix" in his entering classes. One of those whom he helped was Novice G. Fawcett (K1931), who was the very successful president of The Ohio State University until his retirement in 1972. Here is a portion of a letter from Dr. Fawcett to Dr. Peirce written February 22, 1958:

> Your warm and friendly letter of February 15 called to my memory an experience on a bright June morning in 1927 when my father and I were graciously received in your office at Kenyon College. As a tall, gangly boy from the country, with almost no resources, I knew only that I wanted an education, but was not at all certain how this goal could be achieved. This incident may long since have passed from your memory, for I could not have impressed you as being worth a substantial calculated risk. The fact remains, nevertheless, that you did see in me some promise, and as a result of that action, I find myself today in this distinguished position.

15

Endowment Drive

The fund-raising thrust of this decade seems to break down conveniently into two periods: a campaign to raise endowment during the first year followed by a drive to finance a tremendous building program.

In 1920 the General Education Board, making use of funds contributed by John D. Rockefeller, offered $150,000 to the College contingent upon Kenyon raising an additional $450,000. The money was to be used for an endowment fund, half of which was for the specific purpose of increasing the salaries of the professors, and half for the College proper.

The General Education Board set a deadline of July 1, 1921 for the collection of the funds, and an ambitious campaign was launched to contact alumni, undergraduates and churchmen for contributions. Albert C. ("Ace") Whitaker (K1888) offered to contribute $5000 for each $50,000 collected after the first $200,000 had been pledged. The response was excellent and the deadline was met with a little to spare: the grand total was $606,139.

The great building program of the College during the Twenties dried up most of the sources of further gift funds, but the National Church continued to supply yearly contributions ranging from $10,000 down to $2,500, and the Dioceses of Ohio and Southern Ohio made regular contributions to the operating funds.

Building Program

Taking advantage of the enthusiasm generated by the Centennial Celebration, President Peirce felt justified in going ahead with a building program which he considered would provide the College with adequate facilities for all time.

The rapid expansion of the student enrollment to the limit of 250 in the early 1920's made the construction of a dormitory the first priority. The result was Leonard Hall, first occupied by students in September 1924. The style is Collegiate Gothic and the exterior walls are of Glenmont sandstone. As originally built, the rooms were arranged in suites and the building housed comfortably a little over one hundred men. Costing about $200,000, Leonard Hall was the gift of Ohio Churchmen "as a tribute of love and devotion to William Andrew Leonard, Fourth Bishop of Ohio, and in reverent memory of his wife."

Ground-breaking ceremony for Samuel Mather Hall. President Peirce with shovel, and from left: Professors R.C. Lord, L.B. Walton, W.H. Coolidge, and E.H. Johnson.

The construction boom continued almost immediately with the planning for Samuel Mather Science Hall. Announced at the Centennial and ready of occupancy at the opening of college in September 1926, "Old Mather," as it is now called, was made possible by a gift of $350,000 by Henry G. Dalton of Cleveland. At his request the building was named in honor of Samuel Mather, for many years his senior partner in Pickands, Mather and Company.

The new building was sorely needed. The quarters of the science departments in the north end of Ascension Hall had become overcrowded, dilapidated, antiquated, and, in some ways, positively dangerous. This was before Ascension was reconstructed and fireproofed. The fume hoods from the chemistry laboratories reportedly vented into departmental offices above them. With additional faculty members being added, more office and classroom space was needed in Ascension.

In order that the building should harmonize with the other buildings of Kenyon, Brier Hill sandstone was used for Mather, with Indiana limestone for the mullions, mouldings, and carvings. Architect Abram Garfield's design was what he called Perpendicular Gothic in feeling, and is reminiscient of the Collegiate Gothic buildings of Oxford and Cambridge.

According to the architect, "The building is as complete as any in the country and should serve as a stimulus and inspiration to the teaching staff and students alike." The first floor contained the two present lecture rooms, along with offices and laboratories for the Physics Department, which also occupied the basement. The second and third floors were devoted respectively to the Departments of Chemistry and Biology.

With the science facilities now moved out of Ascension Hall, work was started immediately on a complete renovation of that building at an estimated cost of $75,000, supplied mainly by alumni and members of the Board of Trustees. Beginning with the just vacated north section, the interior was almost completely torn out. President Peirce's report on June 17, 1927 to the committee in charge of the project states: "Fireproof steel staircases have been installed and all-metal construction for the floors has been adopted. The new-old Ascension will be practically fireproof and the danger which has threatened the work of instruction at Kenyon for many years will thus in the future be averted." The beautiful woodwork in Philomathesian and Nu Pi Kappa Halls was carefully removed, repaired or replaced, and reinstalled. By an arrangement both economical and aesthetic the discarded oak floor joists were worked up into door frames, window sills, blackboard frames, and other trim of the renovated building. The work continued southward through the building as the north portion became usable, and the job was completed in 1928. Over $13,000 was spent in rebuilding the President's Suite, given as a memorial to Campbell Meeker (K1917) by his parents, Mr. and Mrs. Claude Meeker of Columbus.

Certainly one of the most pressing needs of the College by this time was for a new Commons, and to this President Peirce next addressed his attention. The old Commons was located in the building still standing just across the alley south of the Post Office. It was flanked on two sides by a large porch where in good weather the students would gather to await their meals. When the weather was inclement they waited in a large bare room at the front of the first floor. The kitchens were at the rear of this floor, and the food was sent up to the dining room on the upper floor on a dumb waiter. The dining area was crowded and the service inconvenient, with the result that only the men who were served first stood a chance of getting hot food. Sunday night seemed to be cleanup time, and it was said that no two meals at that serving had the same selection of food.

Not only was there need for improved food services, but Kenyon had no social center; thus the new Commons would fill this dual need.

Toward the construction of the proposed building the College had accumulated the following amounts of money:

1. From the Diocese of Ohio, about $70,000 for the construction of the Philander Chase Memorial Tower.
2. From the Class of 1895, $2500 for a memorial fireplace.
3. An equipment fund of $39,000.

As announced at the Hundredth Commencement in 1928, Frank H. Ginn (K1890) of Cleveland, and William Nelson Cromwell of New York, gave the amount — nearly $300,000 — necessary to complete the building according to the designs of Alfred H. Granger (K1887) of Chicago. The donors stipulated that the new Commons should be named Peirce Hall in honor of the man who had been President of Kenyon College since 1896.

Constructed of Ohio sandstone with Indiana limestone trim, the architecture of the building within and without is in the style of the buildings at Oxford and Cambridge. Of particular interest are the stained glass windows by Charles J. Connick of Boston, reputedly the greatest artist in stained glass in America at that time. The windows of the Tower are decorated with medallions illustrating the life of Bishop Chase; those in the middle of the west wall of the Great Hall symbolize American authors and poets, while the others represent significant English poets, novelists, and dramatists. Above the fireplace at the south end of the dining hall was placed a life-size portrait of President Peirce in academic robes. This was painted by the eminent artist, Karl Anderson, and was another gift from Mr. Ginn.

Great Hall of Perice. This photograph shows the original ceiling construction, before tie-beams were installed in 1941-42.

In addition to the Great Hall, the structure at the time of its building also housed the first floor lounge at the northeast corner. On the second floor were a billiard room, a card room, and a women's lounge, while on the third floor there were six bedrooms to be used for guests of the College. A small coffee shop was provided in the basement.

When Peirce Hall was occupied in the Fall of 1929 it brought the college's $1,100,000 building program to a close, and President Peirce announced proudly, "We now have all the buildings we will ever need."

One of the notable events in the early 1920's was the installation of electric lights in the dormitories during the summer of 1921. According to the *Collegian* for October 26, 1921: "Current is obtained by a special line which is connected to the Ohio Power Company's line east of Mt. Vernon. In addition to the regular current, the College has installed a large dynamo from which current can be used in case of an emergency." The *Collegian* reported that the emergency equipment had to be used several times within the first few months of operation. Prior to this time gas was used for lighting, with kerosene lamps preceding gas.

Social Life in the Twenties

With the completion of Leonard Hall, a social living pattern emerged which was to remain stable for about two decades. The six national fraternities and one local each had a separate division in the dormitories, and the non-fraternity men, with a few exceptions, were all quartered in Old Kenyon and were bound together in a social organization known as the Middle Kenyon Association.

The Betas "singing in" on the Middle Path. About 1951.

Tuesday night was fraternity meeting night, and absence from meeting was considered inexcusable. After dinner the men, by groups of two or three or four, would stroll out to the fraternity lodges located in wooded areas on the edges of the village. When the meeting ended, the brothers would link arms and march four abreast all the way from Bexley Hall to their dormitory division, singing the songs of their fraternity as they moved along. About four songs were spaced along the Middle Path: one as the group approached Harcourt Place School for Girls, one going through the village, one just south of the gates; and the final one starting at the north end of Ascension. Sometimes a traffic problem came up when two fraternities arrived at the Bexley gates at about the same time, but the utmost courtesy was shown, with the second group waiting until the others were out of earshot. Walkers on the Path would stand at attention at the side while the groups marched past. The fraternities took great pride in their singing, and it was good. Visitors would sometimes make it a point to come to Gambier on Tuesday evenings just to listen. This custom was one of the most pleasant traditions which has ever existed at Kenyon.

Fraternity rushing procedures changed considerably during this decade. Traditionally newcomers had been pledged "right off the train," or were signed up by upperclassmen from their hometown even before coming to Gambier. This system had its obvious disadvantages, and dissatisfaction began to crop up with the *Collegian* reporting on March 16, 1925 that a new system was coming about gradually, with more and more men waiting until later in the year before pledging.

Finally a completely new system was reported in the *Collegian* for December 1, 1926:

> This plan calls for a period of eleven days following the opening of college year, during which fraternity men and new men may not converse with each other under any circumstances. On the twelfth day, which will always be a Sunday, fraternities are permitted to rush new students between the hours of two in the afternoon and ten at night. The names of new men whom fraternities wish to entertain are handed in to the Pan-Hellenic Council, and a schedule by which each man shall visit, for an hour, each fraternity to which he has been invited is arranged. For the next three evenings, between seven and ten, this schedule continues. During this period, understandings between new

22

men and fraternities may be reached, but decisions are not binding on either side. On Thursday evening, the fraternities, through the Pan-Hellenic Council, send bids to the men whom they wish to pledge. Those students who appear between the hours specified at the fraternity of their choice will be pledged.

Although the death of Stuart Pierson in 1905 in connection with a fraternity initiation had put a stop to most of the out-and-out hazing which had gone on, the tradition of strict discipline for freshmen was still strong in the 20's. From the day of arrival on the campus, the newcomers were required to wear hats or caps, which were doffed to the upperclassmen met on the Path. A little later freshman caps arrived, varying in color and shape from year to year, and they were the standard head covering from that time on. It was mandatory that all freshmen leapfrog over the center gatepost whenever they went through the College Gates. On pajama parade night during the first week of school they were called out in front of Old Kenyon and forced to crawl in a line while singing, "There is a Hell for Freshmen." This was followed by a parade through the village to Harcourt School where impromptu performances were demanded. Other events of the first weeks were the freshman-sophomore fight and the cane rush. The latter event sometimes took place between the halves of a football game on Benson Field and sometimes on the lawn north of

Cane Rush, 1948.

Ascension. A cane was placed upright in the middle of the field and the sophomores and freshmen lined up at opposite ends. At a given signal there was a rush for the cane. The class having the greater number of hands on the cane at the end of a certain time interval was declared the winner. If the freshmen won, the restrictions on them were relaxed. Various tactics were employed to outwit the opposition. One method was for the first person reaching the cane to throw it backwards over his head to the other members of his class, who would immediately fall on it in a pile, resisting the efforts of the opposition to peel off the bodies until time was called.

Every Monday noon after lunch there was a lineup of freshmen on the lawn north of Ascension. Here they were harangued by the president and other members of the sophomore class about the correct behavior of Kenyon men and called to account for their real or imaginary misdeeds. Most of the restrictions ceased about Thanksgiving.

In the fraternity and non-fraternity divisions, however, freshman discipline was continued throughout the entire year. The tradition of paddling freshmen for infractions persisted, and they were required to run errands for the upperclassmen. Every evening one or two freshmen from each division were scheduled to take orders for food to be brought back from The Bakery, a village restaurant. The term "Bakery order" persisted for years after The Bakery burned down and the food came from the Peirce Hall Coffee Shop.

So strong was the tradition of freshman discipline that an administrative proposal for a freshmen segregation plan met with an overwhelming storm of protest. A special edition of the *Collegian* was published on June 15, 1928; the gist of the editorials was that with the segregation of the freshmen it would be impossible to enforce discipline.

Although the use of alcohol by students had been banned at Kenyon since its beginning, the advent of national prohibition created an additional vexing problem for President Peirce and the other members of the faculty, since now it became necessary to cope with the efforts of the agents enforcing the dry laws. Typical of such problems was the dry officers' raid during the Sophomore Dance on May 11, 1923, which caused an eruption of newspaper headlines such as, "State Officers Arrest Youths In Booze Revel." Dr. Peirce felt called upon to answer in a letter circulated to newspapers throughout Ohio:

Rooms of the President
Kenyon College, Gambier, Ohio
May 14, 1923

Dear sir:

The newspapers have published a very sensational account of the sophomore hop at Kenyon College. May I present through your columns the actual facts in the case?

On the night of May 11, during the course of a large ball, at which four or five hundred persons were present, four dry officers, after a quietly conducted search of several hours, arrested seven men, and brought them before the mayor's court. Three of these men were strangers, who had never been in any way connected with Kenyon. Of the four Kenyon students involved, two had manifestly been drinking; a third had been found with liquor in his possession; while the fourth paid no fine, as it could not be established that he had either been drinking or had liquor in his possession. I was myself present in the court room, and know these to be the facts.

As to the attitude of the college authorities, which has been greatly misrepresented, let me say that, in the first place, the rules of Kenyon College, which forbid the use and keeping of intoxicants either in the buildings or on the grounds of the College, long ante-date national prohibition, and that, in the second place, far from protesting against the action of government officers, we welcome any aid in enforcing law and order among our students.

The college faculty has already expelled the two students who were found to have been drinking and has dismissed the man who was found with liquor in his possession. Against the fourth man, as no misconduct was established, no action was taken.

Yours faithfully,
William F. Peirce
President of Kenyon College

The Faculty was quite sharply divided as to drinkers and non-drinkers, and the intolerance of one group for the other inevitably caused some friction in that august body. There always seemed to be two or three "bootleggers" or suppliers of liquor among the students, with sales mainly in beer, corn whiskey, and gin. The principal source of supply for beer was Newark, while a great deal of the whiskey came from New Straightsville, where the closing of the coal mines had driven the residents to operating illicit stills in the abandoned mine shafts. "Bathtub" gin was made by mixing pure grain alcohol with water and oil of juniper, with a few drops of glycerine added for smoothness. The aging time was as long as it took to make the mixture. One of the favorite spots for beer parties was Arbutus Glen, a couple of miles east on Wiggin Street.

It had been the custom at Kenyon for several years to conduct a mock political convention in the spring of the year during which the national political conventions were held. The 1924 Mock Political Convention was a comparatively mild affair, since the energies of the College were funneled into preparations for the Centennial of 1924. However, the 1928 Republican Convention was one of the most hilarious affairs which have occurred in Gambier. Leon A. ("Moon") Mullen (K1928) organized a brass band to lead the parade of all the delegates; there were the usual nominating and seconding speeches; the party planks were outlined (one of them was Free Beer For Bexley); and, just to show how prescient were the students, the nominee was Herbert Hoover. The delegates were assigned to their states by lot in advance of the convention, and arrived at Rosse Hall dressed in appropriate attire for their state. The girls from Harcourt School traditionally represented the Virgin Islands, Virginia and West Virginia.

Student Government

During this decade student government was in the hands of an organization known as the Kenyon College Assembly, of which the students became members upon payment of the compulsory athletic fee. The four officers were elected yearly, and regular meetings were held on the first Monday of each month. The constitution provided for two standing committees: the Senior Council and the Executive Committee. Consisting of one Senior from each fraternity division and two from the non-fraternity group, the Senior Council dealt mainly with discipline problems, typically those involving enforcement of the rule against liquor in the dormitories. The Executive Committee was chosen in a manner similar to the Senior Council, but it functioned as the controlling body over athletics, publications, dramatics, and the Glee Club.

The headline, "Little Business Transacted by the November Assembly," in the *Collegian* seems to typify Assembly activities during this period. In reading the minutes and newspaper reports it becomes obvious that most of the attention of the organization was given over to athletics, with much time devoted to such weighty discussions as whether the basketball letters should be surrounded by a circle. There were moments of diversion: the *Collegian* reports that Patrick Anthony ("Pat") Mulvey (K1926) took advantage of the fact that Assembly fell on St. Patrick's Day to sing his National Anthem, but, all in all, there did not seem to be any Great Issues.

Student Fees and Faculty Salaries

Student expenses at Kenyon did not show a great increase during the 1920's. Tuition was raised from $140 to $300 per year during this decade, but the estimated total yearly expense rose only from $500 to $700. Before Peirce Hall was built students were charged a Commons fee of $70 per year, and paid $5 a week for board at the Commons. If they wished they could eat at one of the restaurants in Gambier, and many did this when they became tired of the college food or were short of funds (no credit was extended at the Commons). However, they inevitably came back to the Commons, since the cost was less and they were forced to subsidize the college eating hall anyway through the Commons fee. With the opening of Peirce Hall, all students were charged a flat rate of $300 per year for board. The result was that most of the restaurants in Gambier went out of business for the following reasons: the food was better at the new Commons, it was more conveniently located, and most students could not afford to pay twice for their meals.

During the twenties the average salary for a full professor was about $3000 per year, while assistant professors got about $2000. Housing or a housing allowance was provided in addition to the regular salary. In 1921 the president's salary was increased from $3600 to $5400 per year.

Admissions

Fifty years ago admission to college was a much simpler procedure than the hectic scheming which is connected with finding the right college today. Strangely enough, the basic secondary school course requirements were almost identical with those of now, but there the similarity ends. The grueling battery of College Board tests was not required at Kenyon. High school and preparatory school records, coupled with the recommendations of the principal or the headmaster appeared to be the main determining factors for admission, but it was suspected that a good family social background, wealth, and membership in the Episcopal Church were a great help.

Course Offerings

As might be expected in a men's liberal arts college which had been in existence for one hundred years, the course offerings were quite traditional. During much of this era the program for all four years was laid out in a "Conspectus of Courses of Study," which appeared to allow for considerable election of courses, but in reality did not give the student much choice once he had decided on which course — classical, philosophical, or scientific — he wished to follow. The catalogue for 1927-28 reflected a change, stating:

> Flexibility is secured by offering a wide choice of electives while continuity and proportion in selection is insisted on. Some ancient language is required for the Arts degree, while the philosophical course emphasizes modern language.
>
> All courses aim at general training in preparation for business or professional life. The scientific course is planned especially to meet the needs of students who expect to pursue engineering, medical or graduate scientific studies.

In spite of this liberalization the list of required courses was loaded. Courses amounting to 128 semester hours were required for graduation, but to be included were: Four years of English (Junior and Senior English were one hour courses), three year courses in language, three year courses in science and mathematics (in addition to freshman mathematics), three year courses in social sciences and psychology, and year courses in mathematical analysis (freshman math), American history ("Fat's" history) and Bible. Completing the list were one semester courses in freshman lecture, and physical training, required of all freshmen and sophomores. The Bachelor of Arts degree was granted if Latin and Greek were included, the Bachelor of Science if the major were in science, and the Bachelor of Philosophy was granted to all others completing the course requirements. A typical catalogue listing included offerings in: English, Greek, Latin, French, Spanish, German,

Mathematics, Chemistry, Biology, Physics, Geology, History, Political Science, Economics, Sociology, Philosophy, Psychology, and Religion and the Bible. Except for English, the courses listed were mostly basic courses, and did not often reflect the scholastic specialties of the members of the faculty. For example, Professor Radford, a renowned Latin scholar, taught Greek during his entire career at Kenyon. On the other hand, surveying was still being offered, a remnant of a previous course in civil engineering taught by Professor Allen, who was expert in the field of surveying.

The required course in mathematical analysis was the rock upon which scores of Kenyon men foundered. It was common to find Juniors and even Seniors still trying to fulfill this requirement. The *Collegian* for May 21, 1930 contains this poignant news article:

> Robert Swanson, '32, has received the appointment from the College and the Department of Mathematics for the position of instructor in the mathematics summer school of six weeks during the coming vacation. As a means of last resort this school is to be attended by those who have encountered difficulty in making the required hours in mathematical analysis during the regular college year. The school was conducted with great success last summer under Tom Jenkins, '28, and several men were able to work off the lacking credits by means of the intensive instruction. Six hours a day are spent in the classroom on the subject, and a final examination on each semester's work is taken by the student under Dr. Allen.
>
> Swanson should find no difficulty making a "go" of the proposition this summer, since he has not only had a splendid record in the first year course, but has had two semesters of advanced work along somewhat the same lines. Several men have already signed up for the course.

Extra-curricular Life

It would be an oversimplification and an exaggeration to say that no cultural activities in this period took place outside the classroom, but certainly in comparison with today, the number of concerts, lectures, plays, and exhibits was minimal. One or two "big" lectures were given each year, and during this era there were appearances by such scholars as Carl Sandburg, Bertrand Russell, John Dewey, and Will Durant. Except for the fine musical comedies put on by the Puff and Powder Club in the early Twenties, there were only one or two plays given a year, and they were reputed to have been poorly-staged and poorly-costumed affairs. Kenyon had always had a great tradition of informal group and choir singing, and this continued during this decade, but there was little effort made to promote instrumental music outside of the chamber music quartets organized by Professor Reeves and the dance band known as the Campus Owls which flourished in 1928-30. This latter group achieved some measure of notoriety during the summer of 1929 by playing its way to Europe on the Cunard liner *Aquitania* and back on the *Caronia*. The leader was G. Russel Hargate (K1930), and the other members were James M. Irvine, Jr. (K1930), Donald G.L. Henning (K1931), Louis D. Strutton (K1931), and Thomas B. Greenslade (K1931).

Since there were no honors programs, seminars or student forums at this time, extra-curricular life was carried on in a limited, loosely organized fashion. Of course, foremost among these activities were the incomparable and interminable "bull" sessions which went on far into the night under the stimulus of bootleg beer. However, the more serious discussions were engendered by the revival of the old literary societies, Philomathesian and Nu Pi Kappa, just prior to the Centennial. The *Collegian* for March 31, 1924 editorialized:

> The rejuvenescence of these old organizations is a healthy symbol of the good old days returning and that the rich fulness of old-time Kenyon life is slowly settling over the campus.
>
> Both of these societies have had long and honorable records in the history of the college; their founding is associated with a world of picturesque details of days gone by. Philomathesian was founded in 1827, and Nu Pi Kappa a few years later by a group of Southern students who became offended at the stand Edwin M. Stanton, then a student at Kenyon and a member of Philo, took on South Carolina's threatened secession. One of the main events of the college year in the days gone by was the contest held on Washington's Birthday, on which date the rival orators of the two societies were pitted against each other in a contest. The rivalry between the two societies threatened at times to culminate in actual personal contact.
>
> The plans which these societies have adopted in regard to membership will be a source of strength to both. Philomathesian has its membership limited to Kenyon students who are not members of Greek Letter Social Fraternities; Nu Pi Kappa has restricted its roll to only those men in college who are members of the Fraternal groups. (These restrictions were hotly denied in the next issue of the *Collegian* by John Carr Duff (K1924), president of Philo).

> Literary societies all over the country were hard hit by the war and also by what seemed a lack of student interest. This lack of interest, we feel, is more apparent than real; this year there is a movement spreading over the country which is more favorable to them.

Apparently the two literary societies were still not on a firm footing: the *Collegian* for May 7, 1927 reported still another reorganization of Philo.

One organization which appears to have been quite successful all during the Twenties was the Science Club. Held together by the strong leadership of Professors Walton, Johnson, Coolidge, Lord, and Allen, it reported a full membership of twenty-five all during this decade. Regular meetings were held, papers read and discussed, addresses given by faculty and outside speakers, and social events such as banquets and visits to faculty homes took place.

Let the casual reader of the *Reveilles* of that time beware lest he be misled by the great numbers of clubs listed: the Woolworth Club, Kappa Beta Phi, Kappa Lambda Mu, the Ivy Club, and the Chess Club. They were all drinking societies. Particularly confusing was Kappa Beta Phi, whose members sported on their watch chains a key which was an exact replica of a Phi Beta Kappa key with the letters reversed.

The Faculty

One of the most stable foundations of this decade at Kenyon was the faculty. Men who were strong in scholarship, strong in character, and strong in their devotion to the College were at the helm of each department: Henry Titus West in German; William Peters Reeves in English; Lee Barker Walton in Biology; Richard Clarke Manning in Latin; Reginald Bryant Allen in Mathematics; George Francis Weida, later Walter Hatheral Coolidge (K1912) in Chemistry; Elbe Herbert Johnson in Physics; and Raymond DuBois Cahall (K1908) in History. Joining the faculty during this period were William Ray Ashford, Philip Wolcott Timberlake (K1917), Charles Monroe Coffin, and Stuart Rice McGowan (K1928), all of whom became familiar and beloved figures in the Kenyon family. Included among this faculty were many who served the College for thirty or more years, and several who were at Kenyon for more than forty years. Such continuity in a small faculty would be hard to match anywhere in the United States.

College instruction in that time was strictly teacher-oriented. Even though small classes could have made possible much discussion and evaluation by students, in general a strict lecture system prevailed, with the students taking notes and regurgitating the information on examinations. This was not unique at Kenyon, but was true of virtually all American colleges. Even in the language classes, where a little informality might be expected to develop, recitation and drill were conducted by some professors with meticulous precision. Professor West, for example, a very critical person even out of the classroom, became positively tyrannical when he faced a class. His method of teaching in first year classes involved the exact memorization of short stories (Geschichten) in German, with which he would illustrate the various points of grammar. So painfully were these stories drilled in that even today if one of his students of fifty years ago would hear the command, "Erzählen Sie die erste Geschichte, Herr Jones!" Herr Jones would snap to attention and begin, "In einem Gericht, befahl der Richter ... " As a comparatively young man, Professor West's eyesight had become seriously impaired, and by the 20's he was almost totally blind, so that he conducted his classes in German literature by relying completely on his remarkable memory. The students in obvious ways tried to take advantage of his handicap, but it was an unequal battle right from the beginning, and the few times "Tite" West was caught in an error were subjects of campus discussion for days.

In the Reeves Room of Chalmers Library there is a bronze tablet, dedicating the room to: "William Peters Reeves, Teacher of English, who for more than a third of a century has kindled the love of books in the hearts of Kenyon men." This is the second Reeves Room; the first was provided through the generosity of Wilbur L. Cummings (K1902) on the second floor of the old Alumni Library, now Ransom Hall.

The Rev. Harry F. Truxall (K1931) wrote of "Pete" Reeves in the *Alumni Bulletin*:

> On that Fall day in 1927 when I first entered his classroom, he was wearing a salt and pepper tweed suit. His knickers revealed two legs scarcely larger than pipe-stems. Gray and dark hair mingled on his head, while a well-cut mustache set him apart from other men. A black

bow tie contrasted sharply with spotless linen. In his left breast pocket was a nice clean handkerchief, which served for show and also an occasional blow. This thin man always entered class with quick steps and as soon as the period ended his exit was immediate. Clang! the bell! it is time for class. Spectacles were pulled forth by a black cord; they were set upon a small nose. Pen in hand, he produced a roll book. "Pete" called only our last names in a staccato style, and we snapped quickly, "Here, sir! Here, sir! Here, sir!" There was something about the way in which he called the roll that, if a man did not answer instanter, he felt himself condemned.

After a semester of digging up sources, we read Chaucer. "Pete's" interpretation of Chaucer was unique; he held that Chaucer, like Dante, wrote many things with a double meaning; that the words could be interpreted in an innocent manner, but at the same time there was a subtle undertone by which Chaucer was laughing up his sleeve at abuses in the church. Reeves would say, "Now Kittredge of Harvard says, 'Let no man say that Chaucer was not a good churchman,' but gentlemen, look at these lines . . . "

On the other hand, "Pete" did not live completely in a world of books. He was credited with being the founder of the Ohio Athletic Conference and was its president for many years; he was a crack rifle and pistol shot; he was a good violinist; he loved to direct plays; he played some bridge. He was always interested in social affairs, plays, concerts, and lectures. His versatility was amazing.

Professor George M. Kahrl, who taught at Kenyon early in his teaching career during the 1930's, remembers Reeves well:

Professor Reeves, while other faculty were concocting learned annotations and cultivating academic eccentricities, made his personal life and his teaching effective from a cultivated sense of style.

He dressed in character, not fashion, with a masculine taste for quality. He commanded respect by approaching each class as an important occasion to be accompanied by good taste and ceremony as well as learning.

He was an old hand at academic politics, resolving impasses simply with the laughter of sharp, objective wit. He had all the faculties of a good actor in animating his wit with his facial expressions; one could almost anticipate some good comedy was in the making when Professor Reeves began agitating his eyes, mustache, chin, pursing his lips, and shaking his head. He put on a good show. On the other hand his concentration on form in poetry and prose occasionally slowed up his deliberate progress through the centuries; try as he might he never got much beyond Chaucer in the year survey of English literature (English 11-12).

33

Remembered above all else by a young instructor, were the occasional long winter afternoons as a guest of Professor Reeves, before the woodfire in his elegant study, his informed and leisurely conversation drawing on the great range of his interests. I shall never forget how he surprised me by specifying the Buck Brothers of Connecticut as making the best wood-carving chisels.

All that Professor Reeves did became not part of a record, a biographical entry, but a manifestation of his great sense that life was the present moment that grew out of a past, that rather than power or prestige or work done, the style counted for more than all else in human relations.

Professor Richard C. Manning taught Latin at Kenyon for 35 years until his retirement in 1937. He continued to live in Gambier after leaving active teaching and here he died in 1957 at the age of 89. Of him Dr. Philip W. Timberlake, McIlvaine Professor of English, wrote in the Autumn, 1953 issue of the *Kenyon Alumni Bulletin*:

Before Nu Pi Kappa Hall had been made in a huddle of what Dean Swift calls "little nests and burrows," its south door opened majestically into space, and what promised to be a grand exit from a noble apartment could in fact be accomplished only by scrambling eight feet down a wooden ladder fastened to the wall. At the foot of this ladder was a desk, on a low platform. And behind the desk for a good part of every morning sat a quiet black-bearded gentleman, the Benson Memorial Professor of Latin, Richard Clarke Manning, facing classes scattered around four long tables. That room is now nests and burrows — faculty offices; and the very spot where I now write is at one of its western windows, near the vanished end of one of those tables.

Richard Manning came to the Benson Chair of Latin with undergraduate and doctoral degrees from Harvard and after further studies in Germany. For the next thirty-five years he was one of the notable group of teachers whom so many Kenyon men studied under with profit and remember with affection; and to the satisfaction of his friends he has continued to reside in Gambier since retiring from active instruction.

In background and heritage Dr. Manning is a thorough New Englander. His family is an ancient one of Salem, with its traditions of seafaring, witches, and seven-gabled houses; and indeed the chronicler of those traditions, Nathaniel Hawthrone, was on the maternal side a Manning.

What one remembers about a teacher is his teaching, and many a Kenyon man will remember with me the strict and profitable hours of introduction to Roman literature in the old room at the foot of the ladder: Livy, Ovid, Horace, Sallust, and the rest, not to mention Allen and Greenough's *Latin Grammar*, in which it is desirable to know also the fine print. I shall not recount the many tales, largely apocryphal, of the wit and soft sarcasm which flicked the young asses along the road to learning. Let the interest and the delight be recorded instead; for it may be said of Dr. Manning, as Horace said of the poet: *Omne tulit punctum qui miscuit utile dulci*, which translates to something like, "The one who mixes the useful with the aesthetically pleasing is sure to get all the applause."

Robert C. Hyde (K1925) recalls that "ponies" or "trots" were commonly used in those days and tells this story: One day a recitation was so clearly a pony translation instead of that of a student that Professor Manning said: "Mr. _____, surely you know that a pony and a donkey don't consort well together." Student: "Yes, sir, and the pony is leaving right now."

Dr. R.B. ("Gummy") Allen was another of the faculty stalwarts of this period. A tall, athletic man, he was a fussy dresser who was annoyed when he did not get elected by the students "Best Dressed Faculty Member" but instead was voted "Thinks He Is." Early in his career at Gambier, Dr. Allen took in a number of Delts as roomers (the College was short of dormitory space), and so in order not to disturb the students in their studying hours he would tiptoe through the house. About that time people were enjoying a comic strip in which one of the principal characters was "Gumshoe the Sneak Thief," from which Professor Allen acquired his nickname, "Gumshoe" — later shortened to "Gummy." Even his assistant, Dr. Bumer (rhymes with bloomer), was called "Bumeshoe." Whenever students placed an alarm clock in the font of the Chapel and timed it to go off during the service, it was Dr. Allen who would tiptoe up to the font to the rythmic accompaniment of thumping feet, silence the alarm, and later announce that the owner of the clock could have it back if he came to his office and claimed it. He left quite a collection.

The Rev. Benedict ("Ben") Williams (K1927), who was Dr. Allen's student assistant in college and who taught Freshman Math during his first year at Bexley, has some fond recollections of Professor Allen:

> My father was a classical scholar (K1878) and prided himself that his boys were trained in Latin, Greek and Hebrew. He protested that "Gummy" made his boys mathematicians. Chuck (Charles, Jr.) and Bob and I became entranced with "Gummy's" enthusiasm for Math and became his followers.

35

"Gummy's" enthusiasm for calculus led him to calculate every curve. He missed one coming back from Mount Vernon by making too short a turn and wrecked his car, but he corrected his calculating and used his mistake as a lesson to students.

When I assisted him in the Math Department he insisted that we cross each other's path at every stair landing in order to "equalize the distance."

One of the real faculty "characters" of the Twenties was Professor Robert S. Radford, known as "Oomphah" or "Uncle Bobbie." The name of "Oomphah" was derived from the sounds he made when he was annoyed or pretended to be.

Although he taught Greek at Kenyon from 1924 until his death in 1936, he was regarded as the leading Ovidian scholar in America. He was universally loved by the students and respected for his outstanding scholarship, but the temptation to make him the butt of student pranks was too much: alarm clocks would go off in the middle of a lecture; cats (he disliked them) would start wandering around his classroom on the second floor in the southwest corner of Ascension Hall; and the student assistant showing slides in his course in Greek Art would somehow accidently slip in a slide showing a voluptuous nude female. Dr. Radford had his classroom desk placed close to the door so that when the bell announcing the end of the period rang he could move toward the door and defend it by waving his blackboard pointer in the faces of the students edging out, in order that he might get in a few more words of his lecture.

According to his contemporaries, Dr. Radford was a faddist in many directions, mostly in matters of diet. He regularly ate eight slightly cooked eggs a day; three at breakfast, two at noon, and three in the evening. At times he would ask for milk toast instead of eggs for breakfast; once he consumed seventeen slices before his appetite was satisfied. He was a hearty eater, and along with his eggs would consume large quantities of bread, baked potatoes, and vegetables such as lettuce and canned peas; he rarely touched meat or desserts, except unsweetened applesauce.

His students could always tell when he had been invited out to a formal dinner, because he would wear his formal evening trousers all day long, accompanied by a regular suit coat. Occasionally he would put on complete dress clothes in the morning and wear his overcoat while teaching. He was known to telephone his hostess before six in the morning to ask what clothes to wear. His extreme corpulence made the changing of his trousers a very difficult task. He regularly ate a hearty meal at home before going out to a dinner party.

Bexley Hall

Up at the north end of the village, Bexley Hall, the theological seminary, started the decade of the Twenties on a dismal note with only six students in attendance. Since student housing at the college was at such a premium, selected students from Kenyon were housed at Bexley for several years. During this decade enrollment in Bexley Hall went up markedly, until in the school year 1929-30 there were 24 in attendance. The financial picture at Bexley was also dim in the early Twenties, with records showing yearly appeals to the Dioceses of Ohio and Southern Ohio for funds to meet the annual deficit. A successful endowment drive to raise $300,000 for the principal purpose of increasing professors' salaries put the institution back into a solvent financial state, and President Peirce was able to report in 1926-27 that the endowment fund had reached $445,811.33, and that surpluses had been attained for the last two years.

During this period the office of Dean of Bexley Hall was held by President Peirce (temporary substitute), Samuel A.B. Mercer, Jacob Streibert (acting), Frederick C. Grant, and Charles E. Byrer.

Although the main impact was yet to come, the stock market collapse on Black Thursday, October 25, 1929, signaled the end of an era at Kenyon. The College had always been peculiarly vulnerable to nationwide depressions, with their attendant drops in enrollment and financial droughts, but this greatest depression of all, followed closely by World War II, brought on some of the most trying years in the history of Kenyon College.

CHAPTER III

Days of Depression and War

Colleges tend to be reflecting microcosms of the world in which they exist. Kenyon in depression days was no exception. For the first years of the Thirties the hopelessness and apathy which swept the nation pervaded the student body. The faculty and trustees vacillated among policies of retrenchment, violent change, and muddling through. It was not until the middle of the decade that the fortunes of the nation and the College took a turn upward.

The Pinch of the Depression

By the school year 1931-1932 the college began to feel deeply the pinch of the depression. The squeeze came from several directions: the drop in enrollment with its attendant loss of revenue from student fees; the drastic cut in the return from holdings in the college endowment funds; and the drying up of gift funds from alumni and friends of the College.

Fortunately the physical plant was in good shape, and for the time being no new buildings were needed. Since no great financial bonanza seemed to be in sight, the trustees addressed themselves to two remedies of immediate priority: the institution of a program of strict economy and increasing student enrollment.

Most of the economies effected came as a result of cuts in the salaries of the faculty and other personnel. In 1930 the teaching staff had all received substantial pay increases, but drastic cuts in 1932 wiped out practically all of the gains. In 1933 five assistant professorships were discontinued, the Department of Romance Languages was ordered to make a salary saving of at least $1500, and the Department of Mathematics a similar savings of at least $1000. Later in 1933 a really deep cut in salaries was ordered by the Board of Trustees:

Resolved that the Board does hereby establish in principle the cash salary list for the College year 1933-34 at the following percentages of the cash salaries paid for the year 1932-33; at 65% of such salaries in excess of Four Thousand Dollars ($4000); at 75% of such salaries in excess of Three Thousand Dollars ($3000) and not in excess of Four Thousand Dollars ($4000); and at 80% of such salaries in excess of Fifteen Hundred Dollars ($1500) and not in excess of Three Thousand Dollars ($3000); provided that no salary be so reduced to less than Fifteen Hundred Dollars ($1500).

At the same meeting the Board also authorized its Executive Committee to sell securities to pay salaries of the college employees.

Since the very beginning of the College the trustees have always been exceedingly generous in their financial support, but it becomes apparent from the documents of this period that the College could not have survived without the financial transfusions which the trustees supplied to alleviate the day-to-day crises which came up. Time and time again $5000 or $10,000 was given as a lump sum for such projects as emergency repairs, an advertising campaign to attract students, or to conduct a survey. Wilbur L. Cummings (K1902), Frank H. Ginn (K1890) and Robert A. Weaver (K1912) are among those frequently listed as financial saviors. Not only did the trustees furnish financial aid, but they gave unstintingly of their time in attempting to save the College. Trustee Cummings was said by many to have been "running the College" during this period, and documentary evidence shows him to have been involved in most of the decisions and transactions.

To compound the fiscal difficulties, the bank crises and closings just prior to the first inauguration of President Roosevelt on March 4, 1933 made it impossible for the College to pay its employees on time. In anticipation of the limit on withdrawals from accounts, money had been removed in cash and kept in safety deposit boxes, but with the complete closing of the banks the boxes could not be opened.

Financed by a gift of $1600 from Mr. Ginn, a Faculty Committee for the purpose of increasing enrollment was formed, consisting of R.J. Kutler, Chairman, C.T. Bumer, W.R. Ashford, S.R. McGowan and E.G. Evans. One of the functions promoted by this group was a series of High School Days, when promising secondary school students were brought to Gambier for a visit to the campus.

The Trustees apparently thought that filling the college with students was of prime importance, even though some of them could pay little more than board and room, for the following resolution was passed on June 17, 1933:

> Resolved that for the purpose of increasing the size of the next Freshman Class to one hundred twenty five (125) if possible by awarding scholarships to high school or other preparatory pupils of honor rank and other superior qualifications, the President be, and he is hereby authorized to create not exceeding fifty (50) scholarships (including the twenty (20) already authorized) for the year of 1933-34, for the value of not less than One Hundred Dollars ($100) nor more than Three Hundred Dollars ($300) for each scholarship, as shall be determined by the President in his discretion.

In order to make it easier for students to pay their fees, installment payments due on the first of each month were accepted instead of complete payment at the beginning of the term. In some cases students were permitted to give promissory notes for their fees.

School of Business Proposal

All colleges were searching for some gimmicks which would attract students to the empty classrooms, and Kenyon desperately sought to find those which would be consistent with her ideals and traditions. One of the innovations suggested was to establish a school of business, and Professor Paul M. Titus of the Department of Economics was asked to report on the feasibility of this suggestion to Mr. Cummings. Professor Titus' opinion was that a school of business was not in harmony with the established purposes of the college, and not within the scope of the resources of Kenyon. Mr. Cummings at a trustees meeting cited an opinion by Benjamin M. Anderson, economist for the Chase National Bank: "This demand for 'practicality' is self-defeating. If the institutions of learning will send to the business and banking world men with good general education, with eager and inquiring minds, and with an understanding of the principles of business and banking, the business and banking community will quickly teach them the particular jobs assigned to them." After careful consideration the proposal for business education was dropped.

New Sports At Kenyon

Many institutions of higher learning sought to attract students with elaborate athletic programs, and poured money into the recruitment and development of stellar football and basketball teams. Because of its small numbers, Kenyon could not possibly enter into such competition and decided to concentrate its main attention on four comparatively minor sports activities: flying, equitation (with polo as an intercollegiate sport), swimming, and tennis.

School of Aeronautics.

School of Aeronautics

The beginnings of flying at Kenyon were told in an article by John R. Tunis, a well-known sports writer, in the April 15, 1934 issue of *The Sportsman Pilot*. Some excerpts:

Through the initiative and generosity of Wilbur L. Cummings of New York, a graduate of Kenyon College in 1902, the first college airport in this country to be officially recognized by the Department of Commerce came into existence this month. On April 21 before the student body and the faculty, a fleet of visiting Army and Navy planes, and in the presence of such distinguished guests as Hon. George White, Governor of Ohio; Hon. John Dickenson, Assistant Secretary of Commerce; Hon. David S. Ingalls, former Assistant Secretary of the Navy; Eugene Vidal, Director of Aeronautics for the Department of Commerce; Lieut.-Col. J. Carroll Cone, Assistant Director of Aeronautics; Congressman Charles West; and Professor Alexander Klemin, head of the Guggenheim School of Aeronautics of New York University, the principal speaker, Port Kenyon was to be officially dedicated and recognized by aviation authorities of the United States.

Mr. Cummings generously undertook to find funds to equip the school, to supply the college with two training planes, and to endow a chair of aeronautics. With his aid the faculty was able to engage Mr. Donald McCabe Gretzer as instructor in aviation and flying. Mr. Gretzer has had seven years' experience as a lecturer and teacher, has been a test pilot for aircraft manufacturers, and is himself holder of a Transport Pilot's license.

The new Wilbur L. Cummings School of Practical Aeronautics is divided into two courses: Ground School Instruction, and Flight Instruction. For the former there is a new aeronautical laboratory completely equipped, while the course of study is identical with that required by the Department of Commerce for preparation in taking a Transport Pilot's license. It includes a course of over one hundred hours which is accomplished at the rate of three hours of classroom and laboratory work per week, for which a three-hour credit is given the student successfully passing each semester. No college credit is given for flight instruction. This part of the course, however, requires a minimum of ten hours dual time and twenty-five hours solo for a pass mark.

The Flying School has been equipped with a Fleet biplane powered with a 100-H.P. Kinner K-5, and a Fledgling, powered with a 184-H.P. Wright. Both ships are painted in the college colors with a large "K" in a white circle on either side of the fuselage.

The original airport was located southeast of Gambier just off Wiggin Street. After a year at that location Mr. Cummings purchased the land where the airport was until its abandonment in 1972. He then had the hangar moved to the new location and built another hangar and clubhouse.

On several occasions Mr. Cummings felt called upon to defend the establishment of a flying school at a college such as Kenyon. For example, in an article headlined "Aeronautics As A Liberal Art" in the *New York Times* for May 12, 1935 he is quoted:

42

I conceived the idea that any student who seriously wanted to fly should go at the matter in a thoroughgoing way and follow a ground-school course such as prescribed by the Department of Commerce for transport pilots. This course requires a total of 100 hours of classroom and laboratory work. This amounts to about three hours per week for the college year. The faculty felt that any student who took the course should receive an equivalent college credit. Such subjects as navigation, meteorology and aerodynamics are profound enough subjects to be placed in any liberal arts curriculum.

Intercollegiate competition in flying by Kenyon took the form of participation in the national intercollegiate air meets held all over the country. Teams from Kenyon held the national championship in 1937 and 1939, and tied with Stanford for first place in 1938. Other colleges and universities participating were Akron, California, Detroit, Duke, Harvard, Michigan, Minnesota, M.I.T., Ohio State, Pennsylvania, Smith, and Toronto. Kenyon also held the Eastern, Midwest and Ohio titles. Some of the point-getters in these meets included A. Rodney Boren (K1938), Clark L. Henderson (K1939), Robert H. Legg (K1939), William F. Lieurance (K1939) and C.D. Nichols (K1938). Nichols was reported to be the first student in the program to make a solo flight, and the first to get a pilot's license.

When World War II came, Gretzer went into the war effort and the school was discontinued. Port Kenyon, with its two hangars and clubhouse, continued to be used by the Kenyon Flying Club until the fall of 1972, when the college asked the Federal Aviation Administration to deactivate the airport, citing lack of activity by the Flying Club and the cost of insurance and maintenance as the reasons. Although the landing strips have been plowed up and are now planted in farm crops, memories of the School of Aeronautics are kept alive in the name of the lacrosse team's playing area — Airport Field, and the two abandoned hangars, now used for storage.

Riding and Polo

Perhaps the authorities were trying to establish the image of Kenyon students arriving in Gambier with airplanes and polo ponies, for the next step was horseback riding at Kenyon. At the meeting of June 16, 1934 the Board of Trustees resolved "that this Board approves the establishment of a School of

Equitation by Mr. R.A. Weaver with hearty thanks of the Board." The College provided the use of the old drill hall of the defunct military academy, but Mr. Weaver paid for all the other expenses including the services of an Instructor in Equitation. The man selected to direct the new school was Captain Frederic Eberle, a former officer in a German cavalry regiment who was detained in this country at the outbreak of World War I and who remained to attend Purdue and secure a degree in engineering. He had taught equitation at Culver Military Academy, and French and German at Lakewood High School. At Kenyon he taught also in the Modern Language Department, and stayed as a teacher of languages for many years after the School of Equitation had passed from the picture.

Polo game about 1937.

Within a few years Kenyon's polo teams attracted national attention, and were considered the Midwest indoor champions year after year, defeating such teams as Illinois,

44

Michigan, Ohio State, Culver Military Academy, and various private and National Guard teams. The last team, that of 1937-1938, was the first non-Eastern indoor polo team to participate in the championship tournament in New York. After defeating Cornell, the 1937 champions, twice in succession, Kenyon bowed to the highly favored and superbly mounted (12 ponies to 6 for Kenyon) Harvard trio in the semifinal.

Among the men who figured prominently in this brief golden age of polo at Kenyon were: Merlin E. Ake, Jr. (K1937), Geoffrey A. Cook (K1937), Frederic Eberle, Jr. (K1941), Robert J. McMahon (K1938), George G. Monroe III (K1936), John J. Sted (K1937), James G. Trainer (K1940), and Robert W. Tuttle (K1937).

The *Collegian* for September 19, 1938 reported that intercollegiate polo had been discontinued for lack of financial backing. The final vestige of Kenyon's School of Equitation disappeared in the school year 1968-1969 when the drill hall, by then known as the horse barn, was torn down. It had been located just south of the small pond between the houses at 208 and 212 North Acland Street.

Tennis

Tennis has traditionally been one of the most successful intercollegiate sports at Kenyon, but beginning in 1935 there was a strong effort to make Kenyon known nationally as a tennis power. Four new tennis courts adjacent to Benson Field were built in time for the 1936 season. Constructed by the Har-True Corporation, they were of the most modern design, and the *Collegian* said proudly that "they could be used immediately after a heavy rainstorm."

A great effort to attract tennis players must have been undertaken at this time, for entering in the fall of 1935 were four freshmen who were destined to put Kenyon in the tennis spotlight in short order. They were Morey Lewis, Donald McNeill, George Pryor, and Gordon Reeder. Since freshmen were not permitted to play in intercollegiate competition, they played under the name of the Gambier Tennis Club. They first burst onto the tennis scene as a group in the 1936 North and South tournament at the Pinehurst Country Club, exciting very favorable comments from the sports writers of the *New*

York Times. During the summer of 1936 the Gambier Tennis Club embarked on a crusade of the major tournaments of the East and the Midwest, covering seven states and in eleven cities. The first paragraph of the September 23, 1936 *Collegian* report on the summer's activities reads: "Led by Don McNeill and Morey Lewis, the Kenyon freshman racket wielders made tennis history during the summer when they captured 27 major championships, traveled approximately 8000 miles, and received newspaper notices in 40 states and the District of Columbia."

Thus began Kenyon's domination of Ohio and national tennis until the war years put a stop to intercollegiate athletics. McNeill was abroad playing in tournaments during the 1939 season, but came back for his final year and was graduated in 1940. It was during this season that he won the U.S. Clay Court title, beat Bobby Riggs for the national championship, and was ranked Number One by the U.S.L.T.A.

Coaching during this historic era of tennis at Kenyon were Eugene Lambert, Randall Jarrell (at a salary of $800 per year as an Instructor of English plus $200 as Director of Tennis), and Bruce Barnes.

The College sought to enhance further the image of Gambier as a tennis center by capitalizing on the publicity given the freshman tennis stars and the excellent new courts. In 1936 three tennis tournaments took place at Kenyon: the Ohio High School Invitational Tournament, the Ohio Intercollegiate Tournament, and the National Preparatory School Invitational Tournament. Added to all this activity was a Tennis Clinic for high school students held on April 28, 1936, in which the Kenyon stars acted as instructors.

Shaffer Pool—Swimming a New Sport at Kenyon

The announcement of a gift by an anonymous Kenyon alumnus of funds for the building of a swimming pool was made at Commencement in 1935. The donor was subsequently revealed as Charles B. Shaffer (K1883), a wealthy oil man residing in Chicago. Thus the way was paved for the development of an additional sport at Kenyon — one which has become legendary in its success.

Shaffer Pool

Swimming had been organized as an intramural activity a couple of years before by William H. Thomas, Jr. (K1936). Meets were held in the small "bath tub" sized pool at the old Y.M.C.A. in Mount Vernon. As the school year 1935-1936 progressed a varsity swimming team was organized, and in anticipation of the completion of the Kenyon pool during the winter, practice sessions went on in Mount Vernon coached by Paul Snyder, an instructor in Mount Vernon High School.

On January 11, 1936 Shaffer pool was dedicated and on February 19 the swimmers took on Denison in the first swimming meet ever held at Kenyon. It was an auspicious beginning, with Kenyon beating the Big Red soundly 69 - 21. In addition to Captain Thomas, the other point winners in this historic first meeting were Frank R. Ditmars (K1938), Cecil Durbin (K1938), George W. Eagon (K1938), John G. Long (K1938), Thomas Stewart Matthews (K1938), Paul T. Milliken (K1937), James K. Patterson (K1938), Henry V. Sebach (K1938), Richard L. Shorkey (K1938) and Carl A. Weiant, Jr. (K1937).

The team participated in two other meets that first year, defeating Wittenberg 69 - 27, and being nosed out by Wooster 48 - 45.

The next year Charles C. Imel joined the Kenyon athletic department as the first regular swimming coach. His 1938 team was undefeated and became the Ohio Conference Champions, starting a string of four straight championships which ended with a close defeat by Wooster in 1942. In 1954 the team coached by Robert Bartels started another string of Ohio Conference Championships which swept through the Fifties, Sixties and into the Seventies. The coaches succeeding Bartels during this domination were Thomas J. Edwards, Richard W. Russell, and Richard H. Sloan.

Shaffer Pool was built at a cost of $35,000, a figure which former Coach (now Dean of Students) Edwards has remarked, "wouldn't dig the hole today." It has stood up well under the hard usage given it over the years, and represents one of the best investments the college has ever made.

Deans at Kenyon

Among American colleges, Kenyon was probably the last to appoint a Dean. Dr. Clarence P. Gould came from Western Reserve University to become the first holder of that office in September 1933. The immediate purpose was to lighten President Peirce's administrative burden, but in addition the new Dean took over the duties of Registrar and was also listed as Professor of English History.

At the same time the Board of Trustees decided upon the appointment of an Assistant Dean for the important work of establishing relations with teachers and students of high and preparatory schools. After much consideration the decision was reached that only a Kenyon man could qualify for the position and George B. Schaffer (K1926) was selected. It appears that Mr. Schaffer became the first Director of Admissions.

Upon the resignation of Dean Gould in 1938, Dr. Gilbert T. Hoag came from Amherst to become the next Dean. He left in 1945 to become Dean of Haverford College.

The Honor System

An editorial in the December 16, 1932 *Collegian* begins:

> With a change in the method of conducting examinations, Kenyon has seen fit to do away with an institution in which she has taken just pride for thirty years. The successful use of the Honor System has been one of Kenyon's distinctive features, and the necessity of recognizing its failure leaves a great many people with a feeling of enormous loss.

The original petition for the establishment of the Honor System in 1903 was made by the student body to the Faculty in response to a proposed change in the examination system, and read, in part:

> We do respectfully petition your honorable body that you will at once, not only reconsider the action you have taken, but that you will furthermore adopt the only system of examinations which is consistent with our honor and our pride in our Alma Mater, namely the "honor system": and
>
> We do solemnly pledge ourselves if the "honor system" is introduced to support that system to the utmost of our ability, and not only to act ourselves in accordance with what we conscientiously believe to be its spirit, but to encourage others to do the same.

The 1932 editorial concludes:

> This petition, and original statement of the conception of the Honor System, requires no comment. In 1903 the student body felt the need of the system, earnestly desired its adoption, and felt capable of upholding it if it should be introduced. In 1932 student opinion is that it has outlived its usefulness, and that regard for it has become so weak that efficient maintenance of the system is no longer possible.
>
> With the February examinations the proctor system will be introduced, with all the unpleasantness that goes with such a method of conducting examinations. All the liberties that in the past have been so pleasant will be restricted, and instead of the former freedom we shall be writing under the watchful eye of members of the faculty. But we have no cause for complaint. The change has been brought about by ourselves, by an admission of our own weaknesses. Our only course of action is submission to the inevitable, with the hope that when the trial period of the proctorship is over, we shall find it both desirable and possible to again adopt the Honor System.

Compulsory Chapel

The minutes of the Board of Trustees meeting on June 17, 1933 show a resolution which told the beginning of the end of another old Kenyon tradition:

> Resolved that compulsory attendance at daily chapel and Sundays be reduced to fifty per cent for the coming year and that the question of future compulsory chapel attendance at daily chapel and Sundays be referred to Bishops Rogers and Hobson for recommendation at the next annual meeting.

Revolt against compulsory chapel probably began on the day the College was founded and waxed and waned all through the years. From the very beginning attendance at chapel services had been compulsory. In the early days two services a day were held, and there were very strict regulations requiring attendance. Gradually the requirements were relaxed until by the Twenties there was one daily chapel service at 7:45 a.m. lasting for fifteen minutes and the regular Sunday morning service. The regulations permitted 35 chapel cuts per semester. However, there were double cuts on Sundays with a maximum of twelve Sunday cuts, and double cuts on the days immediately before and after vacations. Overcutting chapel was considered one of the most serious offenses in the college book of rules, and subjected the transgressor to immediate dismissal from college, a fate from which an appeal was rarely successful.

The students sat in the nave of the Chapel. Seats were assigned at the beginning of each year according to classes and the alphabet. At precisely the moment of the beginning of the service the north door was closed by the student monitor, who then proceeded to take attendance. From time to time dark suspicions arose that the monitor could be corrupted in his attendance figures. On Mondays a Chapel List was posted. Each student's name was followed by a figure showing his chapel cut status. For example, 8/24 meant that he had 24 total cuts of which 8 were Sunday cuts.

The daily morning service opened with the singing of a hymn, followed by prayers, the reading of the Lesson, announcements, and closed with another hymn. The announcements were sometimes of a seasonal nature. Every March

President Peirce would admonish the students not to "cut incipient paths across the greensward." Most students adopted a resigned and irreverent attitude toward the early morning service. Some slept, while others used the time to prepare for their 8 a.m. classes. A few men used up all of their chapel cuts immediately and then relied upon their friends to cajole them out of bed and down the Path to the Chapel. Some fraternity pledges were saddled with the task of getting upperclassmen out of bed, throwing on coats over their pajamas, getting them into cars, driving them to the Chapel, putting them in their seats, collecting them after the service, and taking them back to bed. It was said that sometimes there was no recollection of ever being out of bed.

Occasionally there were diversions — once or twice everyone wore bathrobes to the morning service; and sometimes the music was not up to par because several of the organ pipes had been removed and hidden in the gravel pit. However, most of these early services were quiet, contemplative periods which were at least a cohesive force for the College and served as a tranquil beginning for the day's work.

The Sunday services were much more lively, since they were held late in the morning and most of the students were wide awake by that time. President Peirce preached many of the sermons himself and they were masterpieces of composition and oratory. After croaking through the hymns in desultory fashion during the week the choir came alive and burst forth in full voice on Sundays. Egged on by his friends, Organist and Choir Leader G. Russel Hargate (K1930) once performed "Tea For Two" as an offertory solo, so embellishing the piece that only those in on the rendition knew what was going on. Then, too, the presence of the Harcourt girls in the balcony helped to enliven the Sunday service.

The real moments of drama on Sunday came with the passing of the collection plate during the offertory. Professor Allen was in charge of this activity, and although he kept an eagle eye on the plate as it was passed from hand to hand, somehow Lifesavers or other circular objects always seemed to find their way into the plates before they were borne up to the altar. Once or twice a year the word was passed that the next Sunday would be Penny Sunday. Everyone saved pennies and deposited them in the collection plates, with the result that Dr. Allen and his helpers staggered under the weight of the piled up coins, and pennies fell off the overflowing plates and went clanking all over the floor.

In 1935, just two years after compulsory chapel had been reduced to 50% attendance, daily morning chapel was discontinued. Students were still required to attend one-half of the Sunday services. The final chapter to compulsory chapel was a statement by President Lund in the *Collegian* for March 2, 1960:

> Convinced that religion should never be co-erced and that a true spirit of worship can only be voluntary and free, the Board of Trustees voted unanimously on February 27, to revoke any regulations at Kenyon College requiring compulsory church attendance. Effective this date, chapel attendance will be free.
>
> Kenyon College, however, remains staunchly and proudly a college within the communion of the Protestant Episcopal Church for this step is taken not to repudiate our birthright, but to encourage a more positive and forthright witness to our convictions that human dignity and human freedom alike can survive only where is a religious perception of Divine compassion.

Hika

In 1935 *Hika*, a Kenyon literary magazine, was founded by John C. Neff (K1936), who became the first editor. Much time has been spent in trying to find the origin of the word "Hika," but the consensus is that it is a meaningless word used in Kenyon cheers and appears to be unique on this campus.

The first issues of the magazine were unpretentious in content, consisting mainly of Kenyon sketches, anecdotes and jokes, but as time went on the literary makeup improved markedly. Neff was succeeded by David W. Jasper, Jr. (K1938) and in October 1938 David U. McDowell (K1940) became editor.

McDowell had an exceptionally fine staff, which included Robert T.S. Lowell, Jr. (K1940), Peter H. Taylor (K1940) and Robie Macauley (K1940), and his first issue left no doubt that a drastic change of policy had resulted in a new and serious magazine. The publication grew in fame to the point where it attracted contributors from outside the Gambier community, among them W.H. Auden, William Carlos Williams, Ezra

Pound and Andrew Lytle. Pieces by members of the faculty, including Professor Ransom, and other writers in the community appeared regularly along with the student contributions.

Hika was printed for most of its early issues on slick paper, with a surprising number of national advertisements, some in full color, interspersed with local ads. The first issues ran about 25 pages; rarely were there more than 30.

In the spring of 1942 the *Collegian* ceased publication and merged with *Hika* for a few issues. In February 1943 *Hika* alone was published, and this was the last number until publication was revived in October 1946. Since that time *Hika* has been published more or less continuously. Creative photography and drawings have been added, and the publication has become distinguished by its informality and impulsiveness, reflecting the many changes of viewpoint and format brought in by the rapidly changing boards of editors.

Harcourt Place School For Girls

Closing of Harcourt Place School

As the school year 1935-1936 ended, a cherished Gambier institution closed its doors and the old Kenyon song
"So here's to the health of Old Kenyon
And the Harcourt girls so dear!"

soon ceased to have meaning. Harcourt Place School, a resident school for girls, had fallen the victim of the depression.

Opened in 1887, on the grounds of an earlier Harcourt School for boys started in 1852, Harcourt soon became a popular girls' institution of the finishing school type. Although the curriculum was that of a secondary school, many of the girls were older than the average high school student, since families frequently sent girls to schools such as Harcourt for a year after graduation from high or preparatory schools and then on to college.

The original building was McIlvaine Hall, a residence built by Bishop McIlvaine in 1833. Soon Lewis and Delano Halls, large four story brick structures, were built just south of McIlvaine and the three buildings were connected by means of walkways on the second and third floors. The whole complex was situated about where the freshman dormitories were later built and extended northward toward where Watson Hall now stands. At the time of this writing the steps leading to the school from Chase Avenue still exist.

The girls were not permitted to leave the school grounds without a chaperon, but the Harcourt authorities made great efforts to provide a social life for their students, arranging teas, dances, concerts and plays to attract Kenyon students to the gloomy old buildings. The September 23, 1936 *Collegian* lamented the passing of Harcourt:

> The visits ranged in nature from social calls on the head mistresses to stealthy visits via the fire escape. Kenyonites were entertained by the inmates at affairs ranging from formal dances to tete-a-tetes in the orchard.
>
> The last party was given early in June for the Kenyon French Club. The club now have the sentimental memory of having attended a history-making affair. To celebrate the occasion, the guests were allowed to remain until one-thirty in the morning — something unprecedented in Harcourt history. Very much according to custom, however, was the almost universal failure of attempts to abduct the fair hostesses.

On Sundays the girls paraded down the Middle Path to the Chapel, marching in twos, with their eyes straight ahead, but not missing anything in a 360 degree arc. During the service they were seated in the balcony, and one of the inducements for Kenyon men to sing in the choir was that the singers had the best view of the balcony.

During its most prosperous days the school had an enrollment of up to 60, of which about 20% were day students, the daughters of the faculty or other residents of the nearby area. For the first part of the period of this book the headmistress was Miss Harriette Merwin, irreverently known to Kenyon students as "Hank." The last head was Miss Sarah Bedell Mac-Donald. After the closing of the school the College took over the Harcourt property, and in 1937 tore down Lewis and Delano Halls. McIlvaine Hall continued to be used as a faculty dwelling, dormitory, and storehouse until it was demolished in 1956 to make way for the building of Watson Hall.

College Seal

Early in Kenyon history an official seal of the College was adopted with a design which included a book, a scroll, and crosses. Sometime in the early years of the 20th century the attractive seal which is now official began to be used. It is an adaptation of the Kenyon family arms and includes the Kenyon family motto, *Magnamiter Crucem Sustine* ("Valiantly Bear The Cross"). However, it was not until 1937 that the Trustees finally adopted this as the official college seal.

Honors Program

The first mention of the Honors Program was in the College Catalogue for 1935-1936: "Honors work is designed for students of high standing and unusual ability who wish to devote the last two years of their college course to some subject in which they have a particular interest. A program of honors work was begun in 1934 with a few members of the present junior and senior classes. It is still in the experimental stage."

Preparation for the program began during the school year 1933-1934 when a faculty team headed by Professor Titus visited Swarthmore College to study the program which had been so successful there. The 1937 Commencement was the first to recognize graduation with honors, with 17 men receiving this distinction out of a graduating class of 50. After this initial surge the number reading for honors dropped to the point where honors were awarded to about 10% of the graduates. The program was not pursued during the World War II years, but once the College was back to normal the figure rose to about 20%, and has continued at roughly that figure.

Professors Timberlake and Coffin

Two faculty members who were the backbone of the English Department during these troubled years were Professors Timberlake and Coffin. Philip Wolcott Timberlake (K1917) taught at Kenyon from 1926 until his death in 1957 at the age of 61. In his student days he was the editor of the *Collegian* and the *Reveille,* and was one of the founders of the Lambda Chapter of the Sigma Pi fraternity. After service in World War I he taught in a high school for two years, then turned to graduate work at Princeton, where he received his Ph.D. in 1926. His entire teaching career from then on was at Kenyon; at the time of his death he held the McIlvaine Chair of English and was Chairman of the Department.

At his death a friend and former student, Pulitzer Prize Poet James A. Wright (K1952), wrote a tribute to him which was published in the Summer 1957 issue of the *Alumni Bulletin*:

So now fierce, beautiful Philip Timberlake is dead. His contemporaries and colleagues may wonder at the words I use to describe him. It is true that he was the most gentle and the most sad of men. But when I call him fierce and beautiful, I am speaking as his student. Everybody will agree that to hear him conduct a class in one of the great poets was to have an experience that one is not likely to forget this side of the grave. It is difficult to describe that experience, as it is difficult to contend by means of language with any miraculous combination of love and intellect; but at least I can say that his reading and teaching of the great poets was both beautiful and fierce.

Mr. Timberlake published very little in the way of formal scholarship, though he was deeply learned. He belonged to two or three associations of Shakespearean scholars. He always knew what they were doing. He had the humorist's ability to sift out the fools among the Shakespeareans, and anyone who has ever read through much Shakespearean scholarship will realize that without a sense of humor one is doomed to be strangled alive by human imbecility. But Mr. Timberlake devoted his extraordinary skills almost wholly to teaching. To imagine him dominated by the rats of mechanically regular publication is impossible. He was not dominated by any foolishness in the world, academic or otherwise.

Least of all was he tyrannized by time. Several years ago a few friends and I were living with him in a big three-story house in the Gambier woods. Some of us were studying Anglo-Saxon, and Mr. Timberlake was the teacher. Well, he gave us the grammar, and he gave us *Beowulf*, and he gave us the great short poems. But the greatest thing he gave us was the feeling that we could read the old language, and thrash out its syntactical problems, and love its poetry whenever we felt like doing so . . . He taught us, in short, that Kenyon was not a series of schedules pedantically adhered to. He taught us that the soul must be disciplined, and that, unless discipline comes from within, it is worthless.

Charles Monroe Coffin joined the Department of English in 1927. Except for a couple of years while he was studying for his doctorate and two years service as a lieutenant commander in the Navy, his service at Kenyon was continuous until his sudden death in 1956. The team of Reeves, Timberlake, and Coffin *was* the Department of English during most of the Thirties.

He was the author of *John Donne and the New Philosophy*, a definitive work on Donne first published in 1937, but which has been in continuous demand.

Mr. Coffin was the Dean of the Kenyon School of English which brought to Gambier so many outstanding scholars and writers and which achieved attention and recognition in English-speaking countries all over the world.

His friend and colleague, Philip W. Timberlake gave a eulogy of him at the first faculty meeting in September 1956:

> Among us all, Charles Coffin was pre-eminent for the unusual breadth of his goodness and his intelligence.
>
> His was a rare gift for friendship. He had more and faster friends than is common for a busy college professor, and they were equally among the faculty, the students, the trustees, and the alumni; just as he was acquainted more widely with the village people of Gambier, or with the scholars of his profession elsewhere in this State or in the nation at large. He was quick to present himself to those who were sick, or in distress, but his good company was tonic to his friends even at their best. Kindness and steadfastness were native to him, and we would add that he renewed them continually in his faithful attendance upon divine service in the College Chapel.
>
> Charles Coffin's mind was as wide as it was searching. Eminent scholars knew him and honored his books. The most profound and concentrated pursuit was cut short while he was reading in a great library

on the other side of the continent. But here at Kenyon in all its history there cannot have been many professors who were familiar with so many books in the College library. His reading ranged far, as did those casual talks which he was always initiating or entering into.

The goodness of Charles Coffin's heart and the strength of his mind were dedicated to the vocation of being a teacher who never proposed to stop being a student or a man. As we ponder now the many years of his life among us, it is easy to take the strong impression that this was the perfect college professor, insofar as we dare to speak of such a reach in human attainment.

Professor McGowan

Certainly one of the most protean members of the faculty was Stuart Rice McGowan, whose association with the College spans the time from his entrance as a freshman in 1924 through his retirement to emeritus status in 1971. The many hats which he wore included those of assistant to the president, instructor, assistant professor, associate professor, professor, registrar, dean of students, chairman of the Department of Political Science, besides being the registrar of all the special schools, such as the Kenyon School of English. In addition to his administrative duties he insisted on carrying on with his teaching, first in history and later in political science when it became a separate department.

In October 1933 Professor McGowan was a witness to an event which helped to enliven the dreary depression days — the robbery of the Peoples Bank by an offshoot of the Dillinger Gang. As the robbers burst out of the front door of the bank taking with them Banker Ray Brown as a hostage, they loosed a volley of pistol shots in the general direction of the Middle Path to intimidate the spectators. It happened that Mr. Mc-Gowan was almost directly in front of the bank at this time, and it is said that his attempts to hide his 250 pound bulk behind a small tree on the Path were a lesson in futility.

Professor McGowan was one of the few staff members recalled by Jonathan Winters, the fine comedian who had a brief and disastrous career at Kenyon just after World War II. Speaking on national television of his experiences at Kenyon he ended with, "Give my regards to Stu Magoo and Psycho Sam (Professor Samuel B. Cummings)."

At his retirement Mr. McGowan was presented with the degree of Doctor of Laws by Kenyon. His citation read, in part:

> As a teacher, students have sought you out, appreciated your versatile instruction in both History and Political Science, and enjoyed your good-humored banter both in and out of the classroom. When President of the Ohio Athletic Conference, you strongly resisted overemphasis of intercollegiate athletics in Ohio colleges. As a one-time activist in the political party of your choice, you sought, in vain, to woo Knox County voters into the Democratic Party. You have taught us, administered us and smoothed the way for us over the years.

Professor Cahall

Another Kenyon graduate who spent a lifetime of teaching at the College was Raymond DuBois Cahall (K1908). Except for his doctoral studies at Columbia and brief periods of teaching at both Miami and Ohio State Universities, his residence in Gambier was continuous from his arrival as a freshman until his death in 1964. His courses in political science and history were aimed at "teaching the details of the emerging world responsibilities of our country."

Dr. Cahall was a member of the local chapter of Phi Beta Kappa and maintained a deep interest in the affairs of this fraternity. He wrote several articles on the history of the chapter and was regarded as the local authority on its procedures. Dr. and Mrs. Cahall added a complete wing on the south side of their college residence, Sunset Cottage, making it one of the most beautiful homes in Gambier. Here they entertained quite extensively; it was always a great privilege for students to be invited for an evening with the Cahalls. They were especially attentive to the members of Dr. Cahall's social fraternity, Beta Theta Pi.

Upon his retirement from Kenyon in 1953 after 38 years of service, the College honored Professor Cahall with the degree of Doctor of Humane Letters. In the opening words of the degree's citation an assessment of him and a tribute is found: "His early promise at Kenyon College has been amply fulfilled in nearly four decades of teaching and active participation in the life of the college and the community."

On February 29, 1964 the following resolution was passed:

> We, the Trustees of Kenyon College, honor the memory of Raymond DuBois Cahall, a faithful and distinguished son of Kenyon, and dedicated teacher at this College for nearly forty years. As an undergraduate he distinguished himself by leading the choir and the glee club and by his academic excellence and election to Phi Beta Kappa. Memorable to hundreds of students were his courses in the French Revolution and Napoleon, European Intellectual History, and International Relations. His writings in scholarly journals and magazines of public opinion illuminated historical problems and the current issues of the day. In the passing of Raymond Cahall, Kenyon College and the Gambier community have lost a beloved alumnus, teacher, scholar, and friend.

Professor Ashford

Professor William Ray Ashford of the Modern Language Department was affectionately known to most Kenyon students as "Fauncey" Ashford or "Daisy" Ashford. The nickname "Fauncey" is attributed to his favorite expression, "Fancy that!" A fussy little man, with an amused twinkle in his eye, to many Kenyon men and his fellow teachers he became an old, familiar, and cherished companion. He arrived in Gambier in 1924 and during the 30 years of his career at Kenyon he gained the respect and affection of his students and his colleagues through his unfailing interest in their welfare. His love for Kenyon led him to become very familiar with the history of the College, and the many anecdotes and other memorabilia which he wrote and collected are valuable archival pieces. He was an inveterate theater buff, and upon his death in 1954 his treasured scrapbooks of theatrical performances at Kenyon came to the Kenyon Archives.

Dr. Ashford's relationship to the Iota Chapter of Psi Upsilon was an outstanding example of cooperation between members of the faculty and the fraternities. Although he was not a member of Psi Upsilon in his student days, early in his teaching career he was "adopted" by the Iota Chapter and became the guardian and caretaker of this group, especially during the early disturbing days of World War II when the fate of all of the fraternities was in balance.

Science Faculty

During most of the Thirties science instruction in the newly-built and well-equipped Samuel Mather Science Hall was in the capable hands of Professors Lee B. Walton in biology, Elbe H. Johnson in physics, and Walter H. Coolidge (K1912) in chemistry. Professors Charles B. Rutenber and Casper L. Cottrell were added in chemistry and physics in 1928, but their services were lost to the College during the drastic cuts in personnel early in the depression.

"Bugs" Walton came to Kenyon immediately after receiving his Ph.D. at Cornell in 1902. He served the college until his death in 1937 at the age of 65. His specialized interest in biology was in the organisms occurring in water supplies, but his interests were varied — not confined to his biological work — and he was particularly engrossed with outdoor sports for young people. He contended that "more of that kind of emphasis would keep young people in proper condition morally as well as physically." He was a great believer in play as well as work and was very much involved with athletics at Kenyon. Along with Professor Reeves, he was instrumental in organizing the Ohio Conference and was for many years the faculty manager of athletics at Kenyon. Upon his death Professor Charles S. Thornton became the mainstay of the Biology Department.

Professor Johnson arrived at Kenyon in 1914, and was a loyal member of the Kenyon academic community until his retirement in 1955. Early in his teaching career he recognized that there was much in the study of physics which could contribute to a liberal arts education; the content of his courses reflected that conviction, and one of his favorite courses, *History of Physics*, was designed specifically for the non-science student. At the time of his retirement the College awarded him the degree of Doctor of Science. President Chalmers in his citation described Dr. Johnson as having "participated by his writing, teaching, and leadership in the cultivation of the understanding of science as a characteristic and proper human pursuit." At the time of his death in 1967 the Board of Trustees honored him "for his role in expanding the science laboratory from small quarters in Ascension Hall to the Samuel Mather

Science Hall, built largely through his efforts and under his close supervision."

Professor Johnson was also deeply involved in the hobby of horology; his collection of clocks and watches was quite extensive, and he was considered an authority on time instruments.

The third member of this science faculty was Dr. Coolidge. He went directly from graduation from Kenyon in 1912 to graduate studies in chemistry at Johns Hopkins, where he received his Ph.D. in 1915. He was head of the chemistry department at Centre College in Kentucky until 1924, when he and Professor George F. Weida, his teacher at Kenyon, changed places, with Weida going to Centre and Coolidge coming to Kenyon, where he remained until his death in 1950. In addition to being a highly respected and beloved teacher of chemistry, Dr. Coolidge was an accomplished organist, and regularly played the organ in the Chapel when the student organist was not available.

Social Life

The coming of the Thirties brought only a few changes in the social living patterns of the students. The full use of Peirce Hall provided the College with excellent dining facilities and gave the students lounges in which to entertain their visitors outside of the divisions. Rosse Hall had been used for dances for many years, but it was a gloomy place even when clothed in elaborate decorations, and moving the dances to Peirce Hall added greatly to the enjoyment of the two big social occasions of the year, the Fall Dance and the May Hop (the term "Hop" seems to have been dropped about 1935; afterwards the usual name given was the May Dance or the Spring Dance).

During the depths of the depression it was difficult to raise the money to hire well-known bands for the dances, but by the end of the decade some of the bigger names in the musical world appeared in Gambier: Red Nichols (twice), Ted Lewis, Buddy Rogers, and Glen Gray and the Casa Loma Orchestra.

It may have been hard sledding for the fraternities to stay in operation at this time, but there is no indication that any of them were in danger of folding up. There was very little extra cash, but prices went down, dues were reduced, credit was extended, and expenses were cut. All of the fraternities emerged from the depression with their charters intact.

With the end of Prohibition, the drinking habits of the Kenyon students appear to have changed; the consumption of hard liquor went down, beer drinking increased. The *Collegian* for October 12, 1933 announced that beer was now allowed on the campus, and on the Sunday before Christmas vacation that year there was a turkey dinner in Peirce Hall with beer served for the first time.

Resignation of President Peirce

The college year 1936-1937 saw the departure of many of the faculty stalwarts: Professors Lord, Radford and Walton died; Professor West, Professor Manning and President Peirce retired. The Trustees' Minutes for June 13, 1936 record that:

> President Peirce advised the Board that he was submitting his Fortieth Annual Report as President of Kenyon College, and there are only three college presidents in the United States who have served as long as he; that the student enrollment during his term of office has increased from 65 to 228, and the faculty from 8 to 28; that the income from the college students has increased from less than $3,000 to about $99,000 and the assets of the corporation from $587,000 to over $3,650,000, and that after such a long period of service he desired to notify the Board of Trustees that he would like to retire from active duty at the end of the coming college year and receive leave of absence on salary until February 1938, when he will be seventy years of age and eligible for retirement.

This was amended slightly at the Trustees meeting on May 1, 1937:

> President Peirce stated that he felt his successor would have a more free hand and be better able to function if he were given the title of President rather than that of Acting President until February 1938, to which date the Board has already given President Peirce leave of absence pursuant to his request and that accordingly he desired to present his resignation at this meeting to become effective July 1, 1937.

This suggestion was passed by the Board and pay and retirement benefits to February 1938 were granted Dr. Peirce.

Dr. Peirce's last graduating class was the Class of 1937. The *Collegian* for June 12, 1937 presented an editorial:

> Next Monday the Class of '37 graduates. With them will go also the man who has served Kenyon for forty-one years as President. As he puts it, he's graduating also. Yes, Fat's graduating. He's leaving the Hill which he loves so well, and he's leaving a Hill that loves him just as dearly.
>
> Outwardly we have only a few marked remembrances of Fat. There's the Commons, it's named for him. There's his likeness in oil hanging in the Great Hall, no name is needed under it, for we know him well. Then there's the splendid bronze bust given the College by the Senior Class of '37, it seems so much alive — it might speak. These we claim are the outward signs of Dr. Peirce's endearment to Kenyon. But just as the blades of grass and the old trees on the Hill recall Philander Chase to the Kenyon man's mind, so does each structure on Kenyon's Hill recall President Peirce.
>
> It's with great difficulty on this week-end of great celebration which is nevertheless mingled with sadness that we find words to express our feeling and Kenyon's to William Foster Peirce. Words beyond our vocabulary, phrases beyond our ability to harmonize in sentences and paragraphs are being uttered this week-end in tribute to him.
>
> We can simply say that we, too, love him. To him, we dedicate this issue of *The Collegian* — This is Fat's issue.

The main reason for Dr. Peirce's resignation was doubtless his age; he was sixty-nine at the time of his retirement. However, Kenyon was still recovering from its desperate financial straits of the early Thirties, and he may have felt that he lacked the confidence of the trustees that he still had the innovative leadership needed to extricate the College from its difficulties. Then, too, there were personal problems. Mrs. Peirce and he separated in 1933 after 42 years of marriage, and on May 29, 1934 she brought suit for divorce, charging cruelty and neglect. Charges and countercharges flew back and forth across the courtroom prolonging the procedure, but finally on March 2, 1937 Mrs. Peirce was granted a divorce. Since Kenyon was at that time a church-related college, and since the Episcopal Church frowned upon divorce, this decree may possibly have affected Dr. Peirce's decision to resign.

Shortly after leaving Kenyon he married Mrs. Edith Calvert Bruce on July 7, 1937, and moved to an estate called Ladybird Forest, near Bel Air, Maryland, where he died in 1967 at the age of ninety-nine. Upon the death of his widow in 1972, his entire estate, except for a few minor bequests, came to Kenyon College.

Selection of President Chalmers

The machinery for presidential selection had grown rusty after forty-one years of disuse, but fortunately President Peirce had given a whole year's notice and the trustees had plenty of time to get the mechanism oiled up and in good working order.

It is obvious from reading the qualifications which the trustees specified in their search for a new president that they knew exactly what they wanted. They wanted another young and vigorous "Fat" Peirce who would lead the college for another forty-one years. So deeply engraved was the Peirce stamp on the image of the presidency that they felt obliged to explain that the choice was not limited to clergymen or even Episcopalians, that Peirce had been neither when he came to Kenyon.

Although over seventy candidates were considered, the selection quickly narrowed to the man who became the next president, Gordon Keith Chalmers. At the time of his selection Dr. Chalmers was president of Rockford College, Rockford, Illinois. He was 33 years of age. He was graduated from Brown University in 1925, was a Rhodes Scholar at Oxford for three years, obtaining his Master's degree there in 1928. He received his Ph.D. at Harvard in 1933. From 1929 to 1933 he was an instructor of English at Mt. Holyoke College, was promoted to the rank of assistant professor in 1933, and was elected president of Rockford College in 1934. He was the author of a number of articles on 17th century thought and letters and on the subject of education. Mrs. Chalmers was described at that time by President Wriston of Brown University as "a most charming person and a poet of some ability." She was also a teacher at Mt. Holyoke.

On April 1, 1937 Wilbur L. Cummings, who was chairman of the committee for the selection of the new president, wrote a letter to Dr. Chalmers beginning: "You have asked me to write a letter setting forth what the Trustees have in mind for

Kenyon College. I believe that you are entitled to such a letter as a definition of our purpose and as an assurance of our support if you are to undertake that purpose for us." The body of the letter is such a clear and concise position statement that it is worth quoting almost in its entirety:

Kenyon College has a history of which we are all proud, and we believe justly so. It is a history of struggle, almost romantic in its beginnings. If the founder of Kenyon did not leave it with much in the way of material wealth he did leave it with a wealth of tradition even more valuable. His courage and struggles have made him a heroic figure in the minds of Kenyon men, and his example must have been an unconscious inspiration to many a young Kenyon man worth more to him than learning. I believe it is some of that same determination of the old founder lingering about the place and reappearing now in our determination to make Kenyon a leading place of learning. We believe that we can do this. In any event, we are going to try.

Kenyon College, fortunately, has never had a benefactor of such munificence as to offer to rebuild it overnight, or with the temerity to suggest that it change its name. It has taken 115 years to put it together, and every gift that has helped has come from the heart and in the belief in Kenyon's future. The job is not yet done, but no serious mistakes have been made and the result to date is good to look at. But Kenyon has had hard luck. I'm not complaining, but I believe that it has had more than its share. Drawing largely from the South, it almost had to close its doors after the Civil War. It did have to start over again. And then, as other colleges grew up around it in large numbers, its dignity and idealism held it aloof from their methods of competition, either to obtain students or endowments. Particularly as regards the latter, it did not try to organize its church affiliation or ballyhoo a religious appeal for aid. That it refused to do these things is not its hard luck, but that others did. Kenyon still has her ideals and we are now determined to find out whether they are worth while.

Kenyon was doubly hard hit by the depression. It had only two sources of income, its endowment and its students. Never having appealed for public aid or even to its Church, and not wishing to do so, it had to live within its income. Many of its investments were of a character which, while time has proven them sound, suffered from an abrupt and heavy drop in return. At the same time, Kenyon suffered a severe loss of students to her neighbors who were making an appeal to the utilitarian psychology of the times, that state of mind which felt it could not afford the time to get something worth while but must get something quickly which it could use. The utilitarian in education has never appealed to Kenyon and never will.

In the contingency which arose there seemed to be but one thing to do. It was no time to try for largely increased enrollment. The small

66

stream which constantly flowed in was not entirely choked but could have been greatly expanded. Efforts were accordingly bent to increase student attendance. Here Kenyon became practical but not undignified. She appraised herself and her neighbors. Whatever her claims were, others were making the same claims, however justifiably. Tradition, scenic beauty, ivy-covered halls of learning, distinguished alumni, the close association of faculty with students, etc. were all rolled into every package, and the package could only be distinguished by the college colors. And many reduced the price of the package. The kind of thing that Kenyon had over all the rest would have been vulgarized by overemphasis or advertising. In the stress of material considerations our pride in our English ancestry and traditions became, in the eyes of others, mere imitation and was used against us. We were snobs. Perhaps, in truth, we were, but if so, we are and always will be.

I say we appraised ourselves. In doing so we concluded that our goods, while slightly shopworn, were still wholesome. Accordingly, our educational plan was rejuvenated, but with the idea of strengthening, not popularizing it. But as boys who study also want to play, and play well, our greatest handicap was our size. Too much attention had been given to those sports in which by the very nature of things we could not excel. With the two-fold idea of providing more diversified recreation for the boys we had and to attract others to come to Kenyon, we turned our attention to other forms of sport. Our ever-devoted alumni quickly provided the means. The finest daylight swimming pool in the State was built and the finest battery of hard surface tennis courts. Horsemanship and aeronautics were also added, and the best of instructors in all four of these sports soon put Kenyon teams among the leading teams of the country. As Kenyon's reputation began to spread and the interest of prospective students quickened, our methods of approaching them were also reorganized. The result of four years of effort is a college full to overflowing.

We are now ready for the next and more important step, and with the retirement of President Peirce we are looking for new leadership. That next step is the raising of our standards of scholarship. To some extent it will be taken this year in the raising of our entrance requirements and a more careful selection of incoming student personnel. We are at last in a position where we can be selective. We are not diminishing our efforts to attract students, but indeed are increasing them, for we want the opportunity to be still more selective. But we realize that hand in hand with better selection must go better instruction. We not only want the best men to come to Kenyon but we want to educate them better. We want a reputation for scholarship which itself will attract the best men to Kenyon. We cannot take this step without proper leadership. We need someone to show us the way. To the man who can do so we pledge our loyal support.

I emphasize the word "support." We do not expect the man we select to do the job single-handed and alone. And yet we do not expect

67

to intrude our counsel and advice in the very matter in which we expect him to counsel and advise us. We will select him because we believe he can do for Kenyon what we want done, and we will give him all the help he calls for within our ability to help. But the job we want done is outside our knowledge and experience, and we can only cooperate. Our admission that scholarship at Kenyon is not what it should be and our assurance that we want it raised to the equal of any, is both the confession of a fault and a pledge to correct it. We realize the difficulties that may be ahead, but we are ready to share the responsibility of solving them.

At the trustees meeting of May 1, 1937 Dr. Gordon Keith Chalmers was elected President of Kenyon College at a salary of eleven thousand dollars per year.

The *Kenyon College Bulletin*, No. 153, May 1938 stated:

Gordon Keith Chalmers was formally installed as the sixteenth (actually the thirteenth; this figure included three acting presidents) President of Kenyon College on October 23, 1937. The official ceremony of induction was performed in Rosse Hall by Bishop Henry Wise Hobson, Chairman for the year of the Board of Trustees, in the presence of the Kenyon trustees, the Kenyon and Bexley faculties, Kenyon students, representatives of 127 colleges and universities, and representatives of schools, academies, and learned societies.

The *Collegian* for October 20, 1937 commented on the inauguration:

Amid one hundred and thirteen years of tradition, Kenyon College inaugurates her sixteenth president, Gordon Keith Chalmers. Dr. Chalmers comes to the "opportunity of the midwest" a young man with an outstanding record behind him. He heads one of the youngest college faculties in the country, their average age is thirty-five. Yet, the older men of the faculty, although not as young in years, are young in spirit. It is this youthful spirit, this progressive spirit, which President Chalmers will inspire.

Great things are expected of youth — "youth is the opportunity to do something and to become somebody." At Kenyon, President Chalmers has all the facilities to achieve those opportunities to which we all aspire for Kenyon. We, steeped with our heritage, never have permitted ourselves to sit on our Hill and complacently let the world go by. Too often, oldsters are content to watch others progress while they muse over their achievements of the past. But on the Hill with the energy and ability of youth seasoned by tradition and experience, we look to our new president, to lead us along new paths to greater heights in the educational world.

New Faculty Members

Replacements for the faculty members who had died or retired at about the time of the transition from the Peirce to the Chalmers administrations brought many new faces to Gambier. Some of the young and vigorous newcomers remained for many years and were potent factors in President Chalmers' successful efforts to upgrade scholastic achievement. Among those who joined the faculty during this era were Professors John W. Black (Speech), Charles S. Thornton (Biology), Norris W. Rahming (Art), Bayes M. Norton (Chemistry), Samuel B. Cummings (Psychology), and Richard G. Salomon (History). Also arriving at Kenyon at this time were four staff members who were to become the prime movers in the founding and notable success of the *Kenyon Review*: John Crowe Ransom (Poetry), Philip Blair Rice (Philosophy), Norman W. Johnson (English), and Randall Jarrell (English, Director of Tennis).

President Chalmers felt justified in boasting a little about his faculty in his 1939 *Annual Report*:

> The basis of first class college work is a faculty. If anyone doubts the brilliance, the forcefulness, the originality, and the teaching ability of the Kenyon faculty, let him read the list of scholarly and scientific publications, and the participation in learned society meetings of the current year recorded in the Annual Reports. Kenyon's young faculty, with an average age of under 40, is strong and brilliant.

In the same *Report* he continues:

> The morale of the student body, which evidently struck an all-time low in the early nineteen thirties, has been steadily improving. On the whole I should say that the undergraduates have faced like a man the lugubrious implications of rising academic standards throughout the College. As one student was overheard to say at examination time a short while ago, "We'll be proud we graduated from this place yet." Academic standards are not rising rapidly, but they are rising steadily.

Alumni House and Shaffer Speech Building

Although the depressed state of the finances of the College precluded any great amount of building activity in the early Thirties, the picture brightened sufficiently during the latter part of the decade to permit the construction of two buildings which were considered essential.

The January 25, 1937 issue of the *Alumni Council Bulletin* announced:

> Returning Alumni will rejoice in the latest addition to our College property. Through the generosity of Wilbur L. Cummings, '02, Frank H. Ginn, '90, and other Kenyon men, an Alumni Guest House costing over $35,000 is now in the process of erection.
>
> Ground was broken January 9th and it is expected that the House will be completed and furnished in time to celebrate the GREATEST COMMENCEMENT IN KENYON'S HISTORY in June 1937, honoring Dr. Peirce's forty-one years of service as President, and his retirement from active college life at Kenyon.
>
> The House is located on the site of the old Scott store, north of the campus. The exterior is in the Georgian style of architecture, with a two-story porch on the south side facing the campus.
>
> The plans provide for a lounge on the first floor, with three double doors opening on to the porch; also, on this floor are a rest room, general coat room, registration space, kitchenette and other service rooms, and a number of bedrooms. On the second floor are bedrooms and service rooms. In the basement are lavatories, storage rooms, and heating facilities.
>
> The building will have twenty-one bedrooms, with forty-two twin beds. Three of the bedrooms have private baths. The other rooms are in suites of two rooms and bath, with provision for the rooms to be used separately or together. Two of the baths have tubs with showers; the others, showers only.
>
> The building was designed and is being supervised by Harsh and Davies, Architects of Columbus, Ohio, of which Kelley Davies '08 is a partner.

The Speech Building, now commonly referred to as the Hill Theater, was completed just before the entry of the United States into World War II. From the *Kenyon College Bulletin*:

> On Founders' Day, November 2, 1941, the College dedicated the Speech Building, the gift of Mr. Charles B. Shaffer of the Class of 1883. Few colleges have an up-to-date structure designed especially for speech and dramatics; the new building in Kenyon was planned in the light of many years of experience in college play production and public speaking throughout the country and with the special needs of Kenyon speakers, actors and producers in mind. This attractive modern building will give students over a period of years the privilege of working in debates, oratory, and dramatic production in pleasant surroundings and with effective equipment.
>
> Constructed of native sandstone and located on the east slope of the College Hill, the Speech Building is in keeping with the general architectural style of the College. Its dignified Tudor design is the work

of Charles Bacon Rowley Associates of Cleveland. The interior, faced with Pottsco Block, a building material which insures ideal acoustical conditions, has been painted a cream color harmonizing with the turquoise draperies. The auditorium takes advantage of the natural slope of the hill to provide an unusually fine view of the large stage; and the work-rooms, laboratory and conference rooms provide space for the study of speech as an art, as a science, and as an everyday means of communication.

On October 29 and 30 two public performances of Shaw's *Captain Brassbound's Conversion* were given, marking the first play to be presented in the new building. Directed by Dr. John W. Black, the production starred Mary (Mrs. Stuart R.) McGowan as Lady Cicely and Rupert Anderson, Jr. (K1942) as Captain Brassbound. Other players were John Goldsmith (K1942), William Lum (K1945), Edgar McGuire (K1944), Clarence Miller (K1943), Douglas Nichols (K1945), and William Sawyer (K1942). The *Collegian* revue of the play gave great acclaim to the whole production, but was especially ecstatic about the scenic and lighting effects made possible by the equipment in the new theater.

Maintenance Problems

By 1941 the effects of long deferment of maintenance began to show up. The Board of Trustees was forced to allocate a large sum of money for the painting of dwellings and other frame buildings, some of which had not been painted since 1928. The library was filled with books to the overflow point. The excess volumes were stored in odd scattered areas where they were sometimes damaged by water leaking through the roofs. To cap all this, several persons, including Physics Professor Elbe H. Johnson, noticed that settling of the roof of Peirce Hall had begun to force the walls outward. Engineers were hired to consult on the problem, and expensive repairs were required. The alterations were cleverly done, and the beauty of the Great Hall was impaired very little. Professor Joseph F. Slate of the Department of Art has described what was done: "The hammerbeams at the sides were replaced by tie-beams running completely across the room. However, the braces, wall-posts and corbels supporting the hammerbeams were left intact."

Robert Frost with other notable Gambier poets. From left: Frost, John Crowe Ransom, Roberta Teale Swartz (Mrs. Gordon K. Chalmers), and Robert Hillyer.

Robert Frost and Kenyon

Under the headline, "Robert Frost To Have Brief Stay Here In Spring," the *Collegian* for February 14, 1941 reported:

President Gordon K. Chalmers announced last week that Robert Frost, prominent American poet, will visit Kenyon for several weeks during the second semester. Although the exact dates have not yet been set it has been announced that Mr. Frost's visit will not take place until after Spring Vacation. Mr. Frost comes to Kenyon as a result of a grant by the Carnegie Corporation of New York.

Mr. Frost will not teach formal classes but will teach informally during his sojourn in Kenyon. His position is analogous to that of artist-in-residence in a few other universities and colleges in the United States. He has held other similar positions in the University of Michigan, Amherst, and Harvard College, where he is still the Ralph Waldo Emerson Fellow.

During that residence in Gambier the *Collegian* editorialized on the appeal of Mr. Frost as a visiting professor and

72

added, "We think too we are doubly fortunate in having Mr. Frost because we believe that it would be a good thing if many of the Kenyon 'culture-haters' were robbed of their superstitions about poets and men of letters. Mr. Frost is an excellent man to dispel the veil of mystery with which many people have enveloped anyone who writes good literature."

Thus began a series of visits by Mr. Frost which lasted over two decades. He was attracted here by his friendship for Mr. Ransom, President Chalmers, and Mrs. Chalmers, a very able poet who wrote as Roberta Teale Swartz. He usually resided at the Alumni House, but was constantly on the go, leading informal discussion groups, giving lectures and readings, going to baseball games (he was an avid fan) and other athletic events, attending plays, concerts, and lectures, and in general entering whole-heartedly into the life of the community. It was said that he enjoyed Gambier and looked forward to his visits.

In 1945 Kenyon honored Mr. Frost by presenting him with the degree of Doctor of Laws. One of his last public appearances before his death in January 1963 was on October 28, 1962 in Gambier when he was the principal speaker at the dedication of the new library erected as a memorial for his old friend, Gordon Keith Chalmers.

Summer School

By 1941 the conflict in Europe had reached the stage where direct involvement by the United States was imminent. The time had come for the College to put into action some of the plans which had been prepared as the conflict progressed. One of the first of these was the operation of a summer school. Under the eye-catching but irrelevant headline, "Kenyon To Admit Women Students To New Summer School," the *Mount Vernon News* announced:

> Kenyon College's hallowed halls, strongholds of masculinity since 1824, will be thrown open to women students for the first time when the college inaugurates a six-weeks summer program on June 23.
>
> Feminine registration will be limited, however, to day students, which will restrict co-ed enrollment to those in Mt. Vernon and Knox county.
>
> The primary purpose of the college's first summer school will be to enable those students subject to selective service to complete their college courses more quickly, according to the announcement by Dr. Gordon Keith Chalmers, college president.

Registrar S.R. McGowan will head the administration of the new summer session and many faculty members will stay.

According to the records, very few women enrolled in the summer session; most of them were teachers who took the course offerings in art.

War Statement by Faculty

As the United States progressed steadily and inexorably toward entry into World War II, the faculty and staff left no doubt as to where their sympathies stood. In the Archives is a document with this inscription handwritten across the top and signed by Professor Charles T. Bumer: "This statement was signed by members of the Kenyon College Staff on October 11, 12, 13, 14, 1941. Messrs. Ashford, Black, Bumer, Coffin and Hocking offered it for signing." The statement follows:

> We, the undersigned, make known our conviction that the securities and liberties of the United States are in danger until Hitler and his allies are defeated. Consistent with this stand, we demand of our government an unswerving foreign policy which will pursue to the utmost whatever course is necessary for the swift defeat of the allied totalitarian powers. Should this mean a declaration of war, we recommend it.
>
> Furthermore, realizing the grave danger to the nation of the present state of indecision, we are resolved to make known to our fellow citizens the nature and extent of the peril which threatens us, and to make clear our moral and political obligation to meet this peril.
>
> We believe that it is the plain duty of every man sharing these convictions to say so openly.

A check of the signatures to this document against the names listed in the college catalogue reveals that almost all of the staff signed the statement.

An Accelerated Program

The school year 1941-1942 opened with an enrollment of 323, the largest in the history of the College, due mainly to an increase in the size of the freshman class, since the upper classes were already hard hit by the draft and defense activities. The second term started soon after Pearl Harbor, with an enrollment down to 284, and with indications that it would drop drastically still further. The college administration almost immediately adopted an accelerated program, under which there would be four terms per year of eleven weeks each, including a summer term, making it possible for a man to secure his degree in two years and seven months instead of three years and nine months. The same number of hours were required for a degree, but by reason of the summer term and only two weeks vacation between terms the course was shortened.

The proposal must have met with the approval of the students, for the *Collegian* editorialized:

> Kenyon has adopted the accelerated program in its usual manner, with a minimum of fuss and confusion. True, it has been impossible for some students to find the course they want and when they want it, but on the whole, the college has quickly and easily swung over to its war time basis. The ability of the college to take things in its stride, its flexibility, and, above all, its confidence in its own convictions has again enabled Kenyon to keep up with the times, to perform valuable and important service to its students, and add its part to the war effort.

War-Time Kenyon

Early in 1942 President Chalmers reported that the Navy had made inquiries about the use of the College. From the Board of Trustees minutes: "The President informed the Board that the Navy had asked if the entire college plant is available for its use and that he had replied that the Navy could have the plant, but that the faculty felt that the college would be of greater use in trying to prepare men for the armed services and defense work. The Navy appears satisfied."

It is apparent that the administration wanted to preserve the continuity of students and faculty. The president was looking for a program which would keep the staff more or less intact, and yet provide for the continuing education of those civilian students who were still enrolled. The solution finally hit upon was the Army Air Force Meteorology Program. This arrangement probably saved the College, since otherwise the deficits which had been occurring and the almost total loss of students would have forced it to close its doors.

Kenyon was one of twelve colleges selected to give the Basic Premeteorological or "C" course. The course was for men 18-21 who were high school graduates and who had at least two years of high school mathematics. The course was to last for twelve months; upon its successful completion the students were eligible for the Advanced Meteorology Course of eight months which led to a commission in the Army Air Force.

The arrangement with the Army was that the schooling was to be done on a cost basis. The Army expressed its intention that the College would not profit or lose under the contracts. Although it was years after the end of the war before the College finally settled its accounts with the Army, the intent of the original agreement appears to have been carried out.

In December 1942 Secretary and Acting Dean of the College Robert B. Brown announced the plans which were being made for housing the Army detachment: Meteorology would occupy Old Kenyon completely. Occupants of East and West Wings would move to the Alumni House. Non-fraternity men would go into the lower floors of Hanna and Leonard Halls, with the fraternity men occupying the upper floors. Moving day was designated as the Saturday after Christmas vacation, but the meteorology unit did not arrive until the first of February 1943.

This term of the school year started out with an enrollment of 216 in Premeteorology and 247 civilians. However, the civilian population fell rapidly to about 60 as the year progressed. The lowest number of civilians recorded in the college catalogue during the war period was 51 in the Spring of 1945, but the figure might have been even lower, since the official number represents all the men who were in attendance at any time during the term.

At first there was some doubt whether the College could supply housing for the greatly increased number of men, and Dean Brown sent out questionnaires to Gambier residents surveying the possibility of students being housed in private homes. Apparently the rapid fall in the civilian enrollment obviated this plan.

The time schedule for the meteorology students was reported in the *Collegian Supplement* for December 5, 1942: "The Army men will breakfast at 7:00 a.m. and commence classes at 8:00. At 11:00 the morning classes will terminate and an hour of physical training will follow. Dinner will be served at noon, and their afternoon classes will start at 1:00. These will continue until 4:00 when they will have an hour of military drill. Supper at 5:00 will wind up the day for them." Later on evening study hours and lights out rules were enforced.

Army Air Force parade during World War II.

Included among the courses taken by all the military unit were mathematics, physics, English, speech, history and geography. The courses were taught by the regular faculty, augmented by visiting professors brought in to replace temporarily those who were away in the armed services or war work. There were many members of the teaching staff who found themselves teaching unfamiliar subjects, but adaptation and improvisation were part of the war-time spirit.

In charge of the military unit was a permanent party, consisting of the commanding officer, Lt. Donald M. Ryan, and a group of non-commissioned officers. Almost immediately a social life was organized with a mimeographed newspaper, *Meteorite*, reporting dances, parties, athletic contests, plays, variety shows, concerts, and the organization of a military band.

A formal convocation to confer Certificates of Graduation in Pre-Meteorology took place in Rosse Hall on February 12, 1944. The Hon. H.H. Burton, United States Senator from Ohio, gave the address.

Coming to Kenyon in August 1943 was the Army Specialized Training Unit in Area and Language. Its purposes and organization are described well in a contemporary article in the *Mount Vernon News*:

> Methods of teaching some 200 soldiers how to speak and read French and German for service as liaison men when those countries are occupied by American troops were discussed at the Chamber of Commerce lunch today by Lt. Col. West Culbertson, commanding officer of the Kenyon Army post.
>
> The foreign language school activated Aug. 1 is for enlisted men in ranks from private first class up to master sergeant and is divided into three sessions of three months each. Men are "graduated" from the school according to their progress, at the end of one or more of the three-month periods.
>
> Stress is placed on teaching languages in a manner which will enable them to converse with natives of those countries.
>
> "It is conversational French and German," explained Col. Culbertson, "not barroom French and German."
>
> "Barroom" French and German he defined as the type the average American soldier learned abroad in World War I.
>
> The foreign language school men are drawn from the army where they received basic training, or more. Average age is between 27 and 28 and the school includes men who have been bartenders, college instructors, masters of arts, and of many other walks in civilian life.
>
> A 62-hour work week includes classroom work, study, physical training, and military training.
>
> The foreign language school is separate from Kenyon's pre-met school, composed of younger men just entering the army who are destined for training as meteorology officers.

Although the ASTP group also carried on a program of social and cultural events similar to that of the Pre-Mets, it was of a more sophisticated nature, reflecting the maturity and education of this older group. The unit published two excellent mimeographed newspapers, *Kenyon Rundschau*, entirely in German; and *Seminar*, mostly in English, but with some sections in French and German.

For a short time in early February 1944 there were three military units at Kenyon: the AAF Pre-Mets who were just graduating, the ASTP Area and Language Unit, and a new Army detachment sent to Gambier in February 1944. The newcomers took a curriculum, originally designed as basic engineering, which was revised and extended to apply to preparation for all advanced technical work in the Army and was officially known as Army Basics.

Soon after this the Army issued an order for abandonment of most of its courses in colleges and universities by April 1, 1944. Kenyon was hit harder by this decree than most of the Ohio colleges because of its all-male enrollment. By September of 1944 the College was back on what might be called a normal basis, but with an enrollment of only about 80 men, including 23 freshmen.

The supervision of the feeding of this rapidly changing group of soldiers and civilian students was in the capable hands of Miss Lillian G. Chard, dietitian, and Miss Mildred I. Kimball, associate dietitian. These ladies, affectionately known as "The Bobbsey Twins," came to Kenyon from Rockford College in 1938 at the invitation of President Chalmers. They were in charge of food operations at Kenyon until the retirement of Miss Chard in 1956, and Miss Kimball in 1958.

The food shortages and rationing which the dietitians faced during this difficult period are highlighted by the following news item which appeared in the *Collegian Supplement* on November 13, 1942: "Due to the rationing of coffee, it is imminent that Kenyon men eating in the Commons will be allowed only one cup of coffee per day. Coffee will be served at dinner, according to a poll taken of the preferences of the students. By thus cutting down on coffee, it will be possible to save one third of the amount usually consumed in the Commons."

Despite all the difficulties, Miss Chard has proudly proclaimed, "We never had to go to cafeteria style serving!"

Miss Chard and Miss Kimball were honored by the College for their long and valuable service at the Commencement of 1956, when each was presented with the degree of Master of Arts.

Seven special war-time Commencements were held to accommodate those men who finished their requirements for graduation in December, March, or June. President Chalmers apparently was determined that every Kenyon graduate should have his moment of glory, and made sure that all of the formalities were observed, no matter how sparse the number of participants. Here, in part, is his announcement of December 4, 1943:

To the Members of the Faculties:

Six and perhaps eight candidates for earned degrees are expected to complete their requirements by Friday, December 17.

Most of the men are now in military service and will be unable to receive their degrees; two of them, Shields (Thomas W.) and Weaver (Frederick R.), are residents.

Even though but two candidates can receive their degrees in person, we shall confer the degrees. We shall do this because the ceremony has a special meaning for the students.

The ceremony will be brief. It will be held in Philomathesian Hall and will consist mainly of the conferring of the degrees. There will be no formal speech, but a few remarks will be addressed to the two graduates.

I hope that all the members of the Liberal Arts faculty will be present in cap and gown for the ceremony. All the members of all the faculties are cordially invited to be present in academic dress.

Gordon K. Chalmers

Dissension and Revolt

Life in Gambier was turbulent during the war-time period. Comings and goings of faculty and staff members were so rapid that it is almost impossible to get a clear picture of who was on the campus at any one time. During one period the number of visiting faculty outnumbered the regular faculty by two to one. The student turnover was extremely fast also, and the enrollment fluctuated from a mere handful up to almost 500 while both the Army and the Army Air Force programs were in progress, then back to less than a hundred at the departure of the military units. The problems of housing, feeding, instructing, and all the other chores connected with running a school under these conditions were enormous, and taxed to the utmost the stamina and the patience of the small permanent staff. It is no wonder that these mounting tensions led to squabbles which disrupted the life of the school still further.

President Chalmers was considered by most of his associates a charming man, a brilliant scholar, and an able administrator. Everyone conceded that his actions were motivated by his sincere and strong desire to see Kenyon climb the ladder of scholastic attainments. However, some thought that his decisions were not always made with sufficient advice and counsel of his colleagues. For example, he was said to have made appointments to the faculty without consulting the department heads involved. During the fast-moving war years many quick decisions had to be made which were not always popular with all the students, faculty, alumni, and trustees. Consequently there arose mutterings characterizing the president's actions as autocratic, headstrong, and arrogant. The situation built up to a real crisis in October 1944 when two or three students drew up a letter containing a number of allegations condemning the president's behavior. It was understood that the letter was to be sent to the Alumni Council. An investigation conducted later showed that a prominent member of the faculty had been approached with the letter, had furnished some of the information finally used in it, had made suggestions as to its final draft, and had generally encouraged the students in their action. Instead of sending the letter to the Alumni Council, the students mailed it directly to several hundred alumni.

The Board of Trustees went on record as unqualifiedly supporting the administration, and the faculty passed a resolution repudiating the document and condemning it as "scurrilous and intended to reflect discredit upon the Administration" and "went on record as considering it a gross breach of the ethics of our profession if any member of this Faculty has lent himself knowingly to the composition or distribution of this document."

The *Collegian* had just been revived during the summer of 1944. In the October 13 issue it presented a vehement editorial which read, in part:

> Posing as the valiant champion of Kenyon's "Golden Age," an infamous clique of pseudo-playboys has for some time been running rampant with its asinine sneak attacks and self-termed "passive resistance policy." The past week we have seen such childish pursuits of theirs as sign posting and anonymous telephone calls, coupled with offensive parodies of common street songs — all directed against the Administration, and particularly Dr. Chalmers and his family.
>
> The instigators of these actions are known to all, and need not be named. Their wild anecdotes concerning misappropriated funds, salary slashes, faculty favoritism, etc., ad nauseam, formerly harmless and amusing, have now been elaborated upon and circulated past the limits of respectability, sickening the self-respecting Kenyon man.

81

Our complaint is not that there is opposition to the Administration — for an intelligent and healthy opposition strengthens — but that in this particular instance the rebellion has taken the form of cowardly and underhanded methods. Has not this group the backbone to use such approved mediums of arbitration as the Senior Council or open petitions to Alumni, Administration, or student body? IT HAS NOT!

The *Collegian* continued with another editorial on October 26, 1944:

What would be more unpleasant than to review once more the odious events of the last two weeks? Our "family quarrel" has been a most distasteful experience, one which we would like to forget but cannot. For the student body has been maliciously misrepresented by statements of a few, appropriately termed "Kenyon Rabble Rousers."

Not content with creating dissension on the Hill alone, these would-be crusaders at last resorted to distributing a scurrilous letter which contained falsehoods involving Administration, Faculty and student body. We welcome the opportunity to repudiate this group.

The letter implied that it represented "crystalized" student opinion and contained a number of references suggesting organized student support. Actually such backing was neither solicited nor received, the letter being formulated and issued in the strictest secrecy.

We, the editors of the "Collegian," with the authorization of the Student Council, represent Student Opinion on this issue. We REPUDIATE in full all claims, direct and indirect, of this minute fraction of Kenyon Students that it in any way represents popular opinion on the Hill. It is with keen satisfaction that we report that the instigators have been duly tried and justly punished by the Senior Court.

The Senior Court tried the three students involved, severely reprimanding one, and recommending suspension from college for twelve months for the other two. A memorandum of conversation and understanding was signed by the President of the Board of Trustees and the faculty member involved. In it the faculty member asked for a leave of absence and agreed to seek other employment. He finished the school year and left Gambier in July 1945.

Bexley Hall in Virginia

By 1943 the enrollment at Bexley Hall had fallen to the point where it was no longer feasible to continue instruction. President Chalmers announced that for the school year 1943-1944, the College had accepted the invitation of the Virginia

Theological Seminary at Alexandria to make use of its teaching and other facilities for the students of Bexley Hall. The arrangement, a temporary one, began on September 29. Professor Corwin C. Roach, the Dean of Bexley, accompanied the students to Alexandria, continuing his duties as Dean of the Bexley students and Professor of Hebrew and Old Testament. Bexley Hall maintained its identity, accepting students and conferring degrees. The other members of the Bexley faculty took up new duties in the undergraduate college, in the Army programs, and in some parish work of the Episcopal church.

It was necessary to continue this arrangement for the school year 1944-1945, but in October 1945 Bexley opened its doors back on Gambier soil with eleven regular students in attendance, and its former faculty intact plus a newcomer, the Rev. Dr. Oscar J.F. Seitz.

Alumni in War-Time Service

The *Alumni Bulletin* for August 1945 reported that there were 984 Kenyon men in the services during World War II, as follows: Army, 395; Army Air Force, 194; Navy, 330; Marine Corps, 32; Coast Guard, 7; Merchant Marine, 2; Ohio State Guard, 8; American Field Service, 9; and 7 civilians working with the armed forces. Thirty-six Kenyon men are known to have given their lives and three are unaccounted for.

Emergence from the War Years

The *Collegian* reported that in October 1946 the College welcomed an all-time high registration of 181 freshmen. The paper celebrated a return to a peace-time state by printing a survey of Kenyon's war years which read, in part:

> The Army units here since '43 moved away in the spring of '44 and the Alumni House was repaired when the fraternities returned to East and West Wings. Leonard Hall closed down, those divisions having moved into Old Kenyon. In the fall of '44 Hanna closed also. Kenyon was at its war time ebb. To the seventy odd students remaining on the Hill through the winter season, Kenyon seemed a private club. The campus appeared always deserted. Fraternities, encouraged by the administration, managed to survive although the Dekes were reduced to two men, the Betas to one.

Despite lamentations of some visiting Kenyon men that the school would never be the same, the undergraduates held on to traditional Sunday commons singing and pre-game bonfires in front of Old Kenyon.

Reconstruction continuing through '45 brought the college to normality. Societies returned, the college filled to overflowing, dormitories reopened. Overworked faculty and students anticipated the last term of acceleration. Now that is past. The record of war-time Kenyon is for history. Standing on the outer fringe of this Kenyon epoch what may we survey?

Kenyon has met the challenge, believing that the best service to her men results from broad training in thinking, in looking beyond immediate issues to their ultimate significance. Though not yet in full possession of her peace-time composure, Kenyon has emerged from the war years proud of her record, ready to secure for her men the powers to live well.

CHAPTER IV

Alumni and Development

Early in its history Kenyon College began to realize the necessity for keeping strong ties with and among its alumni. There is ample evidence of this in the pre-Civil War Kenyon catalogues which included a cumulative list of all graduates, non-graduates, and faculty members from the beginning of the College. Presumably this was done partly to impress prospective students with the stability of the institution in its early days, but there is no doubt that this was the beginning of some sort of an alumni organization. The practice of making such an annual listing was discontinued after the Civil War, but a triennial list was published in the catalogues until that of 1899. The 1899 catalogue has thus become one of the most valuable reference books in the Kenyon Archives.

Alumni Organizations

The first mention of a general alumni organization in the catalogues is a listing of the officers of the Kenyon College Alumni Association in the 1875-76 issue, naming Lewis Paine (K1858), of Pomeroy, Ohio, as president. However, the Church newspaper, *Western Episcopalian*, printed news items about alumni gatherings in Gambier as early as 1860.

There was a well-publicized banquet of the Kenyon College Alumni Association held in Rosse Hall on June 23, 1880. Attracting nation-wide attention to this affair was the presence, as a speaker, of the President of the United States, Rutherford B. Hayes, the valedictorian of the Kenyon Class of 1842. After leaving the White House in 1881, President Hayes was a frequent participant at alumni functions, and helped to bolster the College during one of its darkest periods.

By 1897 local associations were being listed in the catalogue along with the general association. Among the first to be formed were the Association of Northern Ohio, the Association of Cincinnati and Vicinity, the Association of the

East, and the Association of Chicago. At the present time the list of local associations has grown to about 25.

Manuscript of speech by President Hayes, Kenyon Commencement, June 23, 1880.

During the early part of the 20th century, alumni activities centered around the periodical meetings of the local groups. In order to strengthen the general organization by insuring participation in its activities by the local groups, the Alumni Council was organized in 1926. This was the executive body of the Alumni Association, its members being elected — six from the Association, six by the Council, and one representing each local association with an additional representative for each fifty alumni in excess of fifty — comprising a total fluctuating membership of about fifty.

Giving additional stability to the alumni organization was an arrangement by which Philip T. Hummel (K1923), who was an assistant to President Peirce, became the alumni secretary for the years 1926-28. He was succeeded by Professor Philip W. Timberlake (K1917).

Beginning in February 1931 a quarterly four-page *Alumni Council of Kenyon College Bulletin* appeared and was sent to all alumni. Along with frequent "Messages from the President," this publication included news items of the College and its alumni. The issue of October 1938 was the last of this series.

The establishment of a stable, centralized, and efficient alumni organization dates with the appointment in 1941 of Robert B. Brown (K1911) as Secretary of the College. In that capacity, said President Chalmers, "It will be Mr. Brown's task to pay attention to the alumni organization and activity, alumni of the Seminary and alumni of the College." When Bob Brown arrived on the Hill in May of 1941, he found that the alumni organization consisted mainly of a few boxes of filing cards with the names and addresses of alumni written on them, and some file folders for individual alumni. Records of the local alumni organizations were scattered or non-existent; there was no central repository for alumni affairs in Gambier.

Alumni Bulletin

One of Mr. Brown's first acts was to establish an entirely new file of alumni based on the records of the registrar. He then founded the *Kenyon College Alumni Bulletin* with Volume I, Number 1 coming out in November 1942. Although this publication was launched at the height of World War II, an unpromising time for beginning such a venture, the news it carried of war-time activities of the alumni and the fast-moving events at the College made it a vital cohesive force for the alumni organization. Published quarterly, the *Bulletin* at first always carried a column by the alumni secretary, and frequently there was a report by the president of the Alumni Association or President Chalmers. Since the *Collegian* ceased publication for part of the war period, the *Bulletin* now is one of the best historical sources for this era. Containing from 20 to 40 pages, the issues of this excellent magazine continued until that of October-December 1971. The name became the *Kenyon College Bulletin* beginning in April 1972. The change in name was made partly because the *Bulletin* is intended for parents and friends as well as alumni, but mainly to save costs by putting all college publications under one mailing permit. At that time the *Bulletin* changed to a newspaper format for some issues.

War-Time Alumni Organization

The last full meeting of the Alumni Council for several years to come was on October 17, 1942. At that meeting the Council voted to discontinue homecomings and commencement reunions for the war period and turn over alumni affairs to the Executive Committee of the Council with instructions to hold its meetings regularly and to invite such members of the Council who could be present to sit with the Committee. With the ending of the war, the Council again took over under the leadership of its president, Fred H. Palmer, Jr. (K1922). Saturday, November 17, 1945, was set aside as the first postwar Homecoming Weekend, and at this time the Alumni Council held its first regular meeting since 1942. Normal alumni activities resumed in earnest with a gala Victory Alumni Reunion in June 1946 with 450 alumni present.

New York Alumni Association meeting at the Williams Club, 1955. From left: President Chalmers, James H. Boyd (K1924), Alumni Secretary Brown, and the Rev. John Q. Martin, Jr. (K1928).

Expansion of Alumni Affairs and Development

By 1955 expansion of alumni affairs and development made necessary some additions to the staff and a realignment of positions in these areas. The *Alumni Bulletin* for Autumn 1955 announced: "At its October meeting Kenyon's Board of Trustees approved the appointment of Robert B. Brown, '11, as Vice President for Development. Mr. Brown will retain his title of Secretary of the College which he has held since 1941. In his new capacity he will be concerned with gifts and bequests to the College from all sources: alumni, friends, corporations, foundations, and others.

"Under Mr. Brown's direction all types of fund-raising activity at the College have been greatly increased. Over the period of his membership on the College staff, Kenyon has received a total of $4,878,104 in gifts, bequests, and foundation grants for all purposes."

Just before the confirmation of Mr. Brown's appointment, William E. Frenaye, III (K1950) returned to the Hill as Assistant to the Secretary of the College, and took up the job of Alumni Secretary. He is credited with developing a system of class agents by which a member of each class collects and disseminates news of the class, and acts as a contact for the class with the Alumni Office. When Bill Frenaye resigned in 1960 to become Assistant Director of Development at Smith College, Brent A. Tozzer (K1939) was named Alumni Secretary. He was succeeded in 1965 by John R. Knepper (K1962) who left in 1968 to become Assistant to the President of Wesleyan University.

Bill Thomas Returns To Gambier

When Bob Brown retired to emeritus status in 1958, William H. Thomas, Jr. (K1936) became Vice President for Development. The *Alumni Bulletin*, Winter 1958, quoted President Lund: "Kenyon is fortunate to have secured the services of William H. Thomas, Jr.; for Bill Thomas comes to us to discharge his personal obligations as a staunch alumnus and as a layman dedicated to the Episcopal Church."

Bill Thomas had long been active in Kenyon affairs — as President of the Alumni Council, as first chairman (and only lay chairman) of the Annual Bexley Campaign, and as a loyal supporter of Alpha Delta Phi fraternity. He brought to the College a broad experience in business and industry, first in the institutional kitchen equipment field, later in the die casting industry.

It was Mr. Thomas' intention to emphasize the connection between the colleges of the Episcopal Church and the Church itself. For this he was admirably qualified. Both in his home parish and in diocesan circles he had been very active, serving as a vestryman and working in the diocesan department of Christian social relations. He was president of the Episcopal Churchmen of Greater Cleveland and co-chairman of the Laymen's Conference in the diocese.

During a reorganization in 1971 the offices of development and alumni affairs were divided, and Mr. Thomas became Director of Alumni Affairs and, as such, serves as Alumni Secretary.

Kenyon Fund

Throughout the years since the founding of Kenyon appeals have been made to its alumni for funds to assist in the operation of the College. Before the return of Bob Brown to Gambier these efforts were sporadic and accompanied by varying degrees of success. Probably an average of $1,000 to $1,500 came in annually after the expenses of the campaign were taken out. There were also special drives, such as those of the Kenyon College Athletic Committee for funds to assist in the athletic program.

In the early 1960's the Executive Committee of the Alumni Council decided to consolidate all appeals to the alumni into one drive for the Kenyon Fund. In 1963-64 a goal of $50,000 was set and this was met with contributions totaling $50,891. Contributions to the Kenyon Fund have increased to over $150,000 for 1971-72 and nearly $180,000 for 1972-73. Kenyon Fund chairmen since this consolidation have been Robert H. Legg (K1939), Randolph D. Bucey (K1950), Bill B. Ranney (K1952), Robert W. Mueller (K1936), and Charles R. Leech, Jr. (K1952).

President Caples described the role played by the Fund in

the October-December 1971 issue of the *Alumni Bulletin*: "The Kenyon Fund for current operating expenses is one of the vital forces in the operation of the College. These monies can be used each year where the need of the College is greatest. They can be applied to academic scholarships or physical needs without restriction. This is the kind of flexibility which will enable Kenyon to remain a great institution."

The Class of 1921 Plate is inscribed with the names of the classes which have had the highest percentage of living members contributing to the Kenyon Fund during a given year. The plate was first awarded in 1957, and the winners have been the Classes of: 1921 (6 times), 1916 (3), 1923 (3), 1924 (2), 1918 (1) and 1922 (1).

Kenyon's first alumni telephone campaign was inaugurated in Cleveland in the spring of 1962 with about thirty-five local alumni manning the telephones. Four other cities were added in 1963 and by 1974 the Phonathon, as it came to be called, had spread to a total of nine cities.

Alumni Day and Reunion Weekend

The two big annual alumni gatherings are Alumni Day (formerly called Homecoming) and the Alumni Reunion Weekend. Held in October at the height of the fall tree coloration, Alumni Day activities usually include a soccer game in the morning, a football game in the afternoon, a buffet lunch, entertainment and refreshments in the alumni tent, and receptions in many of the divisions.

The Alumni Weekend, which was formerly held in connection with Commencement, has been held a week later since 1970. Starting with an Alumni-Faculty-Administration Reception on Friday evening, the social program also features an Alumni Dance Saturday night. In 1972 the College instituted an alumni seminar program given by members of the faculty and aimed at giving alumni an experience in continuing education. Other events of the Weekend include class reunions, a golf tournament, theatrical productions, and a complete recreational program for the children of the alumni.

Gregg Cup

Since 1934 the Gregg Cup, the gift of Henry S. Gregg (K1881), has been presented during Alumni Weekend to "the alumnus who has done the most for Kenyon during the current year." Winners are:

1933-34	Wilbur L. Cummings (K1902)
1934-35	Robert A. Weaver (K1912)
1935-36	Charles B. Shaffer (K1883)
1936-37	Edward R. Seese (K1917)
1937-38	William N. Wyant (K1903)
1938-39	Guy W. Prosser (K1916)
1939-40	John C. Drake (K1924)
1940-41	Richard W. Brouse (K1911)
1941-42	Robert B. Brown (K1911)
1942-43	Fred H. Palmer, Jr. (K1922)
1943-44	Carl R. Ganter (K1899)
1944-45	Alan G. Goldsmith (1911)
1945-46	Thomas S. Goddard (K1903)
1946-47	Earl D. Babst (K1893)
1947-48	R. Gale Evans (K1926)
1948-49	Albert C. Whitaker (K1888)
1949-50	Ernest C. Dempsey (K1911)
1950-51	Louis M. Brereton (K1934)
1951-52	Phil Porter (K1912)
1952-53	Herbert T. Perrin (K1917)
1953-54	William G. Caples (K1930)
1954-55	Pierre B. McBride (K1918)
1955-56	David L. Cable (K1921)
1956-57	Robert A. Bowman (K1916)
1957-58	No award
1958-59	John P. Craine (K1932)
1959-60	George Farr, Jr. (K1926)
1960-61	James A. Hughes (K1931)
1961-62	William H. Thomas, Jr. (K1936)
1962-63	Roger A. Houston (K1914)
1963-64	Donald C. Mell (K1921)
1964-65	Fred Barry, Jr. (K1942)
1965-66	Robert H. Legg (K1939)
1966-67	Randolph D. Bucey (K1950)

1967-68	Pierre B. McBride (K1918)
1968-69	William R. Chadeayne (K1950)
1969-70	Robert J. Hovorka (K1925)
1970-71	Edgar G. Davis (K1953)
1971-72	Bill B. Ranney (K1952)
1972-73	Herbert J. Ullmann (K1952)
1973-74	Charles R. Leech, Jr. (K1952)

Peirce Cup

At the same time the Peirce Cup is presented to the class which has the highest percentage of living members present during Alumni Weekend. Multiple winners during the last fifty years: Classes of: 1898 (4); 1914 (4); 1869 (3); 1896 (3); 1888 (2); 1906 (2); 1908 (2); 1921 (2); and 1923 (2).

Alumni Trustees

One of the most important functions of the Alumni Association is the election of representatives on the Board of Trustees. The Constitution of Kenyon College provides that "There shall be six (6) Alumni Trustees elected by ballot by the Alumni of Kenyon College under rules and procedures adopted by the Kenyon Alumni Association." The Constitution of the Alumni Association implements this by stating that two members shall be elected for a three year term each year from nominations made by the Executive Committee. The officers of the Association together with nine elected members make up the Executive Committee. Three members of this committee are elected each year for a three year term. The balloting for this takes place at the same time as the election of the Alumni Trustees.

Alumni Presidents

As listed in the Alumni Directory, the presidents of the Kenyon College Alumni Association were:

1926-28	Matthew Maury (K1904)
1928-30	Thomas J. Goddard (K1903)
1931-34	Robert A. Weaver (K1912)
1935-36	Henry K. Davies (K1908)
1936-38	Edward R. Seese (K1917)
1938-40	Guy W. Prosser (K1916)

1940-42	Richard W. Brouse (K1911)
1942-44	Alan G. Goldsmith (K1911)
1944-46	Fred H. Palmer, Jr. (K1922)
1946-48	R. Gale Evans (K1926)
1948-50	Louis M. Brereton (K1934)
1950-52	William G. Caples (K1930)
1952-54	Pierre B. McBride (K1918)
1954-55	A. Rodney Boren (K1938)
1955-56	James H. Boyd (K1924)
1956-57	William H. Thomas, Jr. (K1936)
1957-58	James A. Hughes (K1931)
1958-59	Henry L. Curtis (K1936)
1959-60	John R. Jewitt (K1944)
1960-61	Paul E. Ayres (K1939)
1961-62	Fred Barry, Jr. (K1942)
1962-63	Frank Mallett (K1934)
1963-64	Chester W. Smith (K1933)
1964-66	Jack O. Doerge (K1945)
1966-68	William R. Chadeayne (K1950)
1968-69	Edgar G. Davis (K1953)
1969-70	Randolph D. Bucey (K1950)
1970-71	Herbert J. Ullmann (K1952)
1971-72	Bill B. Ranney (K1952)
1972-73	Jon P. Barsanti (K1958)
1973-74	David A. Kuhn (K1951)
1974-75	Calvin S. Frost, Jr. (K1963)

Before the officers of the Association and the Council merged, the following alumni also served as president: Arthur L. Brown (K1906), Albert C. Whitaker (K1888), Walter T. Collins (K1903), Edgar G. Martin (K1896), and James A. Nelson (K1898).

Development Programs

The Kenyon Development Program got under way in 1946 with the backing of the Board of Trustees and the Alumni Council. The Program was designed to raise approximately $2,160,000 for the following essential items: $1,000,000 for the maintenance of faculty salaries on a level comparable to that of similar institutions; $700,000 for construction and maintenance of a new library; $300,000 for the construction and maintenance of a new field house or gymnasium; $100,000 for restoration or equipment needs of McIlvaine House, Rosse Hall, the Music Department, the Aviation Department, the College and Bexley Chapels, and the College Infirmary; $20,000 for additional scientific apparatus; and $40,000 for the improvement of faculty houses owned by the College.

In January 1950 Bob Brown announced in the *Alumni Bulletin*: "A year ago we closed a three-year effort to raise a very large sum of money for some of the things which Kenyon needed most. We fell far short of the mark . . ." Mr. Brown went on to say that the Old Kenyon fire brought to an end the last vestiges of that campaign and that the Old Kenyon Restoration Fund was making great progress.

In the fall of 1955 the College hired the New York-based firm of Marts and Lundy, Inc. to make a fund-raising survey and report in connection with the plans and hopes for a capital fund-raising program. The Marts and Lundy report arrived in February 1956. It favored the setting up of a "development program with a goal of $9,000,000; with a shorter range of $4,000,000 within the next six to seven years; and with a 1956-57 goal of $1,000,000 for the most urgent priorities."

The death of President Chalmers just a few months later delayed the drive for several years. The Trustees thought that the new administration should become firmly established before an extensive campaign was launched.

One of Bill Thomas' first jobs as the new Vice President for Development was to formulate plans for the drive. The Kenyon-Bexley Program, as it was called, set as its goal the sum of $1,806,000, with the original designation as follows: new college library ($1,000,000); addition to the science hall ($350,000); completion of field house ($30,000); library for Bexley Hall ($150,000); major repairs to Bexley Hall ($50,000); miscellaneous repairs ($26,000); and working capital to replace annual giving during the campaign ($200,000).

The drive got under way in 1959 and the final *Analysis of the Kenyon-Bexley Program* appeared on February 25, 1961. It showed that the goal had been exceeded by $20,000. About one-third of the total came from the Board of Trustees, one-third from "Friends of the College," one-sixth from the alumni, and the rest from parents, foundations and corporations. The push to provide the final $300,000 was provided by Pierre B. McBride's challenge offer of $100,000 if the other $200,000 could be pledged by December 14, 1960. In all, 2157 pledges came in for the whole campaign.

The expansion of the College by the addition of the Coordinate College for Women made necessary another major fund drive a few years later. The *Program For Expansion Newsletter* for November 1967 announced:

> Members of the Board of Trustees have made initial pledges to the Kenyon Program for Expansion totaling more than $854,000, it was announced Saturday, October 28, by Pierre B. McBride, chairman of the Executive Committee of the Board of Trustees.
>
> Mr. McBride's announcement came at the conclusion of Founders' Day exercises in the Wertheimer Field House to an audience consisting of guests at the Leadership Conference, trustees, faculty, and students. His statement launched the most comprehensive fund-raising program in the history of the College.
>
> "Having played a part in these plans and preparations," Mr. McBride told his listeners, "the Board of Trustees has the responsibility of augmenting them."
>
> He added: "With their gifts the Trustees are leading the way; we know when the time comes our Kenyon family will join us in helping Kenyon to continue its position as one of the country's outstanding liberal arts colleges."
>
> The announcement of these advance gifts of the Trustees was the first in the $18.5 million ten-year Program for Expansion which was approved by the Board at its June 1967 meeting. Board members authorized the long-range program to be fulfilled in two phases.

Details of the objectives of the Program for Expansion and of the Leadership Conference which began it are in the chapter of this book dealing with President Lund's administration.

Vice President Treleaven

In 1973 Lewis F. Treleaven (K1941) became Vice President for Development. After retiring as a colonel in the United States Marine Corps in 1967, he became Assistant Dean of the Northwestern University Law School, then returned to Gambier in 1971 to become Kenyon's registrar. Commenting on his appointment as vice president, President Caples said, "We are fortunate that we can fill this key position from within the Kenyon family. Lew Treleaven has known Kenyon for 36 years as a student, as an alumnus, as a parent, and as an effective member of the staff. His experience here and at Northwestern, and his distinguished military career, give him an excellent background for this job."

During his student days, Mr. Treleaven was a history major, and was co-captain of the football team and a member of Beta Theta Pi. As Vice President for Development he is responsible for the college's fund-raising, public relations, and alumni activity programs.

As the time for the celebration of Kenyon's 150th anniversary approaches, the development office is engaged in preparing a Kenyon Sesquicentennial Program drive to provide for some of the pressing needs of the College.

CHAPTER V

The Third Best Men's College

Dr. Chalmers was beginning his ninth year as President of Kenyon College when World War II ended. At the time of his election the Board of Trustees had charged him with the principal task of raising academic standards and making Kenyon a renowned name in scholastic circles. His frustration must have been very great for almost immediately on his taking office preparations for the war and the war itself closed in on him and throttled his efforts to achieve the goals assigned him. However, before the war put a stop to his plans, he was able to take two major steps: the assembling of a young,vigorous faculty of considerable academic excellence; and the founding of the *Kenyon Review*.

Post-War Recovery

Now he was faced with the job of putting back together the pieces of the College which had come apart during the conflict, principally the student body, the faculty, and the physical plant.

A grateful Government solved the problem of filling the College with students by passing the G.I. Bill for veterans, providing them with tuition and a stipend for living cost, the total of which depended upon their length of service. Thus the college was provided with a student roster filled to overflowing for the next three years or so.

Reassembling a faculty was not as easy. Some of the former members had left for the armed services and were returning at unpredictable times; others were on leaves of absence for government contract work; and many had drifted away when there were no jobs for them, found other work, and were never to return. So President Chalmers faced a difficult task in gathering together his scattered academic flock and adding to it new members to take care of the G.I. influx.

The buildings and other parts of the physical plant were in

deplorable shape. The Army had not been kind to the dormitories, and top-to-bottom renovation was imperative. Extensive repairs were required on Peirce Hall, and in the Alumni House, which had been used for the housing of civilian students during the Army period, a complete redecorating job had to be done before the original furniture was moved back. In fact, maintenance on all the college buildings had been deferred because of war-time shortages of labor and materials.

Strangely enough, the financial picture was not bad. Although it was very slow in its payments, the Army came through eventually with all the funds contracted for. In addition to providing some aid in repairing and refurbishing the dormitories, the Government furnished hundreds of thousands of dollars worth of temporary and surplus buildings during the period immediately following the war. Then, too, with the Government paying most of the cost of instruction during the war period and with the great diminution of civilian population it had not been necessary to draw so heavily on funds from endowments. Although a clear financial picture is difficult to obtain, the College probably went through the war period with little deficit financing.

Post-War Student Life

William R. Chadeayne (K1950), Secretary of The (Kenyon) Corporation, who was a Fulbright Scholar in England before going on to Harvard Law School, has this to say about the post-war era: "This was a very unusual period in Kenyon's history. With the return of World War II veterans starting in the Fall of 1946, the size of the College doubled almost overnight and then continued to grow. The group was unique in that almost all the entering students were veterans and over age 21 — some considerably older. As I recall, in the Class of 1950 there were only ten or twelve of us who were non-vets and of the usual college age.

"In consequence I think that the students by and large were much more mature and serious about their studies than their counterparts in other times. They worked hard and they played hard. A lot of pre-war traditions such as freshman hazing, fraternity pledge duties and hell week fell by the wayside; the ex-GI's simply wouldn't go along with that sort of hoopla.

"While students were certainly serious and inquisitive as far as their studies were concerned, I can recall very little questioning of authority. The grading system, curriculum, examinations and course requirements were simply accepted as normal for college life."

Chadeayne: "They worked hard and they played hard." The Delta Phis in 1949.

From almost total extinction during the war, the fraternities bounced back and soon became dominant factors in campus life. By 1950 almost 80% of the students belonged to fraternities. Aside from athletics, a few plays and an occasional lecture, the College provided almost no social or recreational programs. These were furnished almost exclusively by the divisions or by the student government with such things as dance weekends and the movie series. Even the independents, then housed principally in Middle Kenyon, had well-organized social activities as a division.

Fraternities provided not only most of the social and recreational activities but were largely responsible for handling disciplinary matters and seeing to it that their members met the academic standards. The Dean's Office relied heavily upon the divisions to police themselves and held the fraternities responsible for straightening out their errant members. Division upperclassmen wielded real moral authority over younger students and took their responsibilities seriously.

The relationship between the faculty and the students was very close at this time. Both groups were small enough in number so that it was possible to know almost everyone on the Hill. The faculty and their wives were invited to most division parties, and most students could boast at least one faculty friend. The faculty in turn were generous in inviting students to their homes; Sunday night "at homes" were frequent and most enjoyable events.

The students took great pride in the academic reputation of their faculty, and delighted in "name-dropping" during their vacations with references to Professors John Crowe Ransom, Philip Blair Rice, Virgil Aldrich, Paul Radin, Robert Hillyer, Raymond English, Charles Coffin and the others who were becoming well-known in the scholastic world. The *Kenyon Review* was at the height of its popularity at about this time, and the students loved to make references to it, even though they might never have read it.

The student dress style of this period was casual but quite uniform: crew cut hair, white buckskin shoes which were never cleaned, khaki "chino" pants and sweaters.

This older student group was not too sedate to indulge in some typically collegiate pranks: flour in the Chapel organ pipes; unbolting of the altar rail in the Chapel; blocks of ice in Shaffer Pool just prior to a swimming meet; and a fake edict that all typewriters were to be brought to Dean Bailey's office to be registered.

John Crowe Ransom and the *Kenyon Review*

In 1937 when newly-elected President Chalmers asked Professor John Crowe Ransom of Vanderbilt University if he would come to Kenyon "to write poetry and teach philosophy" he set in motion a chain of events which had a deep effect on the rise of Kenyon's reputation as a literary and cultural center. Mr. Ransom's acceptance of the offer caused havoc at Vanderbilt where there were loud repercussions at having "lost" this eminent poet and teacher. Professor Thomas Daniel Young of Vanderbilt, a biographer of Mr. Ransom, has written an essay on the circumstances surrounding Mr. Ransom's coming to Kenyon which was published in the Summer 1972 issue of *The Southern Review*. In it Dr. Young relates Mr. Ransom's reply to a reporter's question, "Why did you decide to leave Vanderbilt?" From Dr. Young's essay: "The Kenyon position, he suggests, is nearer his training and interest; he is to be Professor of Poetry. Then he comes, finally, to stating as specifically as he ever would his reasons for accepting the Kenyon offer: 'I think that in a smaller college I'll have more time for writing. In a large university there are so many demands upon a person's time — committees and curriculum reform and all of that.' "

The essay concludes: "Regardless of the reasons for his decision, his leaving Nashville, as Allen Tate wrote many years later was a *felix culpa* or a *felix crimen*, for almost immediately upon his arrival in Gambier — accompanied, as Tate had predicted, by Robert Lowell and Randall Jarrell (Peter Taylor followed the next year) — he became engaged in a series of activities that would profoundly affect the course of modern American letters. During his first year there, he and Gordon Keith Chalmers began to formulate plans for the *Kenyon Reivew*, the first issue of which would appear in less than two years after Ransom's leaving Nashville. Shortly thereafter, the first session of the Kenyon School of English was held. Certainly these two developments brought together more distinguished and soon-to-be distinguished poets, critics, and writers of fiction than almost any other of this century, and every student of modern literature has benefited from the achievements of an imaginative and resourceful man who came to the right place at the right time."

Writing many years later in the *American Oxonian* for April 1963, Mr. Ransom described how the relationship between Robert Frost and President Chalmers was one of the factors which brought him to Kenyon: "Robert was like an older brother to Gordon, perhaps like a father . . . Dr. Chalmers was elected President of the College at the mid-winter meeting of the Trustees in 1937. A few months later he called on me at Vanderbilt, made Mrs. Ransom and me come to Kenyon when he was there looking over the scene, and finally called me to a place on his faculty. It was a long time later that I learned he was following Robert's advice. In the fall I sat down in my modest chair at the same time Gordon occupied his throne. That move determined most of my subsequent career."

The article went on to discuss the role played by Mrs. Chalmers in the founding of the *Kenyon Review*: "Let me say that it was Roberta who was the other determinant of my Kenyon history. She was herself an Oxonian, Roberta Teale Swartz, who enrolled in St. Anne's College in 1927, and was already, as she is now, a real poet. It is my understanding that she and Gordon first met at Oxford. A year after my start at Kenyon arrangements were made through the benefactions of individual Trustees whereby a literary publication was to be inaugurated, and in January 1939 the first number of the *Kenyon Review* was issued. I was Editor, and Philip Blair Rice (Indiana and Balliol '25) had been appointed to the double role of Chairman of the Department of Philosophy and Managing Editor of the *Review*. But it was Roberta who really founded the *Review*. During her college days a strong-minded old mistress had enrolled her in an Eighteenth Century course, and made her read the British quarterlies of the period, not without remarking that no Review of such quality had ever appeared in America. Roberta at once resolved to remedy this disaster, and it is now known, though I never had a single word from her, that she early came to an understanding with Gordon that he would bring it about if and when he could. And so he did."

Volume 1, Number 1 of the *Kenyon Review* appeared as the Winter 1939 issue. The principal contributors for this first number were John Peale Bishop, Ford Madox Ford, R. T. S. Lowell, Delmore Schwartz, Paul Rosenfeld, Randall Jarrell, and Philip Rahv. Included also were book reviews by Haakon M. Chevalier, R. P. Blackmur, C. A. Millspaugh, Howard Baker, Sheldon Cheney, Vernon Venable, Yvor Winters, B. H. Haggin, and Philip Blair Rice. The Manufacturing Printers

Co., of Mount Vernon, Ohio, was the printer for this issue and continued to print the *Review* for all but a few of its issues.

The first staff of the *Kenyon Review*. From left: Philip Blair Rice, managing editor; John Crowe Ransom, editor; and Norman Johnson, secretary.

Under Mr. Ransom's guidance, the *Review* quickly assumed leadership in its field, a leadership it maintained as numerous other literary reviews were established in America. It introduced, or published the early works of such American writers as Robert Penn Warren, Randall Jarrell, Jean Stafford, Richard Ellmann, and Eric Bentley, and such foreign authors as Boris Pasternak, Berthold Brecht, Dylan Thomas, and John Wain. So influential was the *Review* that it became a byword in literary publications here and abroad. *The Times* of London devoted a page to the 25th anniversary of the founding of the *Review*, noting:

What do we find on opening the 100th issue of the *Kenyon Review*, in February, 1964? In pride of place, some striking poems by the most admired of contemporary American poets, Mr. Robert (T. S.) Lowell; a fresh and excellent essay on — none other than Yeats, by Mr. Richard Ellmann; a rich, subtle poem by Mr. W. H. Auden, now an American citizen, with a batch of critical essays about it, and an article on "Auden as Critic" by Mr. Cleanth Brooks . . . So the contents list goes on. It is an extraordinary vindication of the *Kenyon*'s insight from the start into what was valuable and rewarding material for a literary journal in the mid-twentieth century.

At a later date *The Times* referred to the *Review* as one of "The American Big Four," the others being *Partisan, Sewanee,* and *Hudson*. However, it saw *Kenyon* as the liveliest of the reviews. *TIME* Magazine also printed several articles on Mr. Ransom and the *Review*.

Certainly the magazine was read more widely abroad than in Ohio. In 1964 it had about a hundred subscribers in Tokyo, but no more than 15 in Cleveland and fewer than a hundred in the state. Its readers included the prime minister of Denmark, the president of India, a labor leader in Australia, and the leading drama critic in Manila. It had subscribers in 57 countries.

The *Kenyon Review* was never self-supporting. A few individual Trustees and friends of Ransom picked up the tab to get the new literary journal started. Among them were: Earl D. Babst, William B. Bodine, Wilbur L. Cummings, George E. Frazer, William G. Mather, Merrill Moore, Laurence H. Norton, Milton Starr and Robert A. Weaver.

Considerably less than half of the expenses were supplied by subscriptions, and it was necessary for the editor to beat the bushes constantly searching for pledges from individual donors and foundations. The College was, of course, the principal financial backer, and pumped more than a half-million dollars into the operation over 31 years. Ransom's salary at the beginning was absorbed by the College and a grant from the Carnegie Foundation. Financial crises were common; in January 1944 a grant of $7,500 from the Rockefeller Foundation saved the magazine.

In 1958 Mr. Ransom retired, and was succeeded as editor by Robie M. Macauley (K1941), who after his graduation from Kenyon had done graduate work at the State University of

Iowa, taught at Bard College and the Women's College of the University of North Carolina, and authored many stories, articles and a novel. In 1967 he resigned to become an editor of *Playboy* magazine, and the last editor of the *Review* was George W. Lanning, Jr. (K1957).

Volume XXXII, 128, Issue 1, 1970 of the *Kenyon Review* contained a printed insert:

> For over 30 years the *Kenyon Review* has represented one of the most important and acclaimed investments in American letters. In money, this investment has reached a total exceeding half a million dollars — the deficit for last year alone was more than $40,000. Aware that costs very likely will continue to rise, and convinced also that Kenyon College, in meeting this deficit will penalize areas in its excellent academic programs, the Trustees have directed that College funds no longer be diverted for the support of the *Review*.
>
> Accordingly, publication has been suspended, effective with this issue. There is some possibility that publication will be resumed if a sponsor is found who will make funds available for this purpose.
>
> We know you share our deep disappointment in this suspension. The loyalty and support you have given the *Review* are sincerely appreciated by Kenyon College and the *Review* editors and staff.

Commenting on the demise of the *Review*, Editor Lanning noted that the cost of the magazine represents only 1.8 per cent of what it costs to run the College. But it had brought Kenyon immeasurable prestige and publicity. Without the *Kenyon Review*, Mr. Lanning felt, Kenyon will be "just one more dumb little Midwestern college."

Retirement of Miss Taylor and Miss Hickin

The school year 1946-1947 saw the retirement of two women who rendered long and faithful service to Kenyon. Miss Philena H. Taylor was employed by the College for over forty years until her retirement in 1947. During the first half of her years at Kenyon she was the only employee for the secretarial, business, financial, and record-keeping phases of the college operation. Officially she was President Peirce's secretary and the College's Assistant Treasurer (a Cleveland bank was the Treasurer at this time), but for many students she was the first person they met when they came to college (to register) and the last person they saw when they left (to settle their final bill). She died in 1967 at the age of 90.

Miss Eleanor M. Hickin was the College Librarian from 1922 until she retired in 1946. She was the only professional librarian at Kenyon during the early days of her service. Under her leadership the book collection increased by some 40,000 volumes, causing a great strain on the facilities of the old Alumni Library and the Stephens Stack Room. Miss Hicken's continual push for more and better library space was frustrated by the war, and her long-cherished dream of a large new library did not come to realization until 1962, four years after her death.

Heritage Conference 1946. From left: Professor Harold Laski, President Chalmers, and Senator Robert A. Taft.

Conferences at Kenyon

Few events have attracted more national and even international attention to Kenyon College than did the conferences which were held in Gambier in 1946 and 1947. Of the 1946 conference *TIME* said, "Last week in its pleasantly isolated, bucolic little community, Kenyon staged a conference on 'The Heritage of the English-Speaking Peoples and Their Responsibility.' Long and lovingly planned by Kenyon's President Gordon Keith Chalmers, the conference attracted such various bigwigs as Senator Robert A. Taft, British Socialist Harold

Laski, Cambridge University's Denis Brogan, Poet Robert Frost." In addition to those named above, the speakers included a host of other scholars, among them Frank Aydelotte, Jacques Barzun, Crane Brinton, Douglas N. Bush, Edwin D. Canham, The Most Reverend Philip Carrington, Ananda Coomeraraswamy, Stephen Duggan, Walton Hamilton, T. S. Matthews, Redvers Opie, John Crowe Ransom, Sir George Sansom, and Lionel Trilling.

Although the presence of this assembly of international thinkers was more than enough to attract wide coverage by the press, what really brought the Conference into the international spotlight was a statement by Senator Taft near the end of his formal address in which he attacked the findings of the Nuremberg war guilt trials which had resulted in the hanging of eleven Nazi war criminals. His condemnation was reported at great length in the national press, but the *Christian Science Monitor* had this to say: "According to most newspaper accounts, Senator Taft protested at the severity of the Nuremberg sentences, and advocated life imprisonment for the Nazi leaders. Actually, Senator Taft protested at the holding of the war guilt trials at all. To him, they were trials for an ex post facto crime, and hence offensive to Anglo-Saxon justice. But he did advocate that the accused should be treated as Napoleon was treated, and incarcerated for life. His sole objection was to the trials for the alleged crime of waging aggressive war."

In the discussion period which followed, Taft was immediately challenged by Laski, who derided Taft's proposals for life incarceration. Somehow the whole affair was garbled to the point where the College still gets requests for copies of the Taft-Laski *debate*.

The sessions of the three-day Conference were divided into topics: "The Press," "Palestine and the East," "Language and Literature," "Government," and "Address and Reading (Robert Frost)." The formal addresses were followed by questions and comments from the floor.

One of the most pleasant features of the Conference was the presence on the Hill of Lord and Lady Kenyon. Lord Kenyon, Fifth Baron of Gredington, is the direct descendant of the second Lord Kenyon, who helped to found the College and whose name was given to the College by Bishop Chase.

Charles McKinley (K1940) who acted as a guide for the occasion, wrote the following account for the *Alumni Bulletin* for November 1946: "From four-thirty until six o'clock on Saturday afternoon, Lord and Lady Kenyon and Mr. and Mrs. Chalmers received some five hundred guests at Cromwell House, found time for a glass of punch, dressed, and made it to Peirce Hall in time for sherry and a formal dinner there.

Lord Kenyon (center), with President Chalmers and students, October 1946.

"If they may be said to have spent any time quietly during the Conference, it was probably on Sunday evening after the excitement died down, when they spent a couple of hours in the Library, looking through the display of Kenyoniana, ranging from an exchange of correspondence between the second Lord Kenyon and Bishop Chase, photographs of the Centennial, to the birth of the *Kenyon Review*."

Lord and Lady Kenyon returned to Gambier two weeks later to meet with the undergraduates and for Lord Kenyon to receive the honorary degree of Master of Arts at a special convocation.

President Chalmers took advantage of the spotlight thrown on Kenyon as a result of the Conference to publicize an endowment drive with a goal of $2,160,000, for the purpose of providing a new library, a new athletic field house, and increased faculty salaries.

Temporary Housing

With the post-war avalanche of veterans descending on Gambier, the College had to face up to the solution of a tremendous housing shortage. The answer was not the building of several dormitories — the administration recognized that the population bulge was temporary, so the College took advantage of the Federal Government's program for temporary G.I. housing.

Under the headline, "Splinterville Adds Its Chapter to a Rich Harcourt History," Charles D. Williams, III (K1949) described the housing arrangements in the May 2, 1947 *Collegian*:

> Sprawled around the old McIlvaine House on the grounds of the once-renowned, oft-mourned Harcourt Place School for Girls, there now stands nineteen frame buildings, collectively named Splinterville (the poor man's "Tobacco Road"). The small village, provided by the Federal Public Housing Authority at a cost of $250,000 to the government and $10,000 to $15,000 to the school, is occupied by the overflow of one hundred and seventy-five bachelor students and thirty-three families. One large "T" barracks houses 63 men, while two 8-man, six 16-man, and nine family buildings accommodate the rest. A recreational hall has just been completed for ping-pong, general lounging, and a small Snack Bar. The area will be given its final polish within the next few days by the addition of several picnic tables and the three rubbish and garbage disposal centers for which the married students have so long waited. As the final touch, Col. Becker, who has so ably handled the planning and construction, dreams of a laundry building with room for several washing machines and a drying room.
>
> Two other buildings have been provided by the government — an infirmary and a music building. The new infirmary, being raised across Middle Path from Harcourt, will be ready for occupancy by the Fall Term, with luck, at a cost of about $50,000. The Music Building, behind the Speech Building, is already about 50% completed on the inside and will be ready for the new Music Department in the fall.
>
> As soon as Congress approves a $25,000,000 appropriation, Ken-

110

yon will receive top financial priority for a temporary field house — a 40 x 75 foot Quonset Hut to be placed beside Rosse Hall. The school is requesting this space so that intramural competition can be held at the same time that the varsity sports hold practice in Rosse Hall. For the sake of those veterans who cringe at the sight of a Quonset Hut, the administration will provide a picket fence which will hide at least the lower part of the structure. (This building later became the Library Annex).

Harcourt Village. T Barracks at lower right, McIlvaine House at center left.

The more elegant name for Splinterville was Harcourt Village. The buildings were spread out over most of the large area bounded by Ward Street, Kokosing Drive, Chase Avenue and West Brooklyn Street. Of the 33 family units, at least seven were occupied by faculty families. The accommodations were fairly primitive, and one wonders why more complaints do not appear in the literature and records of the day. However, it must be remembered that this was shortly after the war, during which both the military and civilian populations became used to fewer amenities.

The Government also provided some of the furniture, heating stoves, cooking stoves, and refrigerators, and paid for the janitors' salaries and some maintenance. The College was permitted to collect a small amount of rental — $60 a semester for a single man and $90 for a married man — but was not supposed to make a profit.

Two of Kenyon's most illustrious graduates were residents of the T barracks — Actor Paul Newman (K1949) and Olof Palme (K1948), who became Prime Minister of Sweden.

As the student enrollment returned to normal, the temporary barracks buildings were torn down one by one. The last to go in Harcourt Village was a family unit at the southeast corner of Ward Street and Kokosing Drive, but the temporary infirmary building was used until it was demolished to make way for the construction of McBride Residence in 1968.

Robert B. Brown

No one was more helpful in seeing Kenyon through the crisis of the war and post-war years than Robert Bowen Brown (K1911). After many years in business activities in Chicago, Mr. Brown intended to retire in 1941, but Kenyon College, in the person of President Chalmers, persuaded him to come to Gambier as Secretary of the College. "Come with us," Chalmers said. "In a few years you can retire completely." Both men supposed that Mr. Brown's duties would be confined to those which had been set forth in a resolution of the Board of Trustees: "That the Office of Secretary of the College be constituted as a College Office . . . The Secretary shall compile and keep a comprehensive catalogue of the alumni of the College, containing such information concerning each alumnus as will assist him, either directly or through other alumni or local alumni associations to make contact with all alumni and revive and increase their interest in the College."

Bob Brown was soon to discover that the resolution was far from a complete description of what he was to do in his "gradual retirement." In 1942 he "temporarily" became Dean of the College, an assignment which stretched out until the end of World War II. For many years he was alumni secretary and director of public relations. He was founder and first editor of the *Kenyon Alumni Bulletin*. He acted as development officer for the College and in 1953 became Vice President for Development. The part Mr. Brown played in establishing a firm and sound alumni organization is told by one of his classmates, Alan G. Goldsmith (K1911), writing in the *Alumni Bulletin* for Spring 1958:

> Kenyon alumni are few compared with those of other colleges and universities. In former days, with the exception of groups in the area accessible to Gambier, only a few found it possible to keep in touch. A handful of Kenyon-spirited men were able to give of their time, their money, and their talents to keep Kenyon alive. Some regional alumni associations made an effort, by sporadic meetings, to maintain a spirit of unity and solidarity among alumni. Graduating classes were so small that no effort was made to establish class organization. Fraternity divisions vied with each other to get their members back for Commencement. Occasionally, for some special purpose or in a great emergency, an appeal was made to the alumni to make a contribution to assist the College.
>
> In 1941, when Bob Brown went back to Kenyon, he had behind him many years as a successful businessman, skilled not only in corporate affairs but in trade association activities. And things began to happen. New life was breathed into the Alumni Association and the local groups all over the country. The Kenyon Development Program, the Kenyon Fund, the organization of classes — these and many other activities were directed by him with outstanding skill and determination. More regional alumni associations were established, until today the alumni organization compares favorably with that of any college of Kenyon's type in the country.
>
> The College and its alumni owe him a debt of gratitude which is greater than any mere words can express. Fortunately for all of us, he will be available in Gambier in an *emeritus* position for consultation and advice. We shall continue to benefit by his wisdom, his knowledge, and his love for Kenyon and what Kenyon stands for.

Mr. Brown's ties with Kenyon were many: In addition to being a member of the Class of 1911 and of Beta Theta Pi, he was the father of two Kenyon sons, Harry W. Brown (K1937) and Robert B. Brown, Jr. (K1941).

He will be remembered by Kenyon men for the thousands of letters he wrote to them during their war-time service, and every parent who lost a Kenyon son during the conflict received a highly personalized letter from Mr. Brown.

In 1958 he retired and was granted *emeritus* status, continuing to live in Gambier until his death in 1960.

Black Students at Kenyon

The first black student to be enrolled at Kenyon appears to have been William J. Alston, who was graduated from Bexley Hall in 1859. A few years later a young prince from the African Gold Coast, Kwaku Lebiete, came to Gambier and entered the Gambier Mission House, a short-lived institution founded in 1864 under the auspices of the College. Soon after he arrived, the little boy took sick and died on February 17, 1865 at the age of 14. His grave is in the college cemetery and one of the Chapel windows is dedicated to him.

Although there appears to have been no recorded ban on the admission of blacks, there were none enrolled at the College until after World War II. Shortly after the end of the war the Trustees began to investigate the possibility of encouraging black students to apply for admission, and the faculties of Kenyon and Bexley on November 26, 1946 "moved and unanimously voted that the Faculties believe that the College should admit Negro students on a equality with white students and that this opinion should be conveyed to the Academic Committee of the Board of Trustees by the Faculty representatives to that Committee." At the Executive Committee meeting of May 22 and 23, 1948 Mr. Chalmers reported, "This year two really outstanding young Negro men have applied for admission in 1948, one of them from Central High School in Philadelphia, and the other from Steubenville. Both are athletes and have unusually promising social and personal records as well as high academic records; both have applied for and received scholarships." The two men referred to by Dr. Chalmers were Allen B. Ballard, Jr. (K1952) and Stanley L. Jackson (K1952).

By the fall of 1949 both Mr. Ballard and Mr. Jackson were members of the football team. On the football schedule that year was the University of the South (Sewanee). About a month before the game was to be played Pat Pasini, the Kenyon Director of Athletics, received a letter from his counterpart at Sewanee stating in part, "It is my understanding that we agreed that Negroes would not be used by either team." President Chalmers immediately replied, "Negro students are regular students at Kenyon College and in no sense second-

114

class students or citizens. Teams which play Kenyon College will play the Kenyon College team or not at all." The upshot of the whole matter was that the game was cancelled. Kenyon did not play Sewanee again until 1964.

From 1948 on, black students enrolled on a regular basis. From time to time fraternities were charged with discrimination not only on the grounds of race, but also on the grounds of religion. The Interfraternity Council in November 1963 found it necessary to issue this statement: "Due to national or external pressures, no Kenyon fraternity shall discriminate on the basis of race, nationality or religion."

Through the years black students have contributed greatly to the academic, athletic, cultural, and social life of the Kenyon community. Their identity as a group was officially established in 1970 with the formation of the Black Students Union, with Roland D. Parson (K1971) as the first chairman. This group has been active in sponsoring the appearance in Gambier of black speakers, poets, musicians, and artists. A Black Library was established in Chalmers Library, and a Black Student Lounge in Peirce Hall. At the time of this writing there are 17 black students at Kenyon.

Harcourt Place Elementary School

In 1947 President Chalmers and certain other members of the faculty became concerned over what they considered to be inadequacies in the elementary school instruction provided by the Gambier Public Schools. Dr. Chalmers reported to the Trustees that those concerned had elected a school committee consisting of Mrs. H. Landon Warner, chairman; Mr. Clement Welsh, secretary; Mr. William E. Camp, treasurer; and Mrs. James R. Browne and Mr. William R. Transue. The Trustees provided $8,000 for the erection of a building on East Woodside Drive directly behind Bexley Hall, and Miss Agnes Sailer was hired as teacher and principal of the Kenyon Grammar School. The name was soon changed to Harcourt Place School in an attempt to procure funds earmarked for the defunct girls' school of the same name. It was thought that Mount Vernon parents would also be interested in enrolling their children, but very few responded, and the school had to be abandoned for lack of pupils after five or six years. The building is now being used by the Gambier Cooperative Nursery School.

Wertheimer Field House

For many years the athletic program at Kenyon had been handicapped by the lack of proper housing facilities. Rosse Hall had been converted into a gymnasium in the latter part of the 19th century, and almost immediately there were complaints about its inadequacies. The *Collegian* in issues of the 1880's and 1890's characterized the building as "Poorly operated," "Unheated," "Repaired," "Unheated," "Closed, Unheated," and "Poor apparatus." Over the years the facilities in Rosse were improved somewhat: a hardwood basketball court was installed, locker and shower rooms were built in the basement, and offices for the coaches were provided on the balcony. But there was still insufficient space for an extensive program, and the locker and shower accommodations were too far from the playing fields: Coach Rudy Kutler once remarked, "We'd win more games if the teams didn't have to save energy for the climb up the Hill."

The student population explosion after World War II made the situation almost intolerable. The temporary building next to Rosse helped to alleviate matters somewhat, but it was too small for basketball and could only be used for such sports as wrestling and volleyball.

Thus it was with great joy that the *Collegian* reported that on March 4, 1948 Dean Frank Bailey turned over the first spadeful of earth and symbolized the beginning of the construction of the Wertheimer Field House.

One half of a Navy drill hall, located at Camp Peary, Virginia, was allocated to Kenyon by the Bureau of Community Facilities of the Federal Works Agency. The building was given as it stood. The cost of demounting at the Virginia site, transporting the tremendous structure to Gambier, preparing the Kenyon site, and erecting the building were all borne by the College. Before it could be used it required interior sealing, wiring, heating plant installation, plumbing, flooring, roofing, and painting. The building was named in honor of Leo W.

Wertheimer (K1888), who left a bequest to the Alumni Council for the improvement of Kenyon. The Alumni Council appropriated $100,000 of the bequest to begin the Field House project. The additional $200,000 needed to complete the structure was supplied through drives of the Kenyon Development Fund.

Unloading the trusses for Wertheimer Field House, March 1948.

The plans called for the main portion of the structure to measure 114 feet by 286 feet. It contains an eight-lap track, and a basketball court placed at the west end. At the east end there is ample space for tennis, volleyball and other activities. During the original construction an annex was built on the south side to house locker and shower rooms; some time later this was extended to provide additional locker space and offices. When the women students arrived at Kenyon, a locker and shower room structure was built for them at the west end of the Field House.

Kenyon School of English

President Chalmers was apparently determined to bolster still further Kenyon's place on the literary-critical map, for not long after the successful Conferences came the Kenyon School of English, which flourished during the summers of 1948, 1949 and 1950.

The School was organized by Professor Ransom, with the aid of F. A. Matthiessen of Harvard, Lionel Trilling of Columbia, President Chalmers, and a grant of $40,000 from the Rockefeller Foundation. The program was devoted to "the imperative and exciting activity of literary criticism."

Staff of the Kenyon School of English, 1950. From left: Philip B. Rice, William Empson, Arthur Mizener, Robert T.S. Lowell, John Crowe Ransom, Kenneth Burke, L.C. Knight, Delmore Schwartz, and Charles M. Coffin.

In the words of *Newsweek*, "The roster of instructors was enough to pop the eyes of any major in English." It included, besides those mentioned above, Jacques Barzun, Eric Bentley, Cleanth Brooks, William Empson, Alfred Kazin, Robert T. S. Lowell, Arthur Mizener, Philip Rahv, Mark Schorer, Allen Tate, Robert Penn Warren, Yvor Winters, and many other notable literary figures.

Each of the teaching fellows, as they were called, was free to conduct courses as he wished, provided he stuck to the general principles of evaluating literary works instead of merely reviewing historical and biographical details.

Aiding in the administration of the School were Professor Charles M. Coffin, Dean; Mrs. Mary Rahming, Secretary; and Professor Stuart R. McGowan, Registrar. Approximately 75 students and 35 auditors were enrolled in the course, which lasted a little over six weeks. The housing arrangements in the dormitories were changed from year to year, but all meals were taken in Peirce Hall. Expenses covering tuition, board, lodging, and fees came to about $250. Many of the students were veterans enrolled under the provisions of the G.I. Bill. The Wednesday night forums, open to the public, were great cultural events and attracted large audiences.

The three year grant from the Rockefeller Foundation ran out in 1951, and the School moved westward to Indiana University, where it became the School of Letters. It has since been discontinued.

Old Kenyon Fire

By far the greatest tragedy ever to strike Kenyon College was the fire which destroyed Old Kenyon, with the loss of the lives of nine students, in the early morning hours of February 27, 1949.

This is the story sent to *TIME* magazine by Lois Chevalier, Director of Public Relations:

> There were two persistent legends about Old Kenyon: one, the ghost in the basement of West Wing, and the other was the legend of the fireplaces. The ghost has been seen by living men, but there was no memory or documentation of the fireplaces. The oldest recollections of the building, before central heating, were of wood stoves. Four huge chimneys rose through the center section of the building, Middle Kenyon. A fireplace was built in the first floor parlor, into one of those chimneys. Last Saturday night, the Middle Kenyon students had a fire

in the fireplace. About 9 o'clock it had burned down to embers. Some-one dumped some wastepaper in it. It burned in a quick flame and sub-sided. About ten o'clock, the students began going to bed. Others came in later in the evening, following a dance on the campus. They sat around in the parlor for a while. Watchman Emerson Billman walked into the east door of Middle Kenyon, walked through the parlor, saw the last few students still sitting around, went upstairs to the third floor and punched his time clock at 3:35. Then he went down to the basement and over to his next station, in West Wing. He punched in at 3:40. The last four students who were still awake left the parlor at 3:45. By 4 a.m. everyone was in bed. The watchman continued through Hanna Hall and Mather Hall. He punched his clock at 4:10 in Mather, came out on the Middle Path, and looked back toward Old Kenyon. The center hallway was in flames.

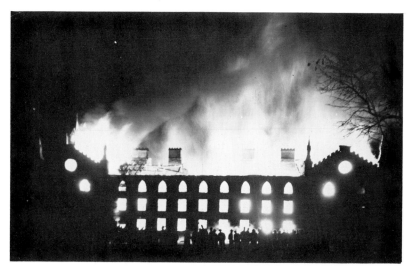

Old Kenyon, February 27, 1949.

Between 4 and 4:10 a number of people discovered the fire. Stu-dents from East and West Wings began calling the Mount Vernon fire department. The two fire hoses in the basement under the first floor entrance were put into immediate use. Someone ran up to set off the village fire siren. Another student tried to phone the college power house, got a bad connection, hung up and ran down the hill to get the college fire truck. Word spread that there were injured men. A student called Mercy Hospital in Mount Vernon and alerted them for emergencies, and asked for ambulances. Meanwhile, people were waking up — some were awakened by the smell of smoke, others by the courageous work of students and volunteer Gambier firemen and Mount Vernon firemen who poured into the burning building, beating on doors, calling "Fire!" No one got up the east stairway to the third floor, and it is doubtful that anyone managed to get up to the third floor in the center section.

Sheets of flame, smoke and hot gasses spread with explosive rapidity through the east and center halls on the second and third floors. None of the survivors mentioned flame in their rooms when they awoke. Most of the second and third floor men went to their doors, opened them a crack, felt the blast of heat, smoke or flame, and slammed them shut. Then they went for their windows. The fire escapes opened out of the halls. Those men whose windows were close enough to the halls managed to jump over to the fire escapes. Others just jumped. One man was met with such a blast of fire when he opened the door that he was practically hurled out of the window without realizing what he was doing. His roommate perished. Only one student came down that flaming staircase. He collapsed on the second floor and was carried out by another student. He died in the hospital the next day. One strong lad who made the fire escape encouraged his roommate to jump, caught him and swung him onto the fire escape; then went down to the second floor and repeated the same feat to save another boy who was unable to make the leap unaided.

Of the 23 boys on the third floor of Middle Kenyon, seven are dead five are in the hospital. Six of the seven never got out of the building at all. Two boys jumped from the second floor, failed to clear the building, and suffered skull fractures. Both died.

On the first floor there were no casualties. One blind student woke, smelled smoke, heard the shouting outside his door. He deliberated a moment, heard the water rushing through the fire hose, and decided that everything must be well enough under control so that he had time to dress. He dressed completely and walked out to safety.

Firewalls separated the two wings from the blazing center of the building. Students in the wings had ample time to wake up, do some rescue work, and go back for their possessions before the flames spread along the eaves and down into their Divisions. Some stopped to outfit Middle Kenyon men who stumbled in, choking with smoke and shivering in their pajamas.

While the fire raged, the Dean's assistant, William Stiles, began checking room lists. Six men were missing, all from the third floor of Middle Kenyon. By Monday noon, hope for them was abandoned. Crews are now searching the still hot rubble for their remains.

Before dawn Sunday morning, the historic Bullfinch tower had burned, the old bell had fallen, Middle Kenyon was gone and the wings were still burning. For the first time in generations, the sixteen fireplaces of Middle Kenyon were visible. The four huge old chimneys, about 25 feet wide at the base, were honeycombed with fireplaces and flues. State, county, and college officials, after making a thorough investigation, decided that sparks from the new fireplace on the first floor had fallen back into one of the forgotten old flues and from there had gone through a break in the ancient masonry into the space between the floors. There they smoldered, building up gasses and smoke in the spaces. About 4 a.m. they burst through the walls into the halls and rooms of the second and third floors.

By Sunday night, each of the 100 Old Kenyon dwellers had been given lodging, most of them in the homes of the faculty. Clothing and contributions for books and personal possessions began pouring into the College from Gambier and Mount Vernon people.

Students who had worked as volunteer orderlies in Mercy Hospital and professors who had been up the greater part of two nights, met their classes at 8 o'clock Monday morning. The *Kenyon Collegian*, student newspaper, came out on time, one page instead of four, with a banner head "Spirit of Kenyon is One of Recovery." The editorial reads, in part: "When catastrophe strikes a weak victim the result is usually ruin, but when catastrophe falls on a strong community like Kenyon College . . . the result is never ruin, never a regression, never a failing, but an ever stronger going ahead."

Expressions of sympathy and support came immediately from all over the country. Well over $50,000 came into the College in the few days following the fire, without any solicitation. The Kiwanis Club of Mount Vernon sponsored a relief fund for students left destitute by the fire. The Mount Vernon Rotary Club raised $11,600 within a few days. The Boy Scouts made a mile of pennies down Mount Vernon's Main Street. Students from Ohio University and Indiana Technical College raised funds and sent checks to Kenyon. In Cleveland, alumni groups of nine fraternities from eleven colleges raised funds and sent checks to Kenyon.

There was never a serious question that Old Kenyon would be rebuilt. The Trustees met on March 5 and voted to restore the landmark building immediately and to raise at once, from all available sources, the funds needed for the work.

According to the first estimates the restoration was to cost about $800,000, and this figure proved to be close to the final cost. There were some insurance payments, but it was thought that at least $600,000 would have to be raised for the work. All other drives were postponed, and resources funneled into the Restoration Fund.

Old Kenyon, October 21, 1949. Facing stones laid out in rows, ready for replacement.

In order that the restored building would copy in every possible respect the exterior of the original, minutely detailed photographs were taken of the remaining walls, and markings put on the stones and on the photographs so that they could be replaced in exactly the same position. The undamaged ivy vine roots were sent to a nursery where special care developed a large root growth, so that when they were replanted they would cover the walls rapidly.

The walls still standing were then leveled, a basement excavated, and by November 1949 a modern steel and concrete "box" had gone up. Then the job of replacing the old stones in their proper places began. The work of fitting the stones together was minimized by exact placement, and little cutting or shaping of stones was necessary. The old fourteen-inch-thick stones were split apart and the halves used to replace broken stones on the back wall. Gone were the four and one-half feet thick stone walls which provided such comfortable windowseat space; the restored building has only a veneer of stone. By the first anniversary of the fire the stones were all in place, the roof was under construction, and the steel framework of the steeple was complete. Students moved back into the new building in September 1950.

Old Kenyon, February 21, 1950.

Although the interior of Old Kenyon was radically re-arranged, from the front the exterior looks identical with the original. Looking at the back old grads with sharp eyes and retentive memories will spot a change — dormer windows have been added on the top floor.

For the historical purist the present building is a replica rather than a reconstruction, but to Kenyon men and women it stands as a symbol of Kenyon College.

Old Kenyon, September 11, 1950. Ready for occupancy.

Inscribed on a bronze plaque on the walls of the new Old Kenyon are the names of the nine students who lost their lives in the tragic fire: Ernest Ahwajee, Edward H. Brout, Albert J. Lewis, Martin E. Mangel, Jack B. McDonald, Marc S. Peck, George L. Pincus, Stephen M. Shepard, and Colin M. Woodworth.

An Air of Apathy

Enrolled as freshmen during the school year 1949-1950 were only 19 veterans, signaling the first year back to a normal post-war regime. The veterans of the preceding years had brought with them an active intellectual ferment which began to be missed. Student morale seems to have been low in 1949-1950. There were complaints of weak student government, boring assemblies, a flaunting of the compulsory Chapel regulations, and a disastrous football season. A miracle happened in 1950, with Kenyon's football team going through an undefeated season, a feat not to be duplicated until 1972. However, an air of apathy seemed to prevail. It was during the 1952-1953 school year that the *Collegian* dwindled to almost nothing.

Advanced Placement Program

In the early 1950's Kenyon College became the birthplace of the Advanced Placement Program of the College Entrance Examination Board. Known at its beginning as the Kenyon Plan, the program helped promote some of the most exciting improvements in secondary school education in the period following World War II. Briefly stated, the program is one in which secondary schools offer work believed to be at the college level and the Educational Testing Service supervises the administration of college-level final examinations. Colleges, on the basis of data made available by the program, may then grant to candidates placement to an advanced section of a subject, or extra credit hours toward graduation, or both placement and credit.

Donald B. Elwell in his Columbia University doctoral thesis, "A History of the Advanced Placement Program," credits Gordon Chalmers with being the instigator and prime mover of this plan. He also names Kenyon's Bayes M. Norton, Professor of Chemistry, as one of the chief developers of the program.

The onset of the Korean War and the accompanying military draft reinforced the desire that many had entertained for some time to create a more efficient educational program by the reduction of repetition and boredom for able students. To this end two programs began to emerge which were in a sense competitors: the Advanced Placement Program which was designed to keep top-notch students in secondary schools while challenging them with college-level courses, and the Program for Early Admission to College which rushed the talented youngsters off to college after the completion of grades ten or eleven.

Always an advocate of upgrading academic achievement in American schools and colleges, Dr. Chalmers rejected the Early Admissions idea. He contended that the secondary schools were better able to provide for the non-academic portion of the education of sixteen- and seventeen-year-old students, and he recognized that many of the better schools might be able to handle their academic education quite as well as a good college.

During 1950 and 1951 the Kenyon faculty engaged in a consideration of the idea of admission with advanced standing, and some of them, Professor Denham Sutcliffe, for example, spoke on the subject at educational meetings. The Kenyon Plan began to get support from other colleges, and the secondary schools of the higher type showed their enthusiastic approval.

By 1951 enough interest in the project had been generated by Chalmers and others that there was a meeting in New York of the representatives of eleven colleges and universities: Bowdoin, Brown, Carleton, Haverford, Kenyon, Middlebury, M.I.T., Swarthmore, Wabash, Wesleyan, and Williams. A twelfth member, Oberlin, came into the group in April, 1952. Joining these representatives were those from twelve high-level secondary schools, led by William H. Cornog, President of the Central High School in Philadelphia, who became the executive director of the study which was undertaken. For several years the program was financed by the Fund for the Advancement of Education.

In September 1953, schools initiated courses leading to the proposed examinations. The first conference for school and college officers was held at Kenyon in April 1954. In addition to Dr. Chalmers, Chairman of the Conference, the speakers from Kenyon included Professors Browne, Fink, Harvey, Norton, Salomon, Sutcliffe, Transue, and Warner.

A little later on that year the first subject matter conference on Advanced Placement in the field of chemistry was held at Kenyon with participants from all over the country coming to the Hill. The meeting was organized by Dr. Norton; assisting him and speaking at the conference were Professors Eric S. Graham and James M. Pappenhagen of the Kenyon faculty.

The College Entrance Examination Board later assumed responsibility for the program pioneered by the twelve schools and twelve colleges. The first examinations given under its sponsorship were administered in 1956.

Advanced Placement has shown tremendous growth over the years: whereas in 1954, 532 students took a total of 959 examinations, present day figures show over 50,000 students taking about 70,000 examinations. However, the numbers have shown signs of leveling off for the past several years.

It is difficult to assess the benefits which Kenyon received in return for the tremendous outpouring of effort by Dr. Chalmers and the Kenyon faculty. It is generally agreed that the College did not get any more than its share of Advanced Placement applicants. In fact it may have received a smaller portion, since the program especially benefited the Eastern colleges and universities, causing the Kenyon Plan to be dubbed the "Kenyon Plan for Admission to Harvard."

The College did gain in more subtle ways. At the onset of the Advanced Placement Program newspapers and educational journals almost always referred to it as the Kenyon Plan; thus the name of the College was connected with a program which had as its objective the upgrading of scholastic achievement.

The members of the faculty sometimes groused about all the time spent on the program, but there can be no doubt that their involvement with the conferences and committee meetings which went on gave them a great deal of professional stimulus and recognition.

However, the chief beneficiaries of the efforts of Dr. Chalmers and his Kenyon co-workers were the secondary schools of America. The Kenyon plan focussed the attention of the nation on the need for early identification of talented high school students and the creation of a challenging program for them. The recognition that secondary schools could do this and do it well provided a tremendous boost for American secondary school education.

The Kenyon faculty has remained active in the program. Among those who have assisted as committee members or readers are Professors Finkbeiner, Harvey, Haywood, Pappenhagen and Roelofs. At the time of this writing Professor Owen York, Jr. is Chief Reader in Chemistry, and Professor Joseph F. Slate is serving as Reader in Studio Art.

Freshmen Dormitories

Early in 1952 the Trustees were informed that there were two main problems which were preventing the College from attracting good students: the bad reputation Kenyon had acquired for drinking, and the lack of dormitory facilities. The Trustees responded by referring the first matter to the Alumni Council. This was distinctly a buck-passing maneuver and nothing could possibly have come of it, since it seems to be the tendency of all alumni, in all colleges, not only to do considerable drinking on their visits back to the campus, but to make blatantly public their own drinking exploits while they were in college. At any rate, nothing further was recorded as heard from the Alumni Council.

The matter of inadequate housing was indeed serious. Although the veterans who had lived in the temporary buildings had not objected too strenuously to the rather primitive conditions, by the early 1950's admissions officers found that prospective students and their parents were turning up their noses at the sight of the dilapidated barracks-like structures

Demolition of Harcourt Village, February 1953, to prepare for the construction of Lewis and Norton Halls.

they encountered on tours of the campus. The College faced the choice of pouring money into poor and rotting temporary frame structures or building a freshmen dormitory. The decision to build anew resulted in not one, but two freshmen dormitories: Lewis Hall and Norton Hall, which were built as duplicates at about the same time in order to cut planning and construction costs.

The dedication ceremonies for the two new buildings took place on October 24, 1953. Unveiled at the same time was the new organ for the Church of the Holy Spirit. The David Lewis Memorial Building was named in honor of David Lewis of Elyria, Ohio, and built with funds provided by the Florence Rauh estate. Mrs. Rauh was the widow of David Lewis. Norton Hall was built in honor of David Z. Norton of Cleveland. This building was constructed largely through the generosity of Mr. Norton's sons, Robert and Laurence, both long-time Trustees and benefactors of the College, and his daughter, Mrs. Fred R. White. The other members of the Board of Trustees also contributed to the construction, notably Mr. and Mrs. Philip R. Mather and members of their family, as well as several other alumni and friends of the College.

The two new dormitories, standing on the site of the Harcourt School, were designed by Charles Bacon Rowley and Meade A. Spencer, architects of Cleveland who had a hand in the design of several other buildings at Kenyon. Originally they housed freshmen and some Bexley students, but after the completion of Watson Hall they were used only by freshmen. The design for each dormitory provided for thirty-two double rooms and twelve single rooms. In each building there was an apartment for a married member of the faculty who acted as a proctor.

Air Force ROTC

The Air Force Reserve Officers Training Corps program came to Kenyon in the fall of 1952 after many months of negotiations by President Chalmers and the members of the Board of Trustees. The *Collegian* for October 1952 reported:

> Due to the fact that on Thursdays the Campus has been deluged by snappy blue uniforms, a word or two on this strange phenomenon is in order. Since many men were having trouble with their draft status

Pres. Chalmers thought it advisable to provide some measure of insurance for the benighted brethren. On investigation it appeared that the Air Force was anxious to try out something new, namely a system whereby Kenyon, Otterbein, and Denison would be given a so-called "satellite" unit to be under the jurisdiction of Lt. Col. Kiefer, who is the Commanding Officer at Ohio Wesleyan, and, Lo — it has come to pass. A summer session was held at Wesleyan to provide the opportunity for Sophomores and Juniors at the three satellite schools to catch up on the first year of the AFROTC program and hence to provide a nucleus of men with some experience around which to build a satisfactory unit.

The program is now in full swing. About 90% of the Freshmen are enrolled in Air Science I and altogether there are 163 men comprising the Kenyon unit. As it is now set up, each man normally has three hours of class work and one hour of drill a week. On Thursdays there is what is known as Common Hour in which the whole unit drills collectively. The Air Force personnel in charge of the unit, namely Capt. Nicholas Tony and M/Sgt. Fred H. Lurding hope to whip it into sufficient shape to defeat Wesleyan in the Government Inspection to be held sometime late in the semester. There are two more groups to be

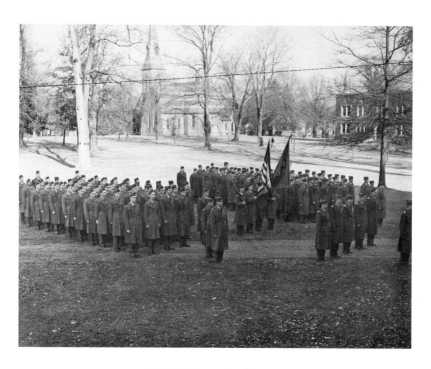

ROTC formation in 1952.

131

organized — the Honor Flight composed of 24 Sophomores in Air Science II, which will be the dress unit of our organization — and the local chapter of the Arnold Air Society, a nationwide honorary organization of the AFROTC which has jurisdiction over such projects as the Military Ball. This Military Ball exposes to the campus the men of the AFROTC in full regalia at a formal dance to be held sometime next spring. It is accompanied by such interesting occurrences as the Queen of the Ball and her date "marching through the sabers." Incidentally, this dance will be open to all by subscription.

On joining the AFROTC the student agrees to complete four years of Air Science and, upon graduation, accept a commission in the Air Force for two years. When this agreement has been signed a deferment request is sent to the student's local draft board, entitling the student to a 1 D classification. The draft being what it is, it is expected that, world conditions remaining what they are, 80-90% of Kenyon men will be in the AFROTC in three years time, all of whom will be trading the assurance that they will complete four years of college for a two-year hitch in the Air Force as an officer. Another added attraction is the fact that when the student joins the Advanced course (Air Science II and III) he receives $.90 a day subsistence pay which amounts to about $82 every quarter. He is also required to go to summer camp in the summer between his Junior and Senior years, at which time he draws $75 a month. In addition, the Air Force sends about 10% of its new officers through graduate school all expenses paid and full pay to boot. All of which seems to indicate that we are likely to be hearing "Hup, two, three, four!" more and more frequently at Kenyon in years to come.

The local chapter of the Arnold Air Society was organized as the Robert Bowen Brown, Jr. Squadron — named for the member of the Class of 1941 who lost his life in World War II. In addition to the social activities mentioned, the AFROTC carried on an active program of swimming instruction for the handicapped children of the Gambier and Mount Vernon community.

As time went on, changing of the draft regulations deeply eroded the AFROTC enrollment. In 1965 the four year program was changed to two years. When anti-war sentiment among American college students became very strong in the late 1960's, there were violent demonstrations against the ROTC programs on many campuses. At Kenyon, however, the attitude of most students was benign; they preferred to let the AFROTC "do their thing."

The commandants of the Kenyon detachment included

Capt. Nicholas Tony, Maj. Joseph F. Hall, Maj. Frank X. O'Brien, Lt. Col. Robert E. Georges, Lt. Col. Charles S. Davis and Maj. Ralph W. Barrett. The last commander was Lt. Col. Roy D. Green; his staff included Capt. Richard M. Higbie, M/Sgt. Frank Morano and S/Sgt. Donald E. Embry. During almost the entire stay of the AFROTC at Kenyon the secretary of the department was Mrs. William Dennis.

The Air Force closed out the Kenyon unit in June 1970 for lack of candidates. The final ceremony at Kenyon was the commissioning of the following graduates of the Class of 1970: Thomas R. Aberant, Jr., Peter A. Fluchere, John J. Foulkrod, Jr., Neil S. Hackworth, Timothy C. Hollinger, Charles H. Matthewson, Donald O. Mayer, William F. Paraska and Rodney L. Wiggins.

President Caples expressed his regret at the AFROTC leaving Kenyon in a letter to Col. Green: "As I stated publicly to the cadets at their dinner this spring, and at their commissioning exercises in May, it is with genuine regret that Kenyon sees this detachment leave. As I stated on those occasions, it is my personal opinion that the most desirable thing for our society is the smallest possible army needed to defend the United States and that such an army should have the largest possible civilian component. It is my belief that without ROTC this ultimately cannot be accomplished."

Operating Deficits

The Executive Committee minutes and the Trustees minutes for the period 1950-1956 read like a damaged phonograph record which constantly repeats. President Chalmers would open the meeting with an enrollment report: There are (typically) 383 students enrolled. The quality of the entering class is good. Scholastic standards are high throughout the entire College. The goal of an enrollment of 500 regarded as the ideal number seems to be eluding our grasp, but we hope to attract more well-qualified students without sacrificing our admission standards.

The Comptroller would then rise to report that the deficit for the year was (typically) $57,000 and that the accumulated deficit was (typically) $312,000. The President would comment glumly that he looked forward to another difficult year, and to a succession of operating deficits from which he saw no relief.

The Chairman of the Committee on Buildings and Grounds then would give his report: Repairs to college buildings and faculty houses will cost $100,000. A start will be made on the backlog with the expenditure of $30,000.

President Chalmers was a scholar, but a businessman and financier he was not. In fact his associates say that he had a disdain — almost a contempt — for money. Instead of relying on the very considerable business and financial judgment of his Trustees and financial officers, he frequently obligated the College to large expenditures without consulting anyone. Time and time again the Board of Trustees were confronted with a fiscal dilemma from which they were supposed to extricate the President, many times by digging down into their own pockets. At least one Trustee resigned in frustration over Chalmers' financial irresponsibility during this period.

While the equity of the College in its total assets went from about $4,000,000 in 1946 to almost $7,000,000 in 1956, during the same period of time the accumulated operating deficit rose from $64,000 to $518,000. Financially, this was a disastrous period in the history of the College.

Bexley Housing

Although the housing for Bexley students had been an acute problem ever since the return of the veterans, it was not until 1955 that definite remedial steps were taken to provide adequate living space for them.

The *Bexleyan* section of the *Alumni News* for Autumn 1955 stated:

> Ground was broken on the morning of November 5 for the new dormitory for students at Bexley Hall. The building, which has been given to the College by the Builders For Christ, has been named the Canon Orville E. Watson Memorial Hall.
>
> Bishop Burroughs turned first ground at the southeast corner of the site, President Chalmers turned ground at the southwest corner, Dean Roach at the northwest corner, and Fred Hanna, a Bexley senior, at the northeast corner. Mr. Hanna, who is attached to the Diocese of Maryland, was selected as a representative student at the Hall.

Ground-breaking ceremonies for Watson Hall. From left: President Chalmers, Bishop Burroughs, and Laurence H. Norton, trustee and chairman of the Bexley Dormitory Building Committee.

The decision to name the dormitory for Canon Watson has been greeted with expressions of satisfaction and pleasure throughout the Kenyon College membership. Canon Watson, a graduate of Ohio Wesleyan University, came to Kenyon in 1890 as a divinity student. He returned in 1903 as professor of New Testament instruction at the seminary. He remained at the College, a member of the faculties of both Bexley Hall and the undergraduate department, until his death in 1951 at the age of 93.

The Chairman of the Bexley Dormitory Building Committee is Laurence H. Norton, Hon. '44, a member of the Board of Trustees and one of the donors of Norton Hall, which stands immediately south of the site of the new Canon Watson building. The other members of the Building Committee, who are also trustees of the College, are the Very Rev. John P. Craine, '32, Bex. '35, dean of Christ Church in Indianapolis, Austin McElroy, '09, and President Chalmers.

Architects for the dormitory are Charles Bacon Rowley and Associates of Cleveland. After receipt of bids for construction, the contract was awarded to the Steward Construction Company, Inc., of Marion, O. Rowley and Associates were architects of Norton Hall and David Lewis Memorial Building, which the Steward Construction Company

135

erected. The Canon Watson Memorial Hall, while smaller than Norton or Lewis, will conform in architecture to them as well as to Bexley Hall. It will be constructed of Santa Barbara Blend brick trimmed with stone, and will contain seventeen single rooms and twelve double rooms.

The new structure is one part of a project intended to provide adequate housing for all students at Bexley Hall. The other part of the project consists of the construction of from twelve to fifteen units for married seminary students. These units will be placed to the east of the Bexley deanery, and will be constructed this winter.

The Canon Orville Watson Memorial Hall will cost about $257,000. The College expects to spend about $128,000 on units for married students and their families. The gift of the Builders For Christ amounted to $375,000. In addition, the College has a gift from the Women's Auxiliary of the Diocese of Ohio for the housing of a married student and his family, and gifts from Christ Church, Winnetka, Ill., and Christ Church, Shaker Heights, O., for the same purpose.

In charge of the construction for the College will be Brig. Gen. Herbert T. Perrin, Ret., '17. The contracting officer for the College is Edson R. Rand., comptroller.

Construction of Watson Hall brought about the demolition of McIlvaine Hall, which stood just south of the Watson site. The Trustees ordered the razing of this handsome but crumbling old brick building with great reluctance after finding that it would cost too much to restore and was not safe in its decayed state.

McIlvaine Hall was erected in 1834 by the Rt. Rev. Charles P. McIlvaine, second president of Kenyon and Bishop of Ohio from 1832-1873. Bishop McIlvaine lived in the house until he moved to Clifton, Cincinnati in 1846. The building served subsequently as a school for boys, and then a school for girls. Still later it was used as a faculty residence and ended its days as a storehouse.

When Bexley Hall moved to Rochester in 1968, Watson Hall was designated as a dormitory for Kenyon students. The married students units mentioned above were laid out along a street named Bexley Place, and are at present used by students for apartment living.

National Recognition

In a survey conducted during 1956 the *Chicago Tribune* rated Kenyon as third among the Ten Best Men's Colleges in the United States. The complete list was: Haverford, Amherst, KENYON, Wesleyan, Hamilton, Union, Bowdoin, University of the South, Washington and Lee, and Williams.

The national recognition given to Kenyon in the survey helped immeasurably to enhance Kenyon's scholastic image. A short time before, Kenyon's reputation was also given a boost in the book *The Younger American Scholar: His Collegiate Origins* in which Kenyon was rated highly for the large percentage of graduates going on to graduate programs.

Although he did not live to see these ratings, there can be no doubt that Gordon Chalmers was the driving force which brought to Kenyon these national recognitions.

Death of President Chalmers

Dr. Gordon Keith Chalmers died suddenly of a cerebral hemorrhage on May 8, 1956 in Hyannis, Mass. He was 52 years of age. The funeral service was held on May 11 in the Memorial Church of Harvard University. The Rt. Rev. Henry W. Hobson, Bishop of Southern Ohio and Chairman of the Board of Trustees, officiated. He was assisted by the Rt. Rev. Nelson M. Burroughs, Bishop of Ohio and also a trustee.

This unexpected blow completely stunned the Gambier community, and sent shock waves through the entire American educational system. Expressions of sympathy poured in to Mrs. Chalmers and their four children and eulogies came from all quarters for the man who had done so much to uplift the academic stature of Kenyon College and the whole American educational structure. Of the thousands of words written by hundreds of people praising Dr. Chalmers' accomplishments it is possible to print just a few. Here is an excerpt from a tribute by Professor Raymond English of the Department of Political Science in the May 25, 1956 *Collegian*:

> His acute awareness of the challenges of our time made him, indeed, especially critical of the anachronistic complacencies which he dismissed as "disintegrated liberalism." His philosophy of education was expressed in many papers and addresses, and crystallized in his book, *The Republic and the Person*, the final words of which transmit his burning message:

"It cannot be too often repeated that nothing is more certain in modern society than that the continuance of the republic is based on the quality of the individual and his education as a person, and that liberty is based upon a belief in and understanding of the moral law."

But it was at Kenyon that his philosophy was incarnate. In this vital little organism all our activities reflected his quality. The deep concern for scholarship, the awareness that education is a delicate mixture of intellectual, emotional and physical development, the conviction that, while the humanities must always be at the center of true education, the sciences were the allies not the enemies of the humanities, the recognition that the opportunity to understand religion must be a part of the training of the full man, and, above all, the absolute commitment to freedom: all these are aspects of Kenyon College which the spirit of President Chalmers fostered and enhanced. He gave a ringing, confident, idealistic tone to the vibrant life of the College, whose members found their own courage and freedom strengthened by his example even when they opposed him.

CHAPTER VI

Fifty Years of Athletics

Kenyon students engaged in athletic activities right from the founding of the College. Early documents telling of life on the Hill speak of foot races and wrestling and boxing matches. Smythe characterized these early activities as "unorganized athletics, languidly pursued." In 1859 the first baseball clubs at Kenyon were organized, and nearly all the students played on one team or another. In the Archives there are box scores of intramural baseball games between eight-man teams (no centerfielder). Baseball was the first intercollegiate sport played by Kenyon teams; all through the Eighties there was a spirited competition with Adelbert (Western Reserve), Buchtel (University of Akron), Denison, Ohio State, Ohio Wesleyan, and Wooster. Track competition began in 1880, and in 1890 intercollegiate football was first played by Kenyon.

Over the years enthusiasm for athletics at Kenyon has ebbed and flowed on the part of both players and spectators, but one cannot say that it has ever reached the win-at-any-cost frenzy which has characterized the "athletic" schools. John McClain (K1927) satirized the low-key character of Kenyon athletics in his column in the *New York Journal American* for November 3, 1962:

How to Wither the Ivies

This is the time of year when I am often sitting around with old Yales or Harvards or Princetons and they all seem to have a common complaint. They are always beefing about the poor seats they get in the various stadia when their football teams meet.

It seems that all the good locations go to the grads who won major letters, and the other seats are doled out on the basis of seniority, starting back of the goal line and working slowly up the field so you have to be about the class of '01 to get anywhere near the 50-yard line.

One old Princeton, whose present seats are down low on about the ten-yard line, was particularly peeved: "By the time I get to where I can see anything, I will be too old and deaf and blind to know what game they're playing!"

I felt sadly left out of these arguments, not having attended any of the effete Big Three, but I got my own back the other night in the presence of several Yales and Princetons and Harvards. I was lucky enough to discover at the same dinner party a younger alumnus of my own alma mater — Kenyon College, Gambier, Ohio.

I don't know how we got the floor, as the men sat over their cigars, but once we got it we had the Ivies speechless.

"I take it you'll be going back to Gambier for the homecoming game with Hiram?" Kenyon '53 said to me.

"I would be," I said, "but the last time I went back — we were playing Muskingum — some upstart and his wife were in my seats at Benson Field."

"You mean, a letter man like you was ousted?"

"Not ousted exactly, but not accommodated in the manner to which I have been accustomed. You may recall that varsity football graduates of my era and their wives were always allowed to climb up and sit in the branches of the oak tree on the hillside right back of the 40-yard line? Well, there was some fellow and his wife, he couldn't have been over 40, sitting on my limb. Drinking out of a flask they were, too."

"I'm glad you mention that," Kenyon '53 said, "because my wife and I had a somewhat similar experience last year. You may not recall, but members of the classes of '50-1-2-3 were given special locations on the roof of the railway station just to the right of the north goal line. It was high enough so that with glasses you could see the opposite end of the field quite well on a clear day. Well, sir, do you know that there was not a square inch of roof left at game time. My wife and I wound up standing on the top of a 1946 Chevrolet parked in the end zone."

"Its a crime the way they let some people drive in and park their cars right near the 50-yard line," he went on, heatedly. "It's perfectly scandalous and there ought to be an investigation!"

"I just took it for granted they were the president and the faculty," I said. "Who are they, anyway?"

"They are rich alumni on expense accounts," '53 said. "They buy phony field passes from a ticket scalper in Loudonville. They don't care if they pay $10 a seat. After all, it isn't their money!"

140

Athletic Staff

At the beginning of Kenyon's second century in 1924, the only faculty member completely involved with athletics was Harold A. Wiper whose title was Athletic Director. Although he exercised supervision over all sports, other team coaches were employed by the Student Assembly with the financial aid of the Alumni Council. By 1924 Wendell C. Love (K1919) had been employed for some years on a part-time basis as head basketball coach and assistant football coach. Other coaches hired on a similar basis included Evan G. Evans (K1925), Rudolph J. Kutler (K1926), Gary Clash, Edward Maloney, and Eugene Lambert. Rudy Kutler succeeded Wiper as Athletic Director in 1928 and continued in that post until he went into the Army in 1944. Bud Evans also was a long-time member of the coaching staff, serving as coach of basketball, baseball, and freshman football for eight years beginning in 1927. Apparently the College took over the responsibility for hiring members of the Department of Athletics in 1938. In that year Dwight L. Hafeli and Charles C. Imel joined the staff and were listed in the catalogue as members of the faculty. Since that

The Kenyon coaching staff in 1925. From left: Wendell C. Love, Harold A. Wiper, and Rudolph J. Kutler.

141

Football coaching staff in 1972. From left: Dick Sloan, Bill Heiser, Phil Morse, Don White, and Tom McHugh.

time this custom has been followed. The members of the athletic staff at the time of this writing are Director of Athletics and Associate Professor of Physical Education Philip J. Morse, Associate Director Thomas F. McHugh, and Assistant Directors Donald E. White, George W. Christman, Jr., Richard H. Sloan, William J. Heiser, James M. Zak, and Karen L. Burke.

Athletic Facilities

In 1924 all gymnasium facilities on the Hill were located in Rosse Hall, and the only outdoor playing areas were Benson Field (later called facetiously Benson Bowl) and the tennis courts behind Old Kenyon. After the burning of Rosse Hall in 1897, the building had been restored as a gymnasium and auditorium, but by the beginning of the third half century it was woefully inadequate for intercollegiate and intramural sports. Team and shower rooms were located in the basement, and although they were constantly improved, their distance from Benson Field made them very inconvenient for most athletic activities.

Benson Field was used principally as a football field, but a track was built around its periphery, and a baseball diamond was laid out each spring. As time went on the following playing areas were added: tennis courts next to Benson and additional courts adjacent to East Woodside Drive; McBride Field, used mainly for football games and women's field hockey; Falkenstine Field, for soccer and baseball; and Airport Field, for lacrosse, informal sports, and picnics. The principal use for Benson Field at present is for outdoor track and football practice.

The building of Shaffer Pool in 1936 and Wertheimer Field House in 1948 has provided adequate but not luxurious housing for indoor athletic events.

End of the Physical Education Requirement

A physical education requirement had long been a part of the curriculum. The Faculty Minutes for May 13, 1968 record the end of this requirement:

> In taking up the question of the Physical Education requirement, the Provost noted that Council was prepared to make a proposal for a requirement and the Senate was prepared to make a counter-proposal for the abolition of any requirement. Therefore, rather than considering a specific proposal for a requirement, the recommended order of business would be to discuss the desirability of any requirement. Professor Banning moved that there be no Physical Education requirement. Extended statements were made by Dean Edwards in favor of a requirement, and by Professor Hettlinger summarizing the arguments of the Senate in opposition to a requirement. After lengthy discussion a motion to table was made, and defeated by a show of hands. Thereupon the original motion was voted on by show of hands and passed, 31 to 24.

With the end of the required physical education, there has been an increase in the intramural sports activities, supervised by Coach Donald E. White. The catalogue lists nine intramural sports for women, and fourteen for men. In addition, the Department provides fifteen coeducational recreational activities for students, faculty, and administration.

Football

According to an old yearbook, "football was first played in Ohio at Kenyon College, where, as early as 1850, groups of students played between two large trees on the campus, using a round ball which custom ruled could not be touched by the hands." Gradually American football developed a character of its own that distinguished it from its European counterpart. During its first few years at Kenyon, football was frowned upon by the faculty. However, in December of 1887, a student editor of the *Collegian* ventured a prophecy that football " . . . is bound to become the great college game."

Perhaps so, but not at Kenyon if one goes solely by statistics: in the 50 years covered by this book, there have been ten winning seasons of football, and five of them came in the last six years when Philip J. Morse was head coach. During this half century Kenyon went through two fourteen-game losing streaks, one in 1954-55, and again in 1963-64-65.

The alumni in bygone days used to hark back to the days when Kenyon played Ohio State — and beat them. The late James Thurber, eminent writer, cartoonist, and holder of an honorary degree from Kenyon in 1950, once wrote in a nostalgic vein about the football classic which took place each year when Kenyon played OSU on Thanksgiving Day.

Says Mr. Thurber:

"You see, when I was 12 years old, the great football event, the annual gridiron classic, was the final game of the season between Ohio State and the powerful Kenyon eleven.

"The Ohio State-Kenyon game had to make up in color and side-show for what it lacked in quality. The Kenyon classic was always held on Thanksgiving Day. Everybody got into his surrey or Thomas Flyer and drove to Ohio Field in a jovial mood, full of Madeira, turkey, and mince pie.

"The color scheme itself was worth driving north to see: Pumpkins and corn and dahlias, hedge apples and scarlet and gray banners and a big turkey cock dyed a deep purple. Perhaps it was this strutting mascot that riled the Ohio State rooters. Anyway, the Kenyon game usually ended in a free-for-all.

"The menfolks would climb out of the stands, or the surrey, or the auto, yelling for Gambier blood, while the womenfolks stayed behind, throwing hedge apples at everything purple that showed its head or wattles.

"In pointing for the Kenyon game in those dear dull days, Ohio State faced such formidable opposition as Otterbein, Wit-

144

tenberg, Denison, and Wooster. 'Why don't those big Ohio State bullies take on their own size,' Aunt Abigail Schwartzbaugh asked me once. 'They do,' I told her. 'They take on Michigan once a year.' And they did, too, but perhaps you would rather discuss something more pleasant."

The records show that 21 games were played between 1890 and 1911, with Kenyon winning five and Ohio State sixteen. Up until 1900 the two teams were evenly matched, with each squad winning five games. After that OSU became much too powerful and ran off eleven consecutive victories until the 1911 season, after which the series was discontinued.

Kenyon played Ohio State once more in 1929: OSU 54, Kenyon 0.

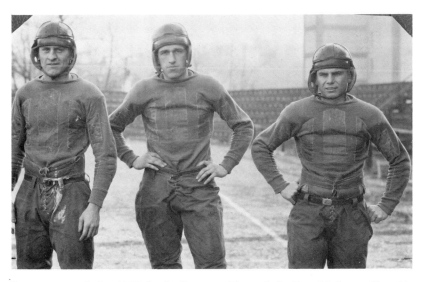

Some stars of the 1925 football team. From left: Pat Mulvey, Harold Peters, and Harold Worley.

Coach Harold Wiper's 1925 squad started this half century of football off on an optimistic note by winning the Ohio Conference title with a record of six games won and two lost. Named to All-Conference teams were Kenyon's Harold H. Peters (K1927), Patrick A. Mulvey (K1926), Robert B. Harris (K1926), Clayton M. VanEpps (K1927), Burchell H. Rowe (K1927), and Frank T. Hovorka (K1928). Team captain for that year was Harold W. Worley (K1926).

Although Rudy Kutler became athletic director in 1928, he was head football coach for only four years, in 1932 and 1941-43. The other head coaches for the period 1928-45 were Gary Clash, Edward Maloney, William Navin, Eugene Lambert, Dwight Hafeli, William F. Lang, and H.F. Pasini.

The first winning season for many years was put into the records by the 1931 team, coached by Ed Maloney. This was the last season of play for stars Martin P.A. Sammon (K1932) and Ralph Dudley Stock (K1932).

On the eve of Pearl Harbor, the *Collegian* for December 5, 1941 editorialized: "We are very proud of the 1941 Kenyon football team; in fact, we are so proud that we can't think of anything to say about them that hasn't already been said. They have been hailed as the best Kenyon football team in many years; they have compiled the best record with regard to wins (5) and losses (2); they rolled up one of the largest scores made by a Kenyon team in many years; they worked harder and liked it more than any other athletic team we have seen for quite a while.

"An immense amount of credit is due head coach Rudy Kutler who in one year instituted a new system and produced a fighting, winning team. His assistants Dave MacDowell, Russ VanWieder, and Freshman Coach Charles C. Imel played very important roles in the forging of a strong varsity."

Led by Captain Gabriel J. Paolozzi (K1942), stand-out players for the 1941 season included Paul Herrick (K1943), Robert A. Weaver, Jr. (K1943), Fred Weaver (K1944), Myron C. Monck (K1944), Edward N. Chamberlain (K1943), Hal Grace (K1943), John A. Goldsmith (K1942), and Donal R. Ross (K1944).

Although many schools gave up football during World War II, Kenyon played some sort of an abbreviated schedule each year. Some of the difficulties of fielding a team are told in an article in the *Mount Vernon News* for July 12, 1944:

Rudy Kutler, Kenyon's athletic director and only coach, wants it clearly understood that while he's determined to field a football team this fall, he may have to change his mind ... Two years ago Rudy operated with only 21 players ... Last fall he had only 14 boys on the squad ... Twenty-five turned out for drill Monday, but unless there are many pleasant surprises among the 25, the 1944 Lord squad will be just as short-handed as last autumn . . . Several of the boys who reported Monday admitted they had never "paid any attention to football games," but all added they are willing to try it . . . Kutler and his squad deserve all the breaks they can get . . . Many larger colleges and universities have quit the sport in face of lesser difficulties.

Dave Henderson became head football coach in 1946, and his first four teams set uninspiring records — in fact his 1949 squad lost all of its games. But in 1950 it finally happened — an undefeated season. Tied by Wooster 13-13 in the first game, the Lords swept triumphantly through the next five games, with a season total of 120 points versus 46 for their opponent. The much-needed boost in student morale resulting from the football team's success is described in a November 8, 1950 *Collegian* editorial:

"Although no one could possibly accuse Kenyon of being anything but a center of higher learning, the success of her fall teams at the present time compares with some other Ohio muscle factories. Kenyon's phenomenal success in football and soccer has certainly given the student body a tremendous boost in spirit and morale — a state of affairs which we would like to see stay around for a long while."

The captain of this team was Ross Haskell (K1951), and some of the other stellar members included Allen B. Ballard (K1952), Dominick M. Cabriele (K1953), Charles F. Coffey (K1954), Grant W. Cooke (K1952), Robert H. Eggert (K1952), F. Ronald Fraley (K1953), Stanley L. Jackson (K1952), David A. Kuhn (K1951), Donald Marsh (K1954), Bill B. Ranney (K1952) (Captain-elect for 1951), and John S. VerNooy (K1952).

The 1950 football season was also remarkable for two other developments: the first use of the two-platoon system by Kenyon, and the eligibility of freshmen for the first time since the early days of the game. Freshman eligibility had been under discussion in Ohio Conference circles for several years, but in May of 1950 Kenyon decided to ease the manpower shortage in Gambier by withdrawing from the Conference in order to use freshman players during the 1950 season. Kenyon was only out of the Conference for one year; the Conference in 1951 decided to permit freshman eligibility, and Kenyon was reinstated.

Although the teams in both 1951 and 1952 posted 3-3 records, it was seventeen years until Kenyon had a winning season. Head coaches during this long dry spell were Bill Stiles (1952-57), Dick Pflieger (1958-60), Art Lave (1961-63), and Henry A. Johnson (1964-66). Phil Morse's first season in 1967 ended with a record of eight straight losses, but in 1968 things began looking up. With end Chris Myers (K1971) leading the Ohio Conference in pass receptions, and Mitchell L. Black (K1972) in punt returns, the Lords achieved a 5-4 record, the first winning season since 1950. The passing team of Bill Christen (K1971) to Myers and a stellar defense led by Edward Grzybowski (K1972) sparked Kenyon to winning seasons in 1969 and 1970.

Dan Handel   **Jim Musbach**

Football co-captains in 1972

Then in 1972 the building years paid off with an undefeated season showing the best record any Kenyon football team has ever put into the books. The 1972 passing attack was based on the throwing ability of Dan Handel (K1973) to Mike

Duffy (K1973) or Jim Myers (K1975), brother of Chris. Standouts for the offense also included Jerry Retar (K1975), Ed Nemer-Kaiser (K1973), Frank Snow (K1973), Tom Samstag (K1973), George Letts (K1974), and Joe Szmania (K1975). This was also the first year of play for the Lord's star soccer-style place kicker, Giovanni DiLalla (K1976). Co-captain Jim Musback (K1973) headed a defense which included such stars as Don Bernsteel (K1973), Charles Contrada (K1973), Mike Gibbons (K1974), Pete Schneeberger (K1973), Dave Utlak (K1974), Matt Valencik (K1973), and John Vrtachnik (K1974).

Baseball

Even though baseball in the past has been considered the national sport, it has never attracted great interest as a national intercollegiate sport. Part of this lack of enthusiasm is the result of the timing of the baseball season, squeezed as it is between the beginning of good weather in the spring and the end of the school year. Bad weather has sometimes knocked out almost a complete season of baseball, and the scholastic pressures of approaching final examinations have had an additional dampening effect. One of the problems at Kenyon is that the College does not appear to attract the type of student who has been a dedicated baseball player from his younger days in the Little League through his high school years. The Lords have usually managed to come up with three or four fine ball players each season, but there has been no depth.

The 1927 baseball team produced a 4-3 record for the first winning season in this half century. The *Reveille* picked pitcher Alden J. Rathbun (K1929) and shortstop Stephen F. Maire (K1929) as outstanding players on this nine. The team's batting average, as given by the *Reveille*, was a phenomenally high .316.

During most of the Thirties baseball was in a state of depression at Kenyon. Some of the *Reveille* reports tell of "players out of their natural positions," "coaching which amounted almost to comedy," and "mediocre material."

The Lords came through the 1939 season with a 5-5 record, largely attributable to good coaching by Chuck Imel and masterful pitching by Raymond Ioanes (K1940). Ioanes' work on the mound so impressed baseball scouts that he was given a tryout with the Cincinnati Reds during the summer of 1939.

In 1941 Imel again coached the team to a tie season. This time the pitching star was Paul B. Herrick (K1943), and fine hitting performances were turned in by Samuel R. Curtis, Jr. (K1941), Ralph L. King (K1944), and Burt C. Johnson (K1942).

In his final year as a baseball coach, Pat Pasini produced a 1952 nine which recorded six wins. The *Collegian* called this "the most impressive record ever accumulated at the College." Led by Captain Richard L. Thomas (K1953), this squad featured the pitching of Joseph P. Pavlovich (K1953), the catching of Hugh J. McGowan III (K1954), and the hitting of Dominick M. Cabriele (K1953) and F. Ronald Fraley (K1953).

Joe Pavlovich   **Joe Adkins**
Two star Kenyon pitchers

Jess Willard (Skip) Falkenstine took over the coaching of baseball in 1953. He loved baseball more than any other sport, but was plagued by generally poor material. It is a credit to his coaching ability that he fielded four outstanding teams in his twelve years as baseball coach at Kenyon. Paced by the brilliant pitching of Allen T. Frost (K1960) and the prudent hitting of Joel F. Holmes (K1959), the 1959 squad posted a 10-10 record. Skip called catcher Harley Henry (K1959), the Phi Beta Kappa-Rhodes Scholarship winner, "the smartest third base coach in college baseball."

Joseph W. Adkins III (K1963) put together one of the finest pitching records ever achieved at Kenyon. He led the Ohio Conference in strikeouts for each of his last three years on the Hill, and for each of these years he was one of two pitchers on the OAC All-Star team. His earned run average in 1961 was 0.38, the lowest in the Conference.

Falkenstine's 1961 nine breezed to a 9-5 record, "the best since 1900," said the *Reveille*. Adkins and Captain Herbert S. Blake III (K1961) were the pitching mainstays, and Calvin L. Ellis (K1963) led in hitting.

As a senior, Adkins pitched the 1963 squad to a 10-10 season, then the 1964 team came along with a best-ever 11-5 record. The star pitcher that year was Douglas L. Morse (K1967), and outstanding other players included Hubert G. Hicks (K1964) and Kenneth R. Klug (K1967).

After Skip Falkenstine died in 1964, Hank Johnson took over the baseball coaching duties. His 1965 nine was 10 and 7 for the season. On this squad Terrence E. Parmalee was the standout pitcher, and good hitting performances were turned in by Klug, Charles S. Hayes (K1968), and John A. Lynn (K1965).

Tom McHugh, who began coaching baseball in the 1968 season, rates the 1971 team as his most competitive nine. It was during this season that Christopher A. Myers (K1971) led the Conference in stolen bases and batted .340. Other outstanding players that year were Mitchell W. Black (K1972), William R. Gorski (K1973), and pitcher Barry B. Direnfeld (K1971).

In 1974 star all-around athlete Mark P. Leonard (K1976) was named to the Ohio Conference All-Star first team as an outfielder.

Track

Track is another spring sport which has suffered from bad timing. Although provision for track activities in the Field

House has helped to alleviate some of the difficulties in recent years, unpredictable weather and the scholastic pressures of the end of the school year have combined to keep down interest in this sport.

The 1924 track team celebrated Kenyon's Centennial with a good season, placing second in the Ohio Relays and sixth in the Ohio Conference Meet. Letters were awarded that year to Captain Sterling E. Rybak (K1925), George T. Brown (K1926), John F. Furniss (K1926), Don J. Gassman (K1926), Richard B. Lyman (K1926), and James M. Reed (K1926). Furniss still holds the Kenyon record for the javelin, although the event has been dropped from competition.

The Lord's track squad was notably unsuccessful during the 1930's. Accounts of the meets note the lack of depth and balance, although there are reports of fine individual performances; the Kenyon record of Philip W. Fox (K1931) in the long jump, set in 1930, stood for more than forty years until finally broken by Perry Thompson (K1972) in 1971. During this entire half century the *Collegian* voiced complaints about the poor condition of the outdoor track on Benson Field.

Under Coach Bob Parmelee, the Lords had outstanding winning seasons in track in 1949 and 1950. Paced by Phil Best (K1951), these teams included such performers as Edward Karkow (K1951), E. Peter Schroeder, Jr. (K1950), Stanley L. Jackson (K1952), Grant W. Cooke (K1952), Thomas J. Davis, Jr. (K1950), and Lloyd C. Hood, Jr. (K1950).

Early in the 1950's interest in track declined to the point that Kenyon did not have a team for several years. Coach Lester Baum revived the sport somewhat, but it was not until 1961, when Don White began his track coaching career at Kenyon, that the sport took on stature again. The 1961 team put into the books a 7-6 dual meet record. Stars of this squad were Dana S. Clarke (K1962) in the 440, James W. Monell (K1963) in the distance events, and Dave Shevitz (K1963) in the sprints. Although the 1962 team did not have outstanding success in dual meets, they were barely nosed out for the championship in the Ohio Conference meet by Baldwin-Wallace. In this meet the stars were Clarke and Shevitz, plus Geoffrey L. Chentow (K1965) and William E. Sweeney (K1965).

Another great performer of the Sixties was T. Arthur Hensley (K1968). He teamed up with Lee P. VanVoris (K1967) and Charles A. Williams (K1967) to lead Kenyon to a respectable 7-8 record in 1967.

Perry Thompson   **George Letts**
Two outstanding track men of the Seventies

The best all-around Kenyon track man for many years was Perry R. Thompson (K1972), who became Kenyon's first track All-American when he placed fifth in the long jump in the NCAA meet in 1971. During this period Kenyon managed to place in the middle or above in the Ohio Conference standings. Other stars during the Thompson era included: Peter J. Galier (K1971), Ulysses B. Hammond (K1973), Gregg E. Johnson (K1969), William M. Lokey (K1969), Arthur K. Vedder (K1970), and David N. Yamauchi (K1970).

A real track stalwart was George B. Letts (K1974). He was track captain for his last three years at Kenyon, and was high point man for all of his four years. During his career as a track star the Lords had their best season in 1972, when the team had a 6-3 record in dual meets. Besides Thompson and Hammond, some of the other track men during this period were Samuel Barone (K1972), Peter W. Schneeberger (K1973), and Jeffrey A. Walker (K1974).

Basketball

An account of the first basketball game ever played at Kenyon appeared in the *Collegian* for February 1899:

KENYON, 18. OHIO WESLEYAN UNIVERSITY, 7.

The basketball game on February 11 was a pleasant surprise to many. It was the first time this game has been played in Gambier, and there was doubt in the minds of some whether it will find sufficient approval to obtain the support which it will require.

The game which took place in the K.M.A. (Kenyon Military Academy) gymnasium began at 4:00 P.M. Mr. Cummings, the referee, gave a short exposition of the principal points of the game. The ball was tossed into the center of the room as time was called. The first half was twenty minutes long and the playing was so brisk and exciting that the time passed quickly. Kenyon made ten points and O.W.U. three.

The second half lasted thirteen minutes and was much the same as the first, except that Kenyon played somewhat carelessly at times, allowing O.W.U. to throw two baskets. Kenyon threw four, making the final score 18-7.

Basketball developed from that point into one of the most popular sports at Kenyon. At times some excellent teams have been put together on the Hill, but basketball cannot be rated as one of the most successful sports.

At the beginning of this half century, the Lords had the best season since winning the Ohio Conference championship in 1915; the 1924-25 squad, coached by Wendell Love, had a record of thirteen wins against two losses. This was the first season of play for Clayton M. VanEpps (K1927), who starred for three years. Other members of this team included Alvin G. Corey (K1925), Evan G. (Bud) Evans (K1925), Burton P. Lewis (K1925), Harold H. Peters (K1927), and Edward H. Stansfield (K1925).

The 1925-26 season was disappointing, but in 1926-27 the

154

Lord basketballers came through with a 15-3 record, and were third in the Ohio Conference standings. The 1927-28 squad, under new coach Bud Evans, posted a fine 12-4 record. The starting five of this team all graduated that year: Barton S. Dempsey (captain), Francis W. Humphreys, Daniel S. Johnson, Virgil R. Muir, and Stephen E. Newhouse. The 1929-30 team under Captain Myron Robinson (K1931) also had a winning season, but the Hill did not see another winning year until Coach Gene Lambert's 1936-37 squad had an 8-5 record.

Basketball practice in Rosse Hall about 1947. From left: Bill Schneebeck, Eppa Rixey, and Dick Hershberger.

The three years from 1946-49 during which Eppa Rixey III (K1949) starred brought back an aroused interest in basketball at Kenyon. H.F. (Pat) Pasini was the coach for the first two of these years, then Dave Henderson took over. Although not

155

considered extremely tall by later basketball standards, the 6'-6" Rixey was the first "big" man to play for the Kenyon Lords. The records he set mark him as the finest basketball player Kenyon had ever had at the time of his graduation. In the 1947-48 season he scored 550 points for an average of 25 per game, and he was the first Kenyon player ever to exceed 1,000 points in his college career. Assisting him in putting into the books a 12-6 record in 1948-49 were David M. Bell (K1950), Leonard H. Burrows (K1951), John D. Mooney, Jr. (K1950), and Perry M. Trinkner (K1950).

Paced by Frank Gingerich (K1955) and Daniel D. Bumstead (K1957), Coach Falkenstine's 1954-55 team had a 9-8 winning season. Then in 1960-61 and 1961-62 the Lords, led by star Jeffrey A. Slade (K1962) and coached by Bob Harrison, had 11-8 and 13-9 records. The *Reveille* said of this team: "Behind unparalleled faculty, student, and alumni support, the Lords turned in the second most successful season in Kenyon's history."

Enthusiasm for basketball in Gambier has probably never reached greater heights than it did during the four playing years of John A. Rinka (K1970). Attendance at the games filled Wertheimer Field House to capacity, with the result that on December 12, 1967, just before the opening of a game with Wooster, the entire main bleachers collapsed, injuring 16 people. The game was cancelled, and new and safer stands were installed within a short time.

Rinka was a cool-headed, durable, sharp-shooting guard, with exceptional ball-handling skills. Although only 5'-9" in height, he was the finest basketball player Kenyon has ever had at the time of this writing. In his four years at Kenyon, Rinka scored 3,251 points for the third highest mark on the NCAA college division record books. He had six 50-point or more performances, with 69 being his highest. In his senior year he received the Ohio Conference's Gregory Award for the third straight year. His uniform number 24 and the ball used in the last game he played are in the Basketball Hall of Fame Museum in Springfield, Mass.

In 1968 Harrison left Kenyon to become head basketball coach at Harvard, and was replaced by Bob Brannum. When

Brannum went to Brandeis University as head coach of basketball in 1970, the newly-graduated Rinka went with him to become freshman basketball coach and assistant athletic director at Brandeis.

Superstar Johnny Rinka.

The only losing season during this Golden Era of basketball was in 1968-69, when Kenyon had twelve wins versus fourteen losses. Scores were very high during this period, since the Lords were essentially a run-and-shoot team, without a strong defense. In addition to Rinka, stars during these four years include Terrence E. Parmelee (K1968), Richard C. Fox (K1968), John A. Dunlop (K1969), Christopher H. Marty (K1969), Larry F. Finstrom (K1969), Martin J. Hunt (K1972), James H. Smith (K1972), and Timothy J. Delaney (K1972).

Jim Zak replaced Brannum in 1970, and is the coach at the time of this writing. He developed his most successful team during the 1971-72 season. Led by stars Marty Hunt and Jim Smith, this squad had a 13-15 record, and were edged by Wittenberg in the finals of the Ohio Conference tournament.

Tennis

Tennis history for this half century began with an undefeated team and ended with an undefeated team. The *Reveille* for 1924 describes how a two-man Kenyon team — Sanford W. Small (K1923) and Hale Sturges (K1924) — swept through the 1923 season for a 7-0 record, and won the Ohio Intercollegiate Doubles Championship. Kenyon's 1974 tennis squad also went through the entire season without a defeat. In between there have been few poor years, and tennis vies with swimming in being the most successful sport at Kenyon.

The Lords were also undefeated in 1927 and 1928, when the stars were Francis W. Humphries (K1928), Daniel S. Johnson (K1928), Joseph W. Scherr, Jr. (K1929), and the Kawasaki brothers, Daijiro and Morinosuke (both K1929).

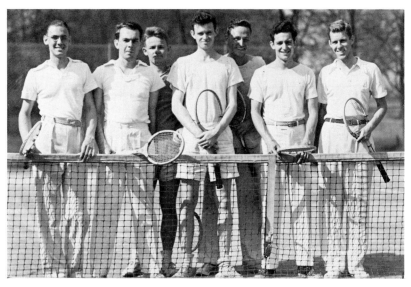

National Tennis Championship Team, 1937-38. From left: Paul D. Graebner (K1939), Robert S. Wuerdeman (K1938), Morey Lewis (K1939), Gordon Reeder (K1939), George Pryor (K1939), M.L. Olds (K1939), and Donald McNeill (K1940).

The story of the successful bid for national acclaim for tennis at Kenyon undertaken by Don McNeill and his team-

158

mates beginning in 1937 has already been told in a previous chapter, but just before that time Kenyon had been a real power in Ohio college competition. Warren Munger (K1935) led the team to a winning season in 1934 and went on to win the Ohio Conference singles championship. The 1935 and 1936 squads were undefeated, and the 1936 team won the Ohio Conference Tournament championship.

After World War II Kenyon tennis teams again took up their dominant place in the Ohio Conference. The 1946 group was undefeated in dual match play, won the Ohio Conference Tournament again, and the team of Bruce Bothwell (K1942V-1946) and Robert J. Derham (K1944V) won the doubles tournament. Other members of this team were Richard W. Hershberger (K1947) and John E. Parker (K1949).

Lloyd Budge was hired as the tennis coach for three seasons beginning in 1948. His teams posted winning records in match play, tied for the Conference Tournament championship in 1949 and were second in 1950. The star of this era was William H. Schneebeck (K1950), who won the tournament singles championship in 1949 and 1950.

History professor H. Landon Warner took over the coaching duties for the next two years, and both of his teams won the Ohio Conference Tournament. Outstanding players were Timothy Ryan (K1952), Ronald R. Ryan (K1953), Tilden H. McMasters (K1953), Robert H. Harrison (K1953), John L. Goldberg (K1952), and William D. Greaves (K1953).

The 1953 team, under Coach Bob Bartels, had a 9-1 record and tied for the championship in the Conference Tournament. Beginning in 1955, Tom Edwards had charge of the squad for four winning seasons, and then Bob Harrison took over tennis coaching for the next ten years. Harrison's first team in 1959 came through the season with fourteen wins versus five losses and won the tournament championship. Members of this group were: Frank M. Coleman (K1959), Guy E. Gibbon (K1960), Douglas B. Hill, Jr. (K1962), J. Duncan Muir (K1960), Eric F. Panzer (K1959), and George J. Russell (K1960).

The 1966 team had an 8-4 season, and in 1967 Kenyon was runner-up in the Conference Tournament. Dick Sloan became tennis coach starting with the 1969 season, and his six teams up until the time of this writing have all recorded winning seasons. The 1970 squad finished the season with thirteen wins and one loss (to Ohio State) and won the Conference Tournament. In 1969, 1973, and 1974 the Lords were runner-up in the tournament, and Kenyon closed this half century of tennis with an undefeated match play season in 1974.

Stars during Coach Sloan's successful era at Kenyon included Andrew D. Stewart (K1970), captain for 1969 and 1970; N. Preston Lentz (K1972), captain for 1972; Mark W. Lowery (K1974), captain for 1974; and David W. Robison (K1973).

Golf

Varsity golf was once described in the *Collegian* as a "little recognized but important sport at Kenyon." It certainly has been important to the members of the team, but to the spectator it is the least attractive of all the sports at Kenyon. In effect, all of the matches are "away" games; this accounts to a great extent for the lack of a supporting gallery of spectators. For the record, however, golf has been one of the successful sports efforts at Kenyon.

The first season of golf as an intercollegiate sport at Kenyon was in 1928, when the team finished the season with a 2-2 record. Members of that first team were Captain Roof G. Gilson (K1929), Gustavus G. Foos (K1928), Donald Bruce Mansfield (K1930), Philip N. Russell (K1930), and Robert M. Weh (K1928). The 1929 squad did not do well, but in 1930 Kenyon achieved a 3-3 record with Mansfield and Robert M. Greer, Jr. (K1930) starring.

Captained by Frank M. Lindsay, Jr. (K1933), the excellent 1933 team recorded the first winning season with ten wins versus three losses.

In the middle Thirties Lord golfers who starred were Robert W. Mueller (K1936) and Charles L. Lord (K1936), but the next winning season (5-2) was in 1941, just before golf was discontinued for the war period.

In the first full season after the war, Kenyon won the 1947 Ohio Conference Championship with the team of Charles W. Ayres (K1947), Donald J. Martin (K1947), Clitus H. Marvin (K1947), and Perry M. Trinkner (K1950). During his four years at Kenyon, Bud Trinkner amassed a series of records: most points in college career, most matches played in college career, lowest 18 hole score, lowest season's average, and lowest college career average. Some of his records still stand at the time of this writing.

Golf team of 1929. From left: William B. McClain (K1929), Rufus L. Page, Jr. (K1931), Captain D. Bruce Mansfield (K1930), Arthur D. Wolfe (K1931), and Philip N. Russell (K1930).

After Trinkner's graduation golf reached such a low level of enthusiasm that it was actually dropped for the 1952 season. However, faculty members Capt. Nicholas Tony and Professor Eric Graham revived the sport in 1953 and assisted with the coaching for several years. The ubiquitous Tom Edwards became the first Athletic Department coach when he took over the 1959 and 1960 teams.

Just as Bud Trinkner had started a new era for golf after World War II, Robert A. Legg (K1965) showed clearly that he was destined to play the same role when he joined the golf team as a freshman in 1962. Playing under coaches Art Lave and Dick Russell, the Kenyon golfers for the next six years were considered leading contenders in the Ohio Conference. Their 1965 season was the best ever at Kenyon up until that time. In that year their record was 14-2-1, and they were first in the Ohio Conference tournament, with Kenyon men placing 1-2-3 in this order: Perry E. Hudson (K1966), Captain Bob Legg, and Michael A. Wise (K1967). The records set by Legg during his four years of golf at Kenyon are comparable only to Bud Trinkner's.

The winning seasons have swept along. Mike Wise and Stephen L. Bartlett (K1969) continued their splendid play under Coach Russell. In 1968 Bob Brannum took over the coaching reins, and the coach at the time of this writing is Jim Zak. During Brannum's two years of coaching he had winning teams, and his 1970 squad had a 9-1 record, the best win-loss record to that time. Zak's 1972 team was undefeated in dual match play and placed third in the Conference tournament. Alan W. Cafruny (K1974) was runner-up medalist in 1972. In 1974 Douglas A. Dorer (K1976) won the Conference tournament title by nine strokes, and the Lords as a team were third. Four-year golfers for this era included S. Ray Rainka (K1970), George L. Thomas, Jr. (K1972), and E. Robert Schellhase (K1973).

Swimming

The story of the beginning of swimming at Kenyon has already been told in another chapter. Chuck Imel's 1938 team was undefeated in dual meets and easily won the Ohio Conference Championship meet. Led by such stars as George Eagon (K1938), Wilbur Griffin, Jr. (K1940), Henry V. Sebach (K1938), William B. Smeeth (K1942V-1946), and Robert R. Tanner (K1941), Kenyon dominated the Ohio Conference for four years. In 1940 every Conference record was held by a Kenyon man. When swimming competition was resumed after the war, Kenyon's 1948 team, coached by Bob Parmelee, went through the season undefeated in dual meets and again won the Conference meet. For the next few years the Lords were second or third in the Conference meet. However, in the fall of

1953, five freshman swimmers arrived on the Hill to herald the beginning of the greatest sustained string of championships in the history of athletics at Kenyon. Three of the new men came from Williston Academy: Edmund F. Fitzsimmons (K1957), Stanley A. Krok, Jr. (K1957), and Theodore D. Kurrus (K1957). This trio was joined by Albert N. Halverstadt, Jr. (K1957) and Philip Payton (K1957). Thus Bob Bartels' 1954 team began the skein of Ohio Conference Championships which has extended for twenty-one years, through 1974, the date of this writing.

Tom Edwards began a ten-year career in swimming coaching in the 1954-55 school year. In addition to the Conference championships, his teams won the Ohio Conference Relays during six of his ten years. Edwards rates Philip L. Mayher (K1962) as the best swimmer he coached at Kenyon, but he is quick to include as stand-outs the five men named above, plus David G. Borman (K1959), James G. Carr (K1966), David S. Gullion (K1964), Louis B. Kuppenheimer III (K1963), Thomas D. LaBaugh (K1964), Eugene D. Ruth (1962), Joseph R. Sapere (K1962), and the Evans brothers, Charles S. (K1966) and David L. (K1963).

Dick Russell coached for four years, taking over for the 1964-65 season, then Dick Sloan, the coach at the time of this writing, came to the Hill in the school year 1968-69.

Some of the fine swimmers of recent years include Richard I. James (K1974), William Koller (K1970), Douglas Neff (K1971), William A. Wallace (K1972), and Lawrence H. Witner (K1969). The team of Koller, Neff, Wallace, and Witner were the Medley Relay Champions in the NCAA meet in 1969, in which Kenyon placed second overall.

Koller, James, and another star swimmer, John A. Davis (K1973), were recipients of post-NCAA scholarships for graduate work.

As the time for the quest of "21" in March 1974 came around, there was considerable evidence of strain among the swimmers. In the *Collegian* for February 28 the following article appeared under the headline, "The Coming of Age."

> The swimming alumni want to extend their best wishes to the team in its quest for number 21.
> Once again it seems we're the underdogs, but then, we've been in that position for twenty years. The seniors will understand and accept

Kenyon medley relay champions in the NCAA-College Division at
Springfield College in 1969. The Lords are easily identified by their
traditional shaved heads. Rear: left, Bill Koller, right, Larry Witner;
front: left, Bill Wallace, right, Doug Neff.

this, but the freshmen may wonder. The initiates must be told the
story.

They must be reminded that it doesn't matter how they are
seeded, that it doesn't matter how the win-and-loss record is compiled.
At conference time the Kenyon squad undergoes a transformation that
may be unique in athletic experience. It is only at this time that the
freshman realizes the compelling force of tradition. From his first day
at practice six months ago, he was impressed with the importance of
number 21. Each day of that six-month period he was reminded of the
necessity of upholding that tradition. By conference time, the idea of
tradition permeates his thinking and fills his veins with adrenalin.
This tradition swells within him until it becomes all-encompassing and
it is at this time that the mental dominates the physical and the
Kenyonite appears to perform the superhuman.

The freshman should be reminded of commonplace occurences like
John Greller's 1964 championship effort. Before the meet John wasn't
seeded in the top 12, but after the preliminaries he had qualified number
one. He should be told of Greg Kalmbach's ten second drop on the
200 breaststroke to come from nowhere to win the conference title. The
stories are endless, but the freshman doesn't comprehend their reality
until he is on the starting blocks; his hands are tingling, he's

emotionally upset with hopes and fears, and he's carrying the burden of twenty years. He's ready, he wants it, and he's scared — that's Kenyon's time-tested formula of success.

The team is ready, it wants it, and it's scared — it's time to come of age. 21!

LARRY WITNER   BILL WALLACE
DOUG NEFF   DICK KOLLER
JIM KILLPACK   CANDY WALLACE (honorary)

29th ANNUAL OHIO ATHLETIC CONFERENCE SWIMMING CHAMPIONSHIPS

**MARCH 4-5, 1966
PFEIFFER NATATORIUM
DELAWARE, OHIO**

The Lords have long been regarded as the "Kings" of the Ohio Athletic Conference in swimming.

165

Sam Barone (K1972), Kenyon's News Director, wrote in the April 1974 *Bulletin* of the winning of "21": "One of the youngest and least experienced teams ever asked to defend a Kenyon swim title, the 1974 Lords saw their hopes for "21" rise and plummet repeatedly during the three-day Ohio Conference championships . . . By the final night of competition, with just two events remaining, Kenyon was trailing Denison. But for Kenyon, a well-timed break occurred in the three-meter diving. The Lords held a solid second and third with seniors Phil Porter and Charlie Jones, but freshman diver Jake Layton had to hold on to ninth place. When the results were announced Layton had withstood the pressure and hung on to ninth place. Then, in another brilliant come-from-behind finish Kenyon's freestyle relay team of Niles Keeran (K1977), Bill Montei (K1975), Bruce Morton (K1976), and Rich James gave the Lords their sixth first place of the meet, and a winning spread of 18 points over Denison."

Kenyon in 1974 was the sole possessor of the NCAA record for consecutive swim championships, having pushed aside the mark shared with Yale. Kenyon's feat, however, is more than just an NCAA swimming record. Never has any college or university in America, large or small, won 21 straight titles in any sport.

Lacrosse

Kenyon College became a pioneer in lacrosse on April 12, 1941 when the Lords defeated Oberlin 9-5 in the first intercollegiate lacrosse game ever played in the Midwest. Since the team at that time was not officially sponsored by the College, it played under the name of the Kenyon Lacrosse Club. The sport was actually brought to Gambier a year earlier by several former prep school players, headed by Robert A. Weaver, Jr. (K1943) and Edward N. Chamberlain (K1943), who had played together on the championship Deerfield Academy team. Oberlin and the University of Michigan formed teams at about the same time, but Kenyon was credited by Midwestern sportswriters as "pioneers" of the game in the Midwest.

By beating Michigan 11-9 in the only other intercollegiate lacrosse game that first year, Kenyon laid claim to the first Midwestern championship.

Kenyon discontinued lacrosse until after the war. But in 1947 another Weaver, Bob's brother, Pete (K1950), organized the first Midwest team to resume play after the war's end. This squad traveled east for games with lacrosse powerhouses at Navy and Johns Hopkins. Roy Styers, who was an assistant in the Kenyon Athletic Department at the time, and who went with the team as coach and trainer, recalls a little anecdote of the trip: "Kenyon played Navy on a Saturday, and were, of course, badly outclassed. During the halftime the referee, Herman Epstein, strolled over to the Kenyon team to offer a bit of advice on changing the defense pattern. Mr. Epstein had formerly coached at Johns Hopkins and was an attorney in Baltimore. He was astounded to learn that this was the first game of lacrosse for most of the Kenyonites. He communicated this information to the Navy coach, who arranged for more time between the halves so that he (the Navy coach) could teach the Kenyon players more of the fundamentals of the game. The Johns Hopkins game took place on Monday afternoon, and Mr. Epstein closed his office so that he could spend Monday morning coaching Kenyon."

Lacrosse became a varsity sport at Kenyon in 1948. The Lords met Oberlin in a game that introduced lacrosse to the Midwest as a varsity intercollegiate sport and came away with a 7-6 victory. Pete Weaver was the high scorer with four goals. Against Eastern teams Kenyon did not have much success losing to Sampson, Hobart, and Penn State. In home territory the Lords did better, beating Ohio State twice before going down to defeat in the final game with Oberlin.

William C. Stiles was Kenyon's first professional lacrosse coach. He had been a lacrosse star as a member of the famous Deerfield Ten, and had gained All-American status at Hobart. During his ten years on the Hill he also assisted in other sports, and for a time was Assistant Dean. Beginning with a winning season, 4-2, in 1949, his teams posted winning but not spectacular records until 1955, when they were undefeated and untied in the eight games played. Led by Captains Richard G. Evans, Jr. (K1955) and Robert A. First (K1955), this team was awarded the mythical Midwestern championship. The *Collegian* called the 1956 season "disappointing," but the 1957 team came back with an outstanding 9-1 record and won the McCormick Cup as the undisputed champions of the Midwestern Lacrosse Association. After the 1958 season Stiles returned to Hobart to be Director of Student Activities and assist on the coaching staff.

The five seasons during which lacrosse was coached by Richard T. Pflieger and Norman Dubiel were classed by the *Collegian* as losing but respectable. However, in his one year at Kenyon, Coach Bill Hess produced an excellent 1964 team, with a record of eight wins, four losses, and one tie. Although the 1965 squad, coached by Dick Watts, posted a record just under the .500 mark, Kenyon's star, Jeffrey B. Ellis (K1967), was tops in the statistics of the MLA. Ellis left school to enter military service, then returned for his final two years and was graduated in 1972. His assistance in coaching contributed greatly to building up the team in 1971 and 1972.

Dave Cronin   Bob Heaps

Two lacrosse stars of the 1970's.

John Dulski coached during 1968 and 1969. then William J. Heiser, who had earned All-American honors at Hofstra University, began his lacrosse coaching career at Kenyon with the 1970 season. His 1972 and 1973 teams were outstanding. With a record of 12-1, Kenyon became the 1972 Midwestern Lacrosse Association champions, and David W. Cronin (K1973) was second in scoring in the Association. The next year Dave Cronin was the Association's high scorer, and Kenyon was second in the league with a record of 11-2. Robert G. Heaps (K1973) attained All-American honors for both the 1972 and 1973 seasons, and Cronin was an All-American in 1973.

Lacrosse has continued to generate great enthusiasm and support among the students. At the end of this third half century it is indisputably the most popular spring sport. Although the games have been played on Airport Field, a location notably lacking in comfort for the spectators, every home appearance has seen the field lined with student spectators.

Soccer

Like so many other sports at Kenyon, soccer began as the result of interest sparked by members of the academic faculty. In the case of soccer, the founders were Professors Andrew E. Hanfman (modern languages) and Franklin Miller, Jr. (physics).

The 1948 *Reveille* tells of the beginning: "One of the more pleasant athletic surprises of the school year 1947 and 1948 was the emergence of soccer as a varsity sport at Kenyon. In the winter of 1946 a few undaunted soccer enthusiasts of whom Swen Swenssen (K1950), Knute Christensen (K1950), and Hank Abraham (K1948) were the core, attempted to establish soccer at Kenyon, but their efforts proved premature. One year later, however, a genuine interest in soccer was conceived, and so many boys came out for the sport that sufficient personnel for three teams was on hand to welcome the coach, Dr. Andrew E. Hanfman.

"Dr. Hanfman was eminently qualified to coach soccer. He has had a wealth of playing experience on some of Europe's leading teams, and is intimately acquainted with each and every finesse of the game."

169

First soccer team at Kenyon — 1947. Coach Hanfman is at the right;
Captain Hank Abraham is number 37; and number 32 is Olof Palme,
who became Prime Minister of Sweden.

There were only four games that first season in 1947. Kenyon lost twice by close scores to Oberlin, the only other Ohio
college playing soccer. The other games resulted in a win over
University School of Cleveland, and a 2-2 tie with Western Reserve Academy. Several of the Kenyon players on that first
team had learned soccer in Europe; one of these was Olof
Palme (K1948) who later became Prime Minister of Sweden.

Professor Hanfman's 1950 team posted a 5-3 record for the
first winning season. Dr. Miller, who played soccer while an
undergraduate at Swarthmore, took over the coaching duties
in 1951. After a 3-3 first season, his teams had winning records
in 1952, 1953, and 1954. Tom Edwards then coached for three
winning seasons; his 1955 squad compiled the best record to
that time for a Kenyon soccer team, 6-1, and brought to
Gambier the mythical Midwestern championship. A high point
of this season was the breaking of Oberlin's skein of forty-two

games without a defeat. Dean Edwards ranks this season among his most satisfying coaching achievements. During the Miller-Edwards era, J. Wilson Ferguson (K1955) was rated an All-American goalie, and other stars of this period include David C. Adams (K1958), Silas Axtell (K1952), Charles C. Opdyke (K1957), Joseph P. Pavlovich (K1953), Donald Peppers (K1958), Michael F. Taddonio (K1956), and the VanDyke brothers, Bill and Bob (K1959).

Bob Harrison came to Kenyon primarily as a basketball coach, but he also produced some very successful soccer teams during his ten seasons in Gambier. His teams compiled their best records in 1962 and 1967. Captained by David B. Dawson (K1963) and David E. McKee (K1963), the 1962 squad wound up with a record of 5-4-1. The 1967 team came through with a 6-3-1 record, and Ned Smyth (K1970) broke every individual scoring record in Kenyon's history.

Bob Brannum coached Kenyon soccer for the 1968 and 1969 seasons, and he was followed by Jim Zak, the coach at the time this is written. Except for the 1972 season, when the record stood at 4-4-2, all of the Brannum-Zak teams posted winning seasons. The 1969 squad was the state scoring champion, and Zak's 1973 team finished the season with the most wins in the history of soccer at Kenyon, eleven victories against two defeats. This squad won the championship of the first Midwest Liberal Arts College Invitational Tournament at Ohio Wesleyan.

Star soccer players of the Brannum-Zak period include Peter Bersin (K1971), Steven E. Block (K1975), Micah T. Bloom (K1974), Neil S. Bloomberg (K1974), Steven N. Bralower (K1971), Douglas M. London (K1974), Eric W. Mueller (K1975), Stewart F. Peck (K1974), Keith Y. Tanaka (K1972), and Robert C. Zoller (K1974).

Wrestling

Although there are reports of wrestling clubs at Kenyon before World War II, there are no official records of this sport before 1954. The *Collegian* for January 15, 1954 reported: "Wrestling has returned to Kenyon. Now, one may hear the standard grunts and groans emanating from the handball court in the basement of Rosse Hall. Led by Coach Roy Styers, the matmen have scheduled three meets this year and plan to send representatives to the Case Interstate Conference Meet in Cleveland this March." On the schedule that year were the University of Akron, Ohio Wesleyan, and Oberlin; the very first match with Akron ended in a 15-15 tie.

After Styers left, the coaching was done on a volunteer basis by Matt Media and Moses Walker, a Bexley student. The Department of Athletics coaches, beginning in 1958, have been Lester Baum, Art Lave, Dick Watts, John Dulski, and Bill Heiser. Baum's 1960 team posted the first (and only) winning season for Kenyon, 5-3.

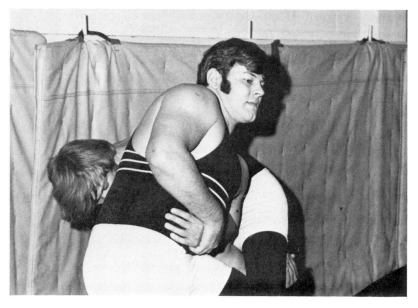

Rick Szilagyi, a four-year wrestler.

One of the most outstanding Lord wrestlers was Richard C. Szilagyi (K1973), who was on the team for all of his four years, and was undefeated in dual meets during his junior and senior years. Many of the wrestlers have been active participants in other sports. For example, David J. Utlak (K1974), wrestling captain for 1973 and 1974, played four years of football and three years of lacrosse.

Excellent facilities have been provided in the Field House for team practice and spectator viewing, but wrestling has not been a popular sport at Kenyon. The squad has lacked depth, and it has been necessary to forfeit many events. The *Collegian* has at various times chided the students for "their lack of support. There has been no more than 30 spectators at any meet."

Women's Athletics

During the first year of the Coordinate College there appears to have been little or no organized activity in women's athletics. At the beginning of the school year 1970-71, however, a memorandum went out from the President's office: "This is to advise that Janet L. (Mrs. James E.) Kelley was appointed on September 8, 1970 as Head Resident in Dormitory No. 2 of the Coordinate College for Women and Instructor of Physical Education and Athletics, half time, during the academic year 1970-1971."

Mrs. Kelley's report for that year shows that many sports were tried out, but the only activities in which there was a fair amount of participation were field hockey, modern dance, folk dancing, and lacrosse. About $500 was spent on uniforms, a record player and records for the dance groups, and equipment for field hockey and lacrosse. Coach Kelley wrote that women participated in two intercollegiate sports — field hockey in the fall and lacrosse in the spring. Some of the opponents were Bowling Green, Denison, Ohio Wesleyan, and Wooster, and records for that year were field hockey, 0-2-1; and lacrosse, 1-0-2.

In 1971-72 fifty-six women played in the two sports, and the field hockey team, playing on Airport Field, posted a 1-4-1 record. Lacrosse was played on McBride Field, and here the results were 1-4.

Esther D. Safford (K1974), writing in the *Collegian* for September 16, 1972, told of the next progressive step in women's athletics:

The biggest oversight in the facilities for the Coordinate College until this year has been the lack of any sort of athletic locker rooms or showers. Fortunately, this has very nearly been remedied. Within thirty days at the most, a women's wing at the fieldhouse will be completed. The wing will include an office for the physical education teacher and women's coach, and shower, locker, and first aid rooms. There will be 110 lockers, both full size and a small size for personal belongings. The shower room will be equipped with both open and stall showers. Also part of the wing is a furnace room, since it requires its own heating and hot water system. Similar remodeling is going on at the swimming pool. However, there the men's old locker room and shower are being redone for the women, and a new wing being built for the men.

Kim Mayhew scores a goal in lacrosse.

Assistant Athletic Director Karen L. Burke came to Kenyon in the fall of 1972 to become the first full-time woman staff member of the Department of Physical Education and Athletics. Her field hockey teams posted a 1-5-1 record in 1972, and in 1973 were 4-3-2. Lacrosse was 1-2-1 in 1973, and 4-3-2 in 1974. Most of the stars of these first teams played both field hockey and lacrosse. They included Virginia F. Buerman (K1974), Kate S. Debevoise (K1974), Ellen W. Griggs (K1977), Jane H. Macintyre (K1976), Dorinda K. Mayhew (K1974), Margaret M. Merckens (K1975), Cynthia A. Merritt (K1976), Elizabeth K. Parker (K1975), and Sally B. Pittman (K1974).

Women's basketball came to the Hill on a club basis in 1972-73; then in 1973-74 the Ladies played their first season in varsity competition. The co-captains of this first team were Liz Parker and Marylen C. Marty (K1974), and the members included Karen A. D'Arcy (K1977), Karin V. Nystrom (K1977), Holly I. Reed (K1977), and Sara A. Washam (K1975).

Intercollegiate tennis began with the 1973 season, when the record was 3-1. Stars included Sally Pittman and Margery E. Artley (K1975).

In 1974 the first Woman Athlete of the Year Award went to Kim Mayhew.

CHAPTER VII

Stones, Bricks, and Mortar

The shock of President Chalmers' sudden death completely paralyzed the College for a time, but work had to go on and provision had to be made for a temporary head. The Executive Committee of the Board of Trustees met on May 19, 1956 and designated Frank Edgar Bailey, Dean of the College, the acting president until the meeting of the full board on June 9. On that date the Board confirmed Dr. Bailey's appointment "for the academic year 1956-1957, or until a new President shall take office within that year."

Acting President Bailey

Frank Bailey came to Gambier in 1947 to serve as the Dean of the College and Professor of History. Previously he had taught history at Mount Holyoke College and M.I.T. After he was graduated from Dartmouth College in 1926, he went on to receive his Master's degree and his doctorate from Harvard University.

Not long after he arrived in Gambier came the tragic burning of Old Kenyon. It is said that his superhuman efforts in assisting the firefighting and rescue of students complicated back injuries which plagued him the rest of his life.

The year during which Dr. Bailey was acting president was a very trying one for the College. President Chalmers had been a strong president, with a reputation for making decisions without much consultation, and the sudden loss of such a dominant person inevitably lowered the morale of the faculty and students. Acting President Bailey elicited firm cooperation from the faculty and administration, and by the fall of 1956 confidently started a new academic year in which he did a fine job of holding the College together.

Professor Daniel T. Finkbeiner was appointed Dean of Students for the school year 1956-1957, and Acting Dean of the

176

College during the following semester while Dean Bailey was on leave.

On his return Dr. Bailey resumed his duties as Dean of the College and held that office until 1963, when he resigned to return to teaching in the Department of History.

Frank Edgar Bailey.

At the time of his retirement from the College in 1968 he received an honorary degree of Doctor of Humane Letters. His citation read:

Scholar-administrator and gentleman-farmer — seeker after truth in the groves of Academe and in the woods and fields: you have now become a son of Kenyon which you have nobly served for twenty-one years. We honor you for bringing the College from the depths of its severest tragedy — the Old Kenyon fire. We are grateful that you shouldered the responsibilities of the presidency of the College during an interim year. But we commend you also for your affection for students during your service as dean, and for the inspiration of your teaching. We admire your forthrightness, your concern for excellence, and that spunky spirit which carried you through difficult periods. The community rejoices that you will continue to be counselor and friend to town and gown.

Dr. Bailey died on Christmas Day, 1972. A portion of the Memorial Resolution of the Board of Trustees, passed on February 17, 1973, reads as follows: "Although it was not until 1968 that he officially became a son of Kenyon, with the awarding of the honorary degree of Doctor of Humane Letters, Frank Bailey was a true son of Kenyon long before that time and gave unstintingly of himself to its betterment. During Kenyon's severest tragedy — that of the Old Kenyon fire — he was untiring in his efforts to aid and to bring solace to those in the College and to the families of the students who had lost their lives in the fire. He had a deep concern and affection for the men of Kenyon, both as Dean and Professor. Of the many fine things we could say of him, we choose to note that he was an honest man and a true and affectionate friend."

Office of the Dean

The *Collegian* reported on September 27, 1957 that what Kenyon has always known as the "Office of the Dean" had been divided into two separate offices. In addition to the office of the Dean of the College, at that time held by Dr. Finkbeiner, "Thomas J. Edwards, long-known and recognized as coach of Kenyon soccer, swimming, and tennis teams, is known as 'Dean of Students.' Dean Edwards will deal with all problems related to the students. All social, personal, and student organizational problems will be handled by his office. The Student Council, Pan-Hellenic Council, and all divisions of student government will be working with Dean Edwards when problems are encountered."

Selection of President Lund

The Trustees' Committee on the Selection of a College President made an exhaustive search during the year following President Chalmers' death for a man who would satisfy the qualifications for the head of Kenyon. The Board at the meeting appointing the new president on June 22, 1957 passed a special resolution expressing its appreciation to Pierre B. McBride (K1918), chairman of the committee, for his unsparing efforts.

Letters connected with the selection indicate that the

Committee was more interested in a man who had successful experience in educational administration, than a brilliant scholar who might take several years to develop proficiency as an administrator. They also wanted a man who appreciated the part religion plays in a liberal arts education, and they preferred a man who had been active as a layman in the Episcopal Church.

The man selected was Franze Edward Lund, at that time president of Alabama College, Montevallo, Alabama. The background material presented to the Board at his election was as follows:

> Born Wuhu, China, (parents U.S. citizens), October 19, 1909: son of Rev. Franze Edward Lund and Augusta Elizabeth (Munn) Lund, Episcopal missionaries; graduated Deveaux Academy, Niagara Falls, New York, 1928; student Trinity College, University of Toronto, 1928-30; A.B. Washington and Lee University 1933, M.A. 1934; Ph.D. University of Wisconsin 1944; LLD (hon) Birmingham Southern College, 1955; married Martha Louise Gray, February 9, 1935; one daughter, Sigrid Gray, student at Randolph-Macon; with Southern Junior High School, Louisville, Kentucky, 1934; Howard Houston Fellow, Washington and Lee University, 1933-34; instructor 1935-38; fellow European History, University of Wisconsin 1938-39, 1943-44; research fellow, Yale, 1944-45; professor history, Wisconsin State College, 1939-46; chairman, department of history and social science, Alabama College, Florence, 1946, dean, 1947-52; president Alabama College, Montevallo, since 1952.

One of the letters attesting to Dr. Lund's ability stated, "In the five years he has been president of what used to be an insignificant, small Southern girls' college, he has built it into an outstanding liberal arts college and made it coeducational. The men he has recruited recently for the faculty are most promising, and he has built the institution physically into a beautiful community."

Other letters refer to Mrs. Lund as an asset to his candidacy. A typical comment was, "Mrs. Lund is just an ideal president's wife, lovely, gracious, intelligent."

Although he assumed office in October 1957, the inauguration of Dr. Lund took place on October 4, 1958. Speaking on that occasion, he made it clear that he recognized the high scholastic standards set by his predecessor and that he intended to maintain them. He stated that the "one social purpose embraced in a concept of liberal education is the training of individual free men and of individual leaders.

"The simple fact remains that a strict adherence to academic standards, to a liberating discipline, produces more men who are leaders — by which I mean simply those who 'make great demand on themselves.' Kenyon has had a proud record of producing Fulbright Scholars, Marshall Scholars, Woodrow Wilson Scholars, Rhodes Scholars, Pulitzer Prize winners, Guggenheim and Rockefeller Fellows."

The Rt. Rev. Nelson M. Burroughs, Bishop of Ohio, performed the induction of President Lund. Receiving honorary doctorates at the same time were Robert Lowell (K1940), Pulitzer Prize-winning poet; Pierre B. McBride (K1918), Kenyon trustee; Carl J. Djerassi (K1943), prize-winning chemist and one of the discoverers of cortisone; the Rev. G. Russel Hargate (K1930), rector of St. Andrews Church in Elyria, Ohio; the Rev. Donald McAdie (K1922), who was about to be consecrated as Suffragen Bishop of Newark (N.J.); and the Very Rev. Roger W. Blanchard, newly-elected Bishop Coadjutor in Southern Ohio.

Problems Confronting President Lund

"Buck" Lund had been made clearly aware of many of the problems which he must face at the beginning of his career at Kenyon. Although his predecessor had left him a priceless legacy of a fine scholastic reputation, the physical plant was in bad shape. The Alumni Library had burst its seams and books were scattered all over the campus; the interiors of Leonard and Hanna Halls were falling down; Peirce Hall facilities needed to be renovated; the power plant was in deplorable condition, with some of its boilers almost inoperative and hundreds of feet of steam line in need of replacement; faculty residences were crying for repairs; — the list seemed endless.

Finances, of course, were Dr. Lund's biggest problem. For many years the College had been enmeshed in deficit financing, and the resulting accumulated deficit was becoming alarmingly large for a college of Kenyon's size. Although the student enrollment reached about 500 at the time of his inauguration, the new president immediately began to feel the pressure to increase the number of undergraduates as a means of narrowing the deficit or eliminating it. However, dormitory space was by now a limiting factor, so decisions had to be made as to the feasibility of erecting new dormitories.

At the time of his election the Trustees had charged President Lund with the responsibility for the rehabilitation of the theological seminary, Bexley Hall. It was being said then that the morale of the Bexley students and faculty was low, that unsuitable candidates were being admitted and that leadership was lacking. It was said that some Bishops were loath to send their candidates to Bexley because of these unsatisfactory conditions. These and a myriad of other problems confronted President Lund in October 1957.

Two More Conferences at Kenyon

A conference on the Essentials of Freedom had been planned by President Chalmers just before his death. The Board of Trustees decided to carry through with his plans, and Professor Raymond English directed the Conference, which took place April 4 - 7, 1957 in Rosse Hall. From the program: "The Conference on the Essentials of Freedom was projected by Gordon Keith Chalmers and made possible by a grant from the Fund for the Republic. Its purpose is to inquire into the meaning and condition of human freedom, to help men to know the truth which makes them free and to recognize falsehoods that may enslave them."

Speakers at the Freedom Conference included Paul G. Hoffman, August Heckscher, Peter Viereck, Isidore I. Rabi, Clarence B. Randall, Gilbert Hauge, J. Donald Adams, Clinton L. Rossiter, Barbara Ward, Hans J. Morgenthau, and Gen. S.L.S. Marshall.

Professor Charles R. Ritcheson of the Department of History directed the Kenyon Symposium on "Communication Between the Arts and Sciences" held on October 27, 1961. The presence of Sir Charles P. Snow, British novelist and scientist, attracted nationwide coverage by the newspapers. Other speakers were Alan T. Waterman, director of the National Science Foundation; Edward Teller, distinguished nuclear physicist; philosopher Brand Blanchard; and James S. Ackerman, art historian. Philip Wiener, editor of the Journal of the History of Ideas, was the moderator.

Cultural and Social Life

The undergraduate days of Professor Ronald E. McLaren (K1958) span the final two years of Dr.Chalmers' administration, the acting presidency of Dr. Bailey, and the first year of President Lund's tenure. He recalls that the students knew President Chalmers as a strong and powerful man, that they had a deep respect for his intellect, and that with the shock of his sudden death came an apprehension over the future of the College.

Looking back on the cultural life of the students, Dr. McLaren feels that the leaders were a small, intellectually vital group whose main goal in coming to Kenyon was to discover and participate in the highest cultural achievement of our society. They saw Kenyon as a place where had been assembled a handful of faculty who were near-great, and they wanted to share in this atmosphere. There was somewhat of a tendency toward bohemianism, and the *Collegian* and *Hika* were used as instruments of social statement.

Professor McLaren says, "We had at Kenyon at that time kind of a preview of the Berkeley free speech movement." He feels that fraternities were a strong force in supplying the social needs of the college, but that they had a polarizing effect because each had its own homogeneous character. During this period the fraternities proved to be of great help to the deans in enforcing discipline.

In 1960 considerable concern arose among some students and members of the faculty and administration over matters of behavior, manners, and responsibility. Student Council President William Reed (K1960) held forth on mealtime behavior in Peirce Hall in the *Collegian* for February 12, 1960:

> . . . If you have ever waited outside Peirce Hall before a meal, you know what I mean. The minute the doors are opened the squeeze begins, and everybody gets squeezed, even your date, perhaps intentionally. It is during these times that one often wonders if there is such a thing as courtesy at Kenyon.
>
> The Archons run to their table, lest they be left to eat alone at some other fraternity's table. The A.D.'s beat the system by sneaking in the back door, infuriating the waiters in the process.
>
> The race has only begun. The waiters rush out with the food, and before you have taken your first bite the seconds start coming around.

182

The next thing you know the waiter is impatiently asking for your plate while the person next to you puts his foot on your pants in order to leave and attend to the many problems of the day. The whole process takes fifteen minutes (time it sometime) and for a really good waiter only ten minutes. During this short fifteen minutes the student consumes a meal that should have taken thirty minutes to eat. He accomplishes this by placing his mouth three inches from his plate. The table conversation is confined to "pass the damned milk." If a stranger approaches the table, the best policy is to ignore him, for he could infringe upon the student's valuable time. So the student leaves and the race is over, that is, until the next meal.

It was at this time that Dean Edwards put forth proposals for fraternity responsibility and self-government. A January 22, 1960 *Collegian* editorial commented:

> At a recent meeting of the Student Council, Dean Thomas Edwards made it clear that he felt the need for a system of fraternity self-government at Kenyon. The immediate reason given for this proposal was the "unhealthy situation" which, at present, exists on campus, manifesting itself in a disregard for the rights and feelings of others by many individuals. Particular examples of this disregard are seen each evening in the respective divisions and dorms on campus, during which time noise reaches a level of distraction which prohibits study and disturbs those who wish to relax or retire.
>
> Foul language seems at the same time to be a habit which cannot be suppressed on weekends or at other times during which women and parents are present in the divisions. General bad conduct and breakage continue to rage unchecked.
>
> The partial solution to this problem, in the opinion of the dean, lies with individual and corporate cooperation with the administration. The situation, he maintains, can best be realized by the institution of some form of fraternity of self-government.

Kenyon was not ready at this time for formal adoption of Dean Edward's proposals, but eyes had been opened by avid discussion, and during the Self-Study Program which followed soon after the proposals, much attention was given to student and fraternity responsibility. The categories of responsibility of the Kenyon fraternities are now spelled out explicitly in the Student Handbook.

Self-Study Program

Beginning in 1961 the faculty, at the urging of President Lund, undertook a two-year Self-Study Program aimed at "showing how Kenyon could become the best men's college in the nation." During the first year Professor Paul M. Titus served as the over-all director of the Program. When he went on leave he was succeeded by Professor Bruce Haywood in the following year. The planning and steering of the Study was the responsibility of the Educational Policies Committee, chaired by Dr. Lund the first year and by Professor Haywood the second year. Members of the faculty were organized into five committees: Committee on Curriculum, Professor Denham Sutcliffe, Chairman; Committee on Instruction, Professor Raymond English, Chairman (first year), Professor Bayes Norton, Chairman (second year); Committee on Student Life, Professor Daniel T. Finkbeiner, Chairman; Committee on Faculty, Professor Charles T. Thorton, Chairman; and Committee on Community Relations, Professor H. Landon Warner, Chairman. In addition, some of the main committees had as many as three sub-committees.

Most of the students had no clear idea of what the study was all about, but as time went on editorials in the *Collegian* became deeply critical of what was considered to be a waste of time and energy of the faculty. Then, too, there were complaints that there was little or no student involvement in the Self-Study Program. These were soon answered by the appointment of student members to the Committee on Student Life.

One of the students who participated in the Study was Perry C. Lentz (K1964), who is now Associate Professor of English at Kenyon. Writing a student comment in the report on the Self-Study Program published in the *Alumni Bulletin* for October-December 1963, he gives a graphic impression of the tremendous amount of organization and effort which went into the Study: "For myself, I found that I was chained to a vast and semi-secret organization: typewritten dates and deadlines came down the chain of command, committees met and debated and drafted during endless afternoons, and sheaves of paper, mimeographed or typed with carbons, were talked over, revised, filed away. As the months went on, the program became more and more time-consuming: meetings were held not only on Monday afternoons but on Thursdays at dinner time and on Fridays after lunch. The work itself — the gradual translation of debate and personal opinion into printed, official commentary, followed by printed, official recommendations — went on with all of the preciousness that is attendant on the committee system . . .

"This was Self-Study: a vague, monstrous, coffee-stained effort to explore opinion and preference, to detail the ideal and to delineate the actual."

In the introduction to the report to the Alumni, Professor Haywood wrote: "Kenyon's future distinction will depend in large measure upon its ability to attract students of excellent promise. The major recommendations of Self-Study seek to ensure that the College's undergraduate programs, both curricular and extracurricular, will satisfy the best. The young man who chooses to spend his undergraduate years in a small college rather than a large university seems to have two governing expectations. First, he seeks a closer relationship with his teachers than a large institution customarily permits. Second, he wishes to be involved in the life of the college and to identify with its purposes."

He goes on, "At the heart of the Self-Study Program has been the work of the Committee on Curriculum . . . The new curriculum adopted by the faculty for introduction in 1964 seeks to preserve what is best in Kenyon's traditional practice while answering the demands of the present hour . . . As a first step toward acquainting Kenyon undergraduates with the major areas of knowledge, the committee recommended the development of five basic courses."

Replacing the traditional diversification, the five basic courses were in science, literature, history, the arts, and in philosophic and religious thought. In these courses the teaching was to seek a high degree of integration.

Looking back ten years, Dr. Haywood, now Provost Haywood, feels that lack of integration was the reason the basic course plan was finally abandoned. However, he believes that one of the most lasting effects the Study had on the future of Kenyon was the departure from the old proscriptive curriculum.

Many of the other faculty members agree with Dr. Haywood that another lasting innovation which emerged from

185

Self-Study was the Campus Senate, in which for the first time students, faculty and administration functioned jointly in a body responsible for extracurricular activity.

Chalmers Library

The story of library building plans for Kenyon is one of frustration. By 1940 the Alumni Library (now renamed Ransom Hall) had become so crowded that its enlargement was regarded as the most urgent need of the College, but with the advent of World War II, building plans had to be abandoned. Again in 1947 plans for a new building were formulated. Professor Paul M. Titus, then Chairman of the Library Committee, recalls that the architect provided three separate exterior designs which could be used to encase one interior arrangement. Workmen actually staked off an area for the new library in 1948, but when Old Kenyon burned in 1949, the money needed for the library went into the reconstruction of Old Kenyon.

Writing in a Kenyon promotional booklet, *First Things First*, Professor Denham Sutcliffe, chairman of the English department, voiced the despair of the faculty over the library situation: "Books are spread all over the campus — in the annex, in the attic of the bookstore, in the old shooting gallery, in department offices. The result is crowding, confusion and discouragement. Books are sometimes hard to find and often irritatingly remote. We are shockingly behind other colleges in the essential matter of a library. The building that ought to be the center of the campus is missing at Kenyon."

The dream cherished by all Kenyonites came to realization with the completion of the Gordon Keith Chalmers Memorial Library in the fall of 1962 at a cost of over $1,200,000. The building was placed between Rosse Hall and Cromwell Cottage, necessitating the moving of the 1911 faculty residence next to Rosse to a location behind Cromwell.

Librarian Edward C. Heintz worked with the architects, O'Connor and Kilham of New York, to ensure that the functional logic of the plans was carried out. O'Connor and Kilham also designed the undergraduate library at Princeton and some twenty other college libraries. The result is a strikingly attractive building which provided Kenyon with library facilities equal to its academic reputation.

Moving Day from the Alumni Library to Chalmers Library.

The *Alumni News* for October-December 1962 reported on the library moving day: "On October 17, students, faculty, staff, and even a few assorted wives joined together to transfer 75,000 books from the old library to the new one. Boxes of books went out of the windows by chutes, were moved across the campus by tractors, and went by conveyer belt to the upper floors of Chalmers Library. There were also walking lines for folio volumes and other items difficult to pack. The job, which was expected to take all day, was substantially completed by mid-afternoon."

Dedication of Chalmers Library. From left: President Lund, Robert Frost, and Mrs. Gordon K. Chalmers.

In his speech at the dedication of Chalmers Library on October 28, 1962, Robert Frost began: "We're here to celebrate the giving of a gift to humanities in honor of a teacher of the humanities, Gordon Chalmers, my friend. The gift is a library, a sanctuary of the humanities, a stronghold of the humanities. And a place of resort for students—young people, older people, but young people particularly, who are having it out with themselves about God and man and sociology and poetry . . ."

In the new library provision was made for the housing, preserving, and safeguarding of the important papers of the College. The Kenyoniana Room, located on the lower floor of the building, is now the home of the Kenyon College Archives. Credit for assembling and arranging the Archives goes exclusively to John B. Hattendorf (K1964). When time came for the "big move" to the new library, Mr. Hattendorf was asked by Edward C. Heintz, the librarian, to assemble the many boxes and files of important papers (at that time in a chaotic state) and see that they were deposited in the specially designed archives room. Mr. Hattendorf spent two years sorting and collecting and once again made the files usable to the community and scholars in need of their contents. For this and for his other contributions Mr. Hattendorf received the Anderson Cup, given to an undergraduate who has done the most for Kenyon during the current year.

In the fall of 1964 Mrs. Denham (Priscilla H.) Sutcliffe became the first college archivist. When she left Gambier in 1967, she was succeeded by Thomas B. Greenslade (K1931).

Mr. and Mrs. Philip R. Mather at the dedication of Philip R. Mather Hall, shown in the background.

Philip Mather Science Hall

The increased enrollment and heightened interest in science of the early 1960's caused serious overcrowding in Samuel Mather Science Hall. At this time Mr. and Mrs. Philip R. Mather of Cleveland took the first step in expanding Kenyon's science facilities by supplying the money to construct a new chemistry building. Philip R. Mather Hall (New Mather, as it soon was called) was placed just north of Old Mather, and connected to it by a plate glass and aluminum walkway. The steel frame structure was faced with Briar Hill sandstone. The architecture of it in no way imitates that of Old Mather, but there is good harmony between the two buildings. The Austin Company of Cleveland were the designers and builders. Dedication ceremonies were on June 1, 1962. The cost of the new science building was over $500,000.

Professor James M. Pappenhagen of the Department of Chemistry played a large part in the design of the educational and research facilities of the building, and in the selection of the equipment. He and Vice President for Development William H. Thomas, Jr. put a tremendous amount of effort into a successful campaign to line up gifts and grants for equipping the building.

The new chemistry building was just one of the many gifts bestowed on Kenyon College by Mr. and Mrs. Mather. Philip R. Mather was an active member of the Board of Trustees for the last twenty-four years of his life. Truly, as cited in his doctoral citation in 1956, "No Trustee has more thoroughly studied the organization and problems of the College nor more richly deserved the respect and affection of the Faculty."

Dempsey Hall

By 1962 it became apparent that the dining facilities in Peirce Hall could no longer accommodate the increased number of students, and the Executive Committee on October 6, 1962 outlined definite plans for an expansion of Peirce. A previous proposal for a dining hall in the freshman dormitories had been abandoned for various reasons, but mainly that of cost of operation. At this time the proposal was made to the Board of Trustees to build an addition to Peirce Hall. Business Manager Lord stated that with the added facilities 864 students could be served at two seatings and that 1000 persons could be served with cafeteria-style service. It is interesting to note that at this point President Lund commented that he had no desire to go beyond an undergraduate enrollment of 700.

On April 1, 1964 a news release went out from Gambier:

Kenyon College President F. Edward Lund today announced that the recently completed addition to Peirce Hall, the college commons, has been named Dempsey Hall.

The two-story annex was named in recognition of the "loyal support of Ernest C. Dempsey, the late James B. Dempsey and other members of the Dempsey family."

Ernest Dempsey, Secretary of the Kenyon College Corporation, is a 1911 graduate and has served on the Board of Trustees for more than 40 years. He is a partner in the Cleveland law firm of Squire, Sanders and Dempsey. Other members of the Dempsey family have been interested in the welfare of the college for over 70 years.

Opened last fall, Dempsey Hall was constructed at a cost of $253,000 and features a dining room with a capacity of 200 on the upper level, along with a lobby, corridor and terrace. The lower level contains private dining rooms and rooms for special events. Vaulted ceilings and panelled walls conform with the style of the older Peirce Hall and the exterior combination of sandstone and limestone is similar.

Although few additions to existing buildings are architectural improvements over the original, the designers of Dempsey Hall did an exceptionally fine job of conforming it to Peirce Hall. The front or west side of Peirce was left intact. One of the most attractive features of Peirce Hall had been the balustraded terrace with its magnificent view over the Kokosing Valley to the hills in the east. The architects simply lifted the terrace, placed it some forty feet east of its original location, and worked it into the Dempsey Hall addition so cleverly that many returning graduates are not even aware of the move. Those with sharp memories will note that the steps to the terrace from the ground, formerly coming up from the south side, are now on the north. The striking profile of Peirce Hall, viewed as one comes up the valley, has not changed.

Gund Hall

Opened in the fall of 1963, Gund Hall, a $404,000 freshman dormitory, was dedicated on October 31, 1964 at the same time the dedication of Dempsey Hall was celebrated. The new building forms the bottom of a "U" between the two other freshman dormitories, Norton Hall and Lewis Hall. The two story structure has 39 double rooms for students, four single rooms for proctors, and an apartment for a faculty adviser.

Gund Hall was named in honor of George Gund of Cleveland, a member of the Board of Trustees from 1948 until his death in 1966, and for many years Chairman of the Financial Committee. Mr. Gund, chief executive officer of the Cleveland

Trust Company and a member of the boards of some thirty major companies, was especially generous to Kenyon, not only in providing funds and expert advice for the building program but in establishing funds for lectures and concerts.

The George S. Rider Company of Cleveland was the architect-engineer for both Dempsey Hall and Gund Hall.

Special Souvenir Program

KENYON vs CAPITAL

25¢   OCTOBER 13, 1962

HOMECOMING

AND

DEDICATION

OF

McBRIDE FIELD

Program cover for the dedication of McBride Field.

McBride Field

On Homecoming Day, October 13, 1962, McBride Field was dedicated. Going into the game with a 2-1 record, the football team provided the only disappointment of the day by losing to Capital, 14-20. On hand to assist in the festivities was Pierre B. McBride (K1918), donor of the funds for the new field and one of Kenyon's most generous benefactors.

Some idea of the students' appreciation of Mr. McBride's generosity, not only in his contributions for improved athletic facilities but those touching every other phase of Kenyon life, may be gathered from the *Collegian* article on October 19, 1962:

> A man who has been a most generous benefactor of Kenyon College for many years was in town last Saturday to witness the dedication of a personally-financed project that spanned 10 years from conception to completion.
>
> The new development, an athletic field first class, is the end result of a $24,000 check which bore the name Pierre B. McBride. This distinguished Kenyon graduate of 1918, a respected Louisville, Ky. business magnate with a civic and a cultural conscience, told the *Collegian* he had visions of a safer and more suitable playing field while a student here, but it wasn't until 1952 that his dream matured into positive action. It was then that he convinced college authorities of the need for improved athletic conditions.
>
> "I talked to a number of people," said the handsome, white-haired Southerner. "I told them I thought improved facilities would be beneficial to hampered athletic teams and to the college as well. I thought it would be a morale booster."
>
> McBride, who made the special gift "about a year ago," seemed quite pleased with the finished product, something which will have to last the school indefinitely. "Whenever you give something, you find it comes back many times over in the form of personal satisfaction. You don't lose anything in giving," he explained.
>
> Without being prodded he went on to say, "I am very conscious that this stipulated grant has deprived the college in other areas." He justified his motive on the grounds that he "just felt that it was a terribly important improvement."
>
> At this point it should not go unmentioned that McBride has invested many thousands of dollars toward the academic amelioration of Kenyon. Such donations have increased faculty salaries and helped to erect new buildings. He initiated and personally subsidized the sabbatical leave program for the faculty. Of most recent importance was his unrestricted $100,000 challenge gift, supplementing his original campaign commitment, that brought the general development drive to a successful conclusion two years ago.
>
> "I don't consider myself an especially wealthy man," he confided modestly, "but I am head of a company (Porcelain Metals Corporation, Louisville) that is doing well. I feel that my contributions are just a partial payment of the debt I owe the college.
>
> "I can thank Kenyon and its fine professors for the motivation they instilled in me," he said. This moral obligation was the "debt" he spoke of earlier. Would that there were more indebted alumni.

The same issue of the *Collegian* printed also a boxed-in column headed "Pierre B. McBride — a Partial List of his Cre-

193

dentials." The items related to Kenyon College were: a Trustee of Kenyon College, and since 1958, chairman of the Executive Committee of the Board of Trustees; served two terms (1954-60) as an Alumni Trustee, and in 1960 was elected to the permanent board; member of the executive committee of the Kenyon-Bexley cooperative development campaign in 1959 and 1960; chairman, in 1956, of the committee of Trustees which successfully undertook to find a successor to Gordon Keith Chalmers; president of the Kenyon Alumni Council, 1952-54; only two-time winner of Kenyon's Gregg Cup Award as alumnus who had done most for the college; member of Delta Tau Delta fraternity; awarded the Kenyon honorary Doctor of Laws degree in 1958.

General Electric College Bowl

The appearance of a Kenyon team on the "General Electric College Bowl" television in the spring of 1963 brought a flood of favorable publicity to the College. The Kenyon group appeared on the NBC prime-time program for five consecutive Sunday evenings, defeating Wake Forest, University of South Dakota, Clark, and Allegheny, before losing to the University of Louisville.

Representing Kenyon were Perry C. Lentz (K1964), Captain; John Gerlach (K1963); Neal M. Mayer (K1963); and Michael P. Underwood (K1965). Professor Paul Trescott, of the Department of Economics, was the coach.

When Kenyon received an invitation to appear on the program, students were invited to take a written examination based on a quiz book put out by the G.E. College Bowl program. About 50 accepted, and the final four were selected as a result of this examination plus other tests.

All told, the team won $7,500 in scholarship money for the College, besides generating a large monetary response from alumni and friends of the College. But the publicity value of the appearances was way out of proportion to the money won. The *Collegian* reported that "someone was tossing around a figure of $300,000 for the publicity and Admissions Director Tracy Scudder has already noticed a difference." As a matter of fact the G.E. College Bowl publicity brochure a year or two later contained a letter from a mother whose son had been influenced to go to Kenyon after the Bowl appearances.

Alvin Beam, writing in the *Cleveland Plain Dealer*, commented: "In educational circles in the nation, the little college in Knox County is practically peerless. In other circles, even in Ohio, there was a serious question as to whether Kenyon was known at all until 'Bowl' came along.

Kenyon's College Bowl Team, whose success brought the College priceless national publicity.

"Especially was Kenyon not known in the spectacular world of television, where a college makes the grade chiefly by the production of a football team. Kenyon does have a football team called the Kenyon 'Lords,' but there is nothing lordly about its play.

"Then here comes TV's 'College Bowl,' providing Kenyon grads with the opportunity to sit before the old tube of a Sunday afternoon and watch Kenyon lads at play."

During the time that the Kenyon team was being selected the students had mixed feelings about the venture. The *Collegian* editorialized: "The College Bowl is . . . or is made to appear . . . as a contest of intellects, despite all producers' disclaimers. General Electric knows it isn't. We know it isn't. The MC says it isn't . . . that it's a fun-type quiz-kiddish quick recall contest, of no real significance in measuring a school's academic quality. But it is doubtful that the five million viewers make such fine distinctions."

The students quickly replaced their apprehension with enthusiasm as Kenyon's team won week after week by large scores. The *Collegian* in detailing the effects the Bowl victories had upon the Kenyon community, emphasized the pride the students developed in their team.

On the Bowl program each college presented a one-minute film and narrative showing life on its campus. The content of this was the subject of much discussion on the Hill. The *Collegian* editors wrote a long editorial full of suggestions, ending with: "What we need to show is Sutcliffe walking to class, Thermos in hand, capped with his Persian lamb hat, and followed by Jack. Only an intellectual would be like that. Or show Feldman and Roelofs riding their bikes, enjoying the hell out of life. Or the students going their indifferent, solitary way. We'd show the buildings, too. Impress the audience with the history of Old Kenyon and the exterior of the library. Scrutinize the interior of Peirce and examine the gulp gullets of the students.

"Come the ides, most of all we'd like to see a film that left us with the impression students feel at Sunday chow. When they arise, face west, and feel, 'By God, this is Kenyon.'"

In the same issue there is mention of some of the people involved in the making of the film, among them: "*Collegian* film critic Jay Cocks has agreed to direct the film, giving his ample critics ample chance to call his work 'bloated,' 'arty,' and 'pompous,'" (John C. Cocks (K1966) is now the film critic for *TIME*).

Professor Denham Sutcliffe prepared the one-minute narration: "Persons who know colleges for their football teams have never heard of Kenyon College. Readers of educational news see it constantly mentioned as one of the best colleges of the liberal arts. Kenyon College, the mid-west's oldest college for men, is beautifully situated in rural Ohio. It is the publisher of the famous *Kenyon Review,* and founder of the Advanced Placement Program, whose tenth anniversary Kenyon celebrates with special scholarships.

"At Kenyon College a faculty of sixty scholars instructs six hundred young men, all chosen carefully from the leading members of their secondary school classes. The faculty can be known and are worth knowing. Independent research is a common enterprise of the students. More than sixty per cent of Kenyon's graduates proceed to graduate schools. New buildings mark Kenyon's conservative expansion and constant improvement.

"Student life is not monastic. There is a vigorous program of intercollegiate and intramural sports. The ladies visit."

Further Ransom Tributes

Long after his retirement from the faculty in 1958 tributes continued to pour in to Professor John Crowe Ransom for his teaching, writing, and his editorship of the *Kenyon Review.* In 1964 two Kenyon undergraduates, D. David Long (K1965) and Michael R. Burr (K1966), edited a handsomely printed 56 page supplement to the *Collegian* entitled, *John Crowe Ransom, A Tribute from the Community of Letters.* Included in it were 55 contributions from students, faculty, and nationally-known poets and writers.

In 1968 Kenyon honored Professor Ransom with a special convocation in celebration of his 80th birthday. In its May 10, 1968 issue, *LIFE* magazine published five photographs of the occasion along with a news story which read in part: "Of the many poets, authors and editors in his debt, an illustrious few had journeyed to foregather with Pappy, as they all call him, and to take part in a special college convocation. Robert Lowell brought along a poem written for the occasion; Allen Tate delivered a prose tribute. At the ceremony Ransom took a bow but said nothing. Later he remarked of few other poets thus feted before death.

John Crowe Ransom died in his sleep on July 3, 1974 at the age of 86.

Faculty Deaths

In 1964 Professor Denham Sutcliffe died at the age of 51. It is probable that no person loved Kenyon more, understood

Kenyon better, and communicated this love and understanding more clearly through writing and speech.

Denham Sutcliffe at the counter of his bookstore.

The *Collegian* for March 13, 1964 devoted a special section to *His Life, His Memory, and His Work*. In the section on his life, Alan R. Vogeler, Jr. (K1965) and Warren M. Iwassa (K1965) wrote:

> Denham Sutcliffe, James H. Dempsey Professor of English, died on February 29, 1964. Though we had known of his illness, the announcement of his death stunned us. The man who had taught here, the man who had instructed and asked in turn to be informed, the man whose abiding concern was the teaching of English, cannot be replaced; and we feel the loss.
>
> Stature was not a gift outright to him. Born in Bristol, Pennsylvania in 1913, soon fatherless, he knew poverty as a youth. His undergraduate education at Bates College was accompanied by an education

of another sort; the desire to win a degree during the depression again
introduced him to privation — and hunger. His attempt was, any man
would agree, successful; in three and one-half years he was graduated
and elected to Phi Beta Kappa. Scholar he was, and also outdoorsman.

From Maine he went to Hereford College of Oxford University,
and in 1938 he received his B.A., taking First Class Honors. To enable
him to begin work on a doctorate, the Rhodes Foundation subsequently approved a third year at Oxford. In 1940 and in 1941 he held Carnegie Fellowships, working independently on his thesis in America. In
1943 he received the degree, D. Phil. from Oxford.

Before he was asked to come to Kenyon in 1946, he taught at Bates
College and at Harvard University. Prior to his Kenyon appointment
he served as president of Education for Freedom, Inc. in New York. In
1956 he was appointed chairman of Kenyon's English department.

Professor Gerrit Roelofs wrote a particularly beautiful
section on his memory, which began: "We all knew him as
Dennie. He would not let the children of the Village call him
Mister Sutcliffe. The title of courtesy was a foreign element in
the relationship between man and child, a positive hindrance
in teaching a small boy how to ride a bicycle. I believe that
every dog and every rabbit in the Village knew him as Dennie,
just as he knew them by their given names. I am sure his students never thought of him as anything else, although proto-
col, and the more Johnsonian the better, required that he and
they salute each other with proper formality. For a man who
was outwardly and formidably formal — a telephone call from
him was an invigorating but sometimes shattering experience
— he was the most sociable and endearing of men. At his best,
he was puckish, merry, splendidly informal. The sonorous formality of Denham was simply a needed device to protect, to
keep spontaneous the innocence of Dennie."

P. Frederick Kluge (K1964) wrote: "I'm certain that to
some of the students — not all of them English majors — Denham Sutcliffe must always represent their experience at Kenyon.

"We were all introduced to Sutcliffe at the same time, at
our class convening banquet in Peirce Hall during the orientation period freshman year. Orientation then was pretty much
as it is now . . . a battery of addresses from the local hierarchs
. . and I suppose we considered ourselves highly sophisticated
critics of the local orators. Yet Sutcliffe's review of the history

and traditions of the College was something special, and half of us walked out thinking it was the greatest thing we'd ever heard."

In 1973 Kenyon College, with The Newberry Library and The University of Chicago Press, brought out a book of ten essays and addresses by Denham Sutcliffe, entitled, "What Shall We Defend?" W. Harley Henry (K1959), a former student of Professor Sutcliffe, wrote the introduction and edited the collection.

Professor Sutcliffe's death occurred during the period when several key faculty members left for other institutions. Some of these were: Virgil C. Aldrich, Chairman of Philosophy; Raymond English, Chairman of Political Science; Charles S. Thornton, Chairman of Biology; Edwin J. Robinson, who succeeded Professor Thornton as Chairman of Biology; and Charles R. Ritcheson of the Department of History.

The loss of these men troubled President Lund very much, and he made numerous references in Trustees' meetings to their departure as weakening the faculty.

Kenyon suffered another tragic loss during the academic year 1963-1964 in the sudden death of Jess Willard ("Skip") Falkenstine, director of athletics. He had been coach of baseball and basketball, and had assisted in football as backfield coach. Following his graduation from West Virginia University and five years in the Navy during World War II, he had coached at R.P.I. before coming to Kenyon. He received his doctorate from Michigan State University in 1957, and had been appointed to full professorship for the school year 1964-1965.

In a tribute to him in the June 5, 1964 *Collegian* Terry Murbach (K1964) wrote: "With the loss of Skip, Kenyon has lost one of its truly outstanding personalities. No one will ever possess his rare combination of abilities and personal magnetism. He has contributed something permanent by giving his athletic teams and the rest of the College a feeling that athletics are and should be a significant part of Kenyon life. We cannot help sensing how inadequate any verbal tribute must be, but there will be a lasting tribute to him in the memories that Skip Falkenstine has left at Kenyon."

In the *Alumni Review* for July-September 1964, Dean Thomas J. Edwards wrote: "It has been said that life consists of what a man is thinking of all day. If this is so, then Skip Falkenstine had a rich and rewarding life. He was never idle; he was vigorous, he was hardy. Mainly, he was interested in people, students particularly, and he used athletics, which he knew and loved so well, as a community for fellowship. Very few have that natural facility for combining technical competence with an authentic fondness for company. Skip did, and Kenyon was the beneficiary."

In the *Collegian* article Professor Edward Harvey had a homey reminiscence of his friend Skip: "No one who knew him will forget him. Each of us will have his own picture, of course. Mine includes his membership in the fraternity which held its brief meetings every morning except Sunday in front of Jim Hayes' grocery store, those of us who have to ingest our daily ration of newsprint even before breakfast. It was a town and gown situation in miniature marked by the greatest good spirits, loud protests against Jim's incessant demands that we do something about his latest indignity, mock anger and flattering insults — men being boys for a few minutes before facing the daily routine."

In the fall of 1955 the Trustees voted to rename the old "Fieldhouse Field," including the baseball and soccer areas, the Jess Willard Falkenstine Field. They directed that all moneys received as contributions in Falkenstine's memory be used for rehabilitating facilities on the field.

On October 27, 1967 Professor Bayes M. Norton was found dead on the floor of the chemistry stockroom where he had apparently gone to make preparations for his morning lecture. He was 64 and had been a member of the faculty for 30 years. A native of Massachusetts, he was educated at Yale and Oxford and was a member of the 1924 U.S. Olympic team.

His friend and colleague, Professor Franklin Miller, Jr., wrote a remembrance of him in the November 2, 1967 issue of the *Collegian*. Some excerpts: "In his wisdom, the late Gordon Chalmers sent me to talk with Bayes Norton when I visited Kenyon in 1948 during the courtship ritual which seems to be required when an academic appointment is to be made. No better choice could have been made; he sold me on Kenyon, and continued to do so during the two decades I knew him. For here was an obvious scholar, a chemist's chemist, who nevertheless radiated an enthusiasm for teaching, a lively participation in the arts, a welcome appreciation of the sports, a sober sense of social responsibility.

"Strangely, it was not until 1962 that the way was opened for Bayes to teach the kind of course he had always wanted to teach. He had been brought in to establish a course that would give non-science students an insight into the aims and methods of 'real science.' He called the laboratory work in his course the 'Nobel Prize experiments' because he knew that students from across the Middle Path could and would respond to the best. He wanted not trivial and sterile exercises, but real contact, face-to-face, with the electron, the photon, the great generalizations of thermo-dynamics.

"We knew him as a teacher and scholar, but his great influence outside the College was in the early days of the School and College Study of Admission With Advanced Standing, known then as the Kenyon Plan.

"The other great push outside Kenyon was Bayes' wartime work as technical administrator for the Office of Scientific Research and Development.

"Bayes Norton served his Church, his profession, his country. Most of all, he served his students and his College."

A Dusty Path

Appearing as a supplement to the *Reveille* for 1964 was a charming one-hundred-page book called *A Dusty Path*. John B. Hattendorf (K1964) compiled the book, the photographs were prepared by William R. Dye (K1967), and John E. Schofield (K1965) did the design and the editing.

Outside of captions the only text written for the publication was its introduction:

> Walking down Middle Path is itself an excursion into Kenyon's history: the names of buildings, streets, and houses along the way remind one of the men who founded and shaped the College.
>
> Their history is one which has not been forgotten. President Bodine randomly collected documents concerning the College and published them in 1890 in *The Kenyon Book*. Professor George Franklin

Smythe wrote a thorough history of the College for its centennial in 1924, and Professor Richard Salomon has published a number of articles on Bishop Chase and the early Church in Ohio. Yet the study of Kenyon's history is not complete; there is much to be done and much to be learned.

What we present here is neither a scholarly nor a complete study of the College's one-hundred-forty years. We have collected some fragments from Kenyon's history; we have chosen them for their historical and pictorial quality and interest. Little of what we have gathered here is new to the historian; but it is our hope that this little book will entertain the reader, encourage interest in the history of the institution, and at least partially capture the spirit of Kenyon College.

Reproductions in the book are of letters and other documents, posters, drawings, and photographs. It is a very pleasant book to read, and the selection of materials reveals an excellent understanding of the history of Kenyon by its editors. The total printing was 1675: bound in *Reveille 1964*, 650 copies; in leather hard grain covers, 25; and in paper binding, 1000. The immediate success of *A Dusty Path* has made it a collector's item.

Departmental Expansion

One of the notably progressive steps taken during the Lund administration was the expansion of the departments of art, music and religion and the elevation of their status to that of major subjects.

During the Twenties and the Thirties the Department of Religion and the Bible gave just one course, Bible 1, 2, which was required of all sophomores and carried with it a one-hour course credit for each semester. Teaching this course was generally one of the duties of the college chaplain, who was also the rector of Harcourt Parish. The college catalogue occasionally listed a member of the Bexley Hall faculty as an additional lecturer.

Just before World War II the name was changed to the Department of Religion and a course in Christian Apologetics was added. After the end of the war the course offerings were expanded with studies in religions other than those of the Bible being given.

The coming to Kenyon of Professor A. Denis Baly in 1956, first as a Lecturer in Political Science, then as a Professor of

Religion, marks the beginning of a permanent Department of Religion with full-time members.

The department now has six members, whose scholarship covers a wide range, enabling the course offerings to include those dealing with most of the major Eastern and Far Eastern religions. In addition, three members of the department are listed in the Department of Classics, where they teach courses in Hebrew, Arabic, and Sanskrit.

The current catalogue has this statement about the Department of Religion: "The department is concerned with the academic and systematic study of religion as a phenomenon of human existence. Its courses are designed to enable students to examine a wide range of religious experience and faiths, the relation of religious to philosophical concepts, and the bearing of religious beliefs upon political actions and social structures."

Farr Hall

In 1964 the Trustees began to see a need for some urban redevelopment of Gambier, particularly with regard to the east side of Gaskin Street at the north end of the business district. Here there was a cluster of small, old buildings, some of them badly in need of repair. The end result of this concern was a commercial building, later named Farr Hall, which was completed in 1966.

It is a tribute to the sensitivity of the students and faculty over the appearance of the Village that the design of this building generated much controversy. The architect submitted three completely different plans before coming up with one which satisfied most of the critics.

The building was named in honor of George Farr, Jr. (K1926), who served as legal counsel of the College for 12 years and who was a member of the Board of Trustees and chairman of the building and grounds committee from 1958 until his death in 1967.

Because of the slope of the terrain, the building is two stories high in front and three behind. The front ground floor at present houses a grocery store, a pizza restaurant, and the college book store. Accessible from the east side, the rear ground floor has at various times been occupied by Kenyon's

FM station WKCO, a beauty shop and a laundromat. On the second floor are 22 single and four double rooms reserved for seniors, plus two apartments for members of the faculty or staff. Farr Hall cost over $500,000 to build.

First to move into the new building was that beloved institution, the Hayes Grocery. The *Collegian* for September 29, 1966 memorialized the event:

> His store decorated by clusters of balloons hanging from the ceiling, Jim Hayes and all of Knox County celebrated the grand opening of Hayes' Grocery. Gambier's answer to Huntington Hartford and the rest of the world of creeping commercialism. Commercialism, in fact, crept not at all, but jumped an entire block from one end of Chase Avenue to the other, as Mr. Hayes moved his store from its former location into newly-built but not-quite-completed Farr Hall.
>
> The new store is bigger, brighter, and better-stocked than the old; Mr. Hayes, Mrs. Temple, and Art Arnold are homey as ever, but there is little else in the emporium that is quaint. Everything is directed toward convenience. There is an IN door and an OUT door. At one of the cash registers, Ardelle (Mrs. Al the Barber) Temple points with pride to Banker Ray Brown's opening day floral tribute as she mentions that, just beside it, Phillips Milk of Magnesia is on sale at a special bargain price. After all, business is business.
>
> Mr. Hayes himself, looking content and prosperous, is "mighty pleased" with his new store. Drinking a Coke and taking an inventory of his lettuce, he spoke to a *Collegian* reporter, his speech punctuated by words like "merchandising" and "competition." Today Jim Hayes thinks in terms of serving the entire Knox County area. His customers include village residents, Kenyon students and faculty, and some of the more liberal element of Mount Vernon's population.

Bushnell and Manning Halls

The Trustees minutes for October 19, 1963 emphasized the need for more upperclass housing: "The anticipated enrollment for the fall of 1964 is 670-675. With all dormitory space used and 29 students living off campus, there will still be a shortage of 14 beds."

To meet this need Philadelphia architect Vincent G. Kling designed two identical "L" shaped buildings to be built just south of the two wings of Old Kenyon. Many architectural buffs contend that the design is not in harmony with Old Kenyon, but occupants of the buildings generally applaud the interior arrangements.

The east building is named Charles D. Bushnell Hall. The name honors the grandfather of Pierre Bushnell McBride, generous benefactor of the College and a long-time member of the Board of Trustees.

The building on the west is called Richard C. Manning Hall in honor of the legendary Benson Memorial Professor of Latin who died in Gambier in 1957.

The characteristic shape of the buildings forms a quadrangle with Old Kenyon. Designed to house 112 students, the total cost for the two structures was $800,000, financed mainly by a $550,000 college housing loan granted by the Housing and Home Finance Agency. The contractors, Albert M. Higley Company of Cleveland, began work during the summer of 1965, and the buildings were first occupied by students at the opening of the fall term in 1966.

Public Affairs Conference Center

The Public Affairs Conference Center, which moved to Kenyon from the University of Chicago in 1967, has provided challenging educational opportunities for the students and has been the source of national recognition. As set up by Professor Robert Goldwin of the Political Science Department, each of three or four Distinguished Visitors are on the Hill for periods of about a week. During that time they lead seminars studying the topic for the year, meet other classes and make public appearances.

At the end of the semester's work the visitors and some 20 other leaders in the fields of national government, mass media, education and industry meet for three days in closed conference. During this period there is an intensive exchange of ideas. Following the annual conference on the Kenyon campus, the proceedings are revised, edited, and published by Rand McNally.

The Ford Foundation furnished the original grant of $71,000 to bring the PACC to Gambier and to assist in its operation for several years. The College is now continuing the Conference operation with the help of gifts and grants.

Following Professor Goldwin's departure from Kenyon, Professor Harry M. Clor was the director for three years. The present director is Dr. Robert A. Bauer, formerly head of the

Foreign Press Center for the United States Information Agency.

The discussions have focussed on such topics as "Civil Disorder and Violence," "Mass Media and Modern Democracy," and "How Democratic is America." The participants have included Saul Alinsky, Edward C. Banfield, Tom C. Clark, James Farmer, Paul Goodman, Sidney Hook, Robert Novak, Senator Charles Percy, and Tom Wicker.

In 1973 the PACC was renamed the Kenyon Public Affairs Forum.

Rhodes Scholars

Three of the seven Kenyon men who have won Rhodes Scholarships brought that honor to the College during this era. They were Eugene Nasser (K1957), William Harley Henry (K1959) and Warren Iwassa (K1965), who was the first candidate from Hawaii to win the honor. During this time there were nine Rhodes Scholarships awarded to graduates of Ohio colleges; thus Kenyon was proud to have received one-third of them.

One of the most prestigious internationally-awarded scholarships, the Rhodes Scholarships recognize academic achievement and physical vigor which may be evidenced by athletics. Established by Cecil Rhodes, the scholarships provide two, possibly three, years of study for 32 Americans at Oxford each year. The Rhodes honor is highly prized by scholars and academicians.

Previous Kenyon winners were William J. Bland (K1909), W.W. Sant (K1914) and Walter Elder (K1942). Recently attaining the honor of winning a Rhodes was Mathew T. Valencic, of the Class of 1973.

There are two Rhodes winners now on the faculty — William E. McCulloh, Professor of Classics, and Peter B. Seymour, of the Department of Romance Languages. Other Rhodes Scholars who have been associated with the College: President Gordon K. Chalmers, English professor Denham Sutcliffe, poet John Crowe Ransom and history professor Charles L. Hamilton.

The excellent showing made by Kenyon graduates in winning national grants and fellowships is highlighted in a typical article in the publication "Along Middle Path" for March 1967. Under the headline, "Seven Kenyon Students Selected Wilson Fellows," the article read:

Kenyon College continues to show outstanding performance in the annual Woodrow Wilson Fellowship competition. The Princeton, N.J. foundation has announced that seven seniors — one more than last year — have been awarded fellowships.

Receiving awards are James W. Ceasar, Shaker Heights, O.; W. Michael Clark, Stockton, Calif.; Lawrence D. Gall, Lakewood, O.; Edward R. Hallowell, Gladwyne, Pa.; James A. Robinson, Chagrin Falls, O.; Mark Savin, Highland Park, Ill.; and Joseph E. Simon, Cleveland, O.

In addition, Robert J. Gibbons, Pittsburgh, and Ronald F. Javorcky, Lakewood, O., received honorable mention.

Kenyon, whose student body represents less than one-half of 1% of the entire full-time, on campus, enrollment in Ohio, received 12.3% of all awards made in the state.

Faculty and Staff Housing

From the early days of Kenyon College it had been traditional for the College to furnish housing for its faculty. Just as traditional was the constant friction between administration and faculty caused by real or imagined inadequacies and inequities in housing. Moving from house to house was almost a yearly affair. Since the choice of a house was based on seniority, a vacated residence resulted in a complete movement of household goods, all down the line, and usually on the same day.

As the faculty began to expand after World War II, the number of college-owned houses was inadequate, and the College rented houses and apartments for its employees. As time went on it became apparent that the College wanted to get out of the real estate business with all of its maintenance problems. College-owned houses were made available for sale to members of the faculty and staff, and the College encouraged them to buy or build by arranging with Mount Vernon banks to guarantee a portion of the purchase or building loan. To those faculty members furnishing their own housing the College gave a cash allowance in lieu of housing of roughly $1000 to $1200 per year.

In 1961 the College offered for sale to members of the

faculty and staff building lots on Kokosing Drive, a newly-built street running through a wooded area from the north end of Ward Street to Kokosing, the "Bishop's Palace." A little later, in 1965, the College laid out the Reeves-Allen Allotment, northeast of Bexley Hall and also in a wooded section. Here were located Reeves Street and Allen Drive, named for distinguished Kenyon professors. Unfortunately, the Gambier Village Council thought it necessary to change the name of Reeves Street to Woodside Drive to consolidate all the names of that street into one.

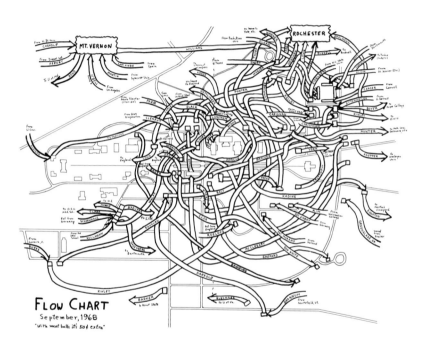

The 1968 "Flow Chart" drawn by Professor Franklin Miller, Jr. shows the faculty moves for that year.

President Lund announced a most drastic change in housing arrangements in a memorandum which went out to the faculty and staff on February 17, 1965:

> The College has recently sought, as most of you know, the opinion of counsel with regard to housing supplied to faculty members as part

of their compensation. The advice of the lawyers is that (except for specific staff positions and clerical members of the Divinity School) such housing cannot be considered tax exempt. They cite two points in particular: first, that such housing can be considered tax exempt "only if it is on the business premises of the employer"; second, that such housing can be considered tax exempt only if an employee's occupancy of a particular residence is "necessary to the proper performance of the duties of his employment."

We believe that the College and its members will be considered to have acted in good faith if it and they embrace a new system with the beginning of the next fiscal year. Accordingly, the Executive Committee of the Board of Trustees adopted the following resolution at its meeting of February 13, 1965:

That effective for the academic year beginning July 1, 1965, and subsequently, all salary contracts for faculty and staff members of Kenyon College will be drawn on a single cash sum basis without separate provision for housing; and further

That faculty salaries, effective July 1, 1965, be adjusted on a common basis so as to provide an increase in income sufficient to cover the cost of reasonable housing, and that said common adjustment be calculated as an increase of 18% on the 1964-65 base salaries; and further

That College-owned residences shall be made available for rental to their present occupants, if they desire, or if vacated, to other members of the faculty and staff, on the existing priority basis, at rental rates to be established by professional appraisers; and further

That all members of the faculty and staff must maintain their regular residences within ten miles of the Gambier Post Office; and further

That the Board of Trustees directs the President (as soon as feasible after the results of this change in housing policy are apparent) to determine whether faculty members possessing tenure or acquiring tenure should continue to enjoy priority in College-owned residences and for what period of years.

As of July 1, 1973 the President's Office listed 20 houses and apartments rented by the College for monthly rents of $59 to $204.

Financial Crisis

By the middle of the 1960's it became clear that the College was in a financial crisis and that only with drastic changes in some educational and financial policies could it hope to survive. Although the equity of the College had increased steadily, doubling in ten years, the cumulative deficit had also increased. In 1964 it was $232,000 and was to rise to a peak of $903,000 in 1970.

In Board of Trustees meetings Dean Bruce Haywood and Treasurer-Business Manager Samuel S. Lord kept the Board constantly informed of the difficulties arising, and Board members Pierre B. McBride and William G. Caples were especially attentive to the situation.

Mr. Lord summarized to the Executive Committee some of the problems in his report of May 23, 1964 on the preliminary budget for 1964-65:

Since World War II, Kenyon College has developed and offered an overall educational program whose cost has produced a cumulative deficit. The extra cash required to support this subsidy has been obtained from (1) liquidation of endowment, (2) by "borrowing" from funds held in reserve for other and special purposes, (3) commercial bank loans. It is anticipated that the cumulative operating deficit on June 30, 1964, will approximate $260,000, with "borrowings" from restricted current funds totaling at least $250,000.

In my opinion, prudent financial management demands the recognition now that the cumulative effects of this policy are such that in the relatively near future, with continuing cash deficits, the sources of these funds may be exhausted and that further operations resulting in an operating cash deficit will be impossible.

More specifically:

1. By the end of the current year we will have fully utilized our *restricted* current funds. We must ultimately reimburse these funds — but even failing reimbursement, there will simply be no more funds to draw upon.

2. *Endowment funds* restricted to specific uses, including the seminary, cannot legally be liquidated or serve as collateral for bank loans. Due to the liquidation of unrestricted endowment to reduce the capital construction loan, and to the commitment of most of the remainder as collateral for the construction and necessary operating loans, this possible source of operating funds will, in the foreseeable future, no longer exist.

3. The remaining source of funds is bank borrowing, but again we are approaching the limit of unrestricted endowment from which to furnish the required collateral, and compounding interest payments would become increasingly burdensome.

I believe that the inescapable conclusion is that policy must be developed and steps taken now to insure that future operations of the college are on a sound financial basis. The goal should be that annual operating costs are covered by (1) income from tuition and fees, (2) endowment earnings, (3) net income from auxiliary enterprises, and (4) special gifts for scholarships.

When this is accomplished, we can utilize our present income from *gifts for operating purposes* (totaling in the years 1957 through 1963, inclusive, over $1½ million) (1) to eliminate the accumulated operating deficit and reimburse the various current outstanding loans and advances; (2) as investments in permanent endowment for the support of increased faculty salaries, the library, and scholarships; (3) in operating and maintenance reserves; and perhaps (4) in current capital facility needs (e.g., the upperclass dormitory and the central heating plant).

Since any substantial increase in either endowment or auxiliary enterprise earnings is highly doubtful, and since any significant reduction in operating expenses is practically impossible, the only conclusion is that we must increase our income from students (by the optimum combination of enrollment and tuition rate) in an amount sufficient to accomplish the desired financial objectives. In this connection, Sidney G. Tickton of the Ford Foundation has said, "I believe that the future of the operating budget at small private colleges (excluding construction, endowment, or scholarships) lies mainly in appealing to willing students rather than to reluctant donors. The students are going to be there, they can afford to go to college, they will be willing to pay a good price for the type of education they need or desire. The future of small colleges depends upon their serving the market."

While a detailed projection of costs and income must be prepared to determine specific necessary action, it is my opinion that, in order to achieve a balanced budget as described above and then to keep pace with rapidly increasing faculty (and other) costs, a substantial increase in enrollment — without a corresponding increase in expenses — is our only possible course. This increase could consist of up to an additional 500 students, over and above the 750 contemplated at the conclusion of our present expansion.

At the Executive Committee meeting of October 17, 1964 Mr. Lord reported that during a visit to Kenyon in April 1964, on behalf of the North Central Association, the representatives of the Association Commission on Colleges and Universities, after viewing all phases of the College's operation, concluded, "*The paramount problem at Kenyon is financial.*"

He went on to note that the operating loss for the year just completed was $49,000, but that $18,000 of that figure was incurred by Bexley Hall, and $24,000 by the *Kenyon Review*. The collegiate operating loss, therefore, exclusive of the *Review*, was $7000.

Mr. Lord further discussed his Paramount Problem theme in the April-June 1965 issue of the *Alumni Bulletin*. Here he states: "We must consider a major expansion in the size of the student body — *without* a corresponding increase in instructional and other operating costs . . . We believe that it is entirely possible to increase the total authorized student body from the present level of 750 to approximately 1250 — an increase of two-thirds — while increasing the faculty by one-third. The resulting student-faculty ratio would not exceed 15:1, a ratio comparable to or lower than that of many institutions of Kenyon's type and program. . . . Thus the student body in total would pay a sufficiently greater share of their educational costs, to reduce significantly the possibility of operating deficits."

In the succeeding number of the *Alumni Bulletin* (July-September 1965) Dean Haywood discussed some of the alternatives which Kenyon might consider: "We have carefully weighed the advantages and disadvantages of three ways of expansion open to us. We have considered the obvious step of adding 500 men, the possibility of Kenyon's becoming a coeducational college, and of creating a college for 500 women which would have its separate campus but which would share Kenyon's program and facilities." Of these proposals, Dr. Haywood favored the third: "We have turned, then, to the coordinate college for women as a way of gaining the advantages we seek while preserving the best features of Kenyon. The arrangement we propose is not novel; it has its antecedents in Harvard-Radcliffe, Brown-Pembroke, Hobart and William Smith, institutions which preserved a character distinct from that of the coeducational university or college. This we expect to do. We propose a scheme which would leave the Hill as it is, with a separate campus for women close so that joint instruction is practicable but separated by its site and architectures from Kenyon sufficiently as to propose separate identities for the two colleges."

The route to financial solvency had been laid out and the signposts erected: (1) Financial separation of Bexley Hall from Kenyon College; (2) Withdrawal of the subsidy to the *Kenyon Review;* (3) Expansion of enrollment by the establishment of a coordinate college for women.

National Leadership Conference

The *Alumni Bulletin* for October-December 1967 predicted optimistically that the weekend of October 27-28, 1967 would go down in Kenyon history as one of the most important dates in the 143 years of the College. The event held on the Hill at that time was a National Leadership Conference, to which had been invited friends of the College, along with alumni, faculty, parents, and students. The weekend marked the transition from a period of study and planning to the start of a program to implement a ten-year period of growth.

President Lund revealed the specific plans for the decade ahead. He reported that a goal of $18.5 million had been set and would be used for eight major projects: residence and dining complex for women ($6,135,000); academic and operating endowment ($5,025,000); fine arts center ($2,715,000); biology building to complete science center ($1,660,000); property improvements and renovations of existing facilities ($1,365,000); physical fitness complex ($1,000,000); health center ($325,000); redevelopment of campus village ($300,000). The list was in the order of dollar value, rather than priority.

Pierre B. McBride (K1918), chairman of the executive committee of the Board of Trustees, outlined the financial campaign plans. He indicated that the drive would be conducted in two phases, with the first step and the first goal, to raise $3 million, to be completed during the academic year 1967-1968. He noted that the Board of Trustees would underwrite one-third of the first phase goal of $3 million.

General leadership for the campaign was announced by Mr. McBride, who was National Campaign Chairman. Co-chairmen were the Rt. Rev. Arthur Lichtenberger (K1923) and Philip Mather. Robert J. Hovorka (K1925) was National Leadership Gifts Chairman, the Rt. Rev. John P. Craine (K1932) was National Special Gifts Chairman, and Dr. John C. Drake (K1924) served as General Gifts Chairman.

Separation of Bexley Hall from Kenyon College

Since Bishop Chase's original purpose in founding a college in Ohio was to train men for the ministry, any suggestion that Bexley Hall be separated from Kenyon College was looked upon by many as a betrayal of the founder's intent. During the

19th century the lack of religious tolerance at times caused a considerable lengthening of the distance between Old Kenyon and Bexley Hall, but there was little talk of an actual separation.

In the depths of the depression, in 1934, Trustee Wilbur L. Cummings proposed the closing of Bexley in a letter to the Rt. Rev. Warren L. Rogers, Bishop of Ohio. Bishop Rogers wrote back a blistering defense of the theological school in reply, and for a time the issue became dormant. With the closing of Bexley for more than two years during World War II, however, the proposals for some sort of separation from the College revived, and there were surveys of Bexley in 1954 and again in 1958 which urged at least separate governing boards.

The appointment of Almus Morse Thorp as Dean of Bexley in 1960 began a new era in the history of the seminary. Under his administration the faculty was strengthened by valuable new members, the quality of the students was upgraded, and the morale of both groups improved. But it became clear that three main factors essential for good theological education were lacking in Gambier:
1. Opportunity for participation in parish life, particularly in urban work.
2. Easy access to graduate studies in related disciplines.
3. Ecumenical contact.

On May 8, 1967 a letter went out from the desk of President Lund:

> In recent months we have received expressions of concern regarding the relationship between Kenyon College and Bexley Hall, our graduate school of divinity. I am writing this letter to report on the actions, directed by the Administration and the Board of Trustees, relating to this historic union.
>
> First, let me state that the concern of the Trustees is and always has been to provide the best collegiate and theological education possible. We are encouraged with the manner in which our undergraduate program is developing. There has been growth and excitement as we have expanded the faculty, and built new facilities and planned for the future.
>
> On the other hand there has not been similar progress with the Seminary. Its fine Dean was appointed in the hope that by building a

strong faculty and providing outstanding facilities for married students as well as for single men the disadvantages of geographical isolation could be overcome. The Board of Trustees instructed me to give Dean Thorp every possible help in building a first-class institution, and made available to Bexley Hall all the material and financial resources necessary to that end. Nevertheless, despite a temporary growth in the size of the student body, the desirable enrollment was never achieved and in 1965 showed signs of declining. Item: the response to our request for funds to build the Lichtenberger Library was a disappointment — despite our best efforts.

It became clear to me that there was no longer a viable role for even the best seminary so far isolated from urban centers. Over the years a contrary trend in theological education has become more and more important. Increasingly the training of our clergy has been most successful in metropolitan centers, where seminarians are exposed to the civic problems they will encounter in their pastorates, and where they can learn to exercise healing ministries in association with psychiatrists, clinical psychologists and the social services. It is now universally accepted that a seminary needs the advantages offered by the library, technical and cultural resources of a university complex, the opportunity to become a true graduate school, and the chance to cooperate with other denominations in an ecumenical dimension. An article, "Winds of Change," written by a dedicated professor of the Seminary (Professor Robert J. Page) appearing in the current issue of the *Kenyon Alumni Bulletin*, confirms and elaborates this opinion.

With great reluctance in the fall of 1965 I came to the conclusion that Bexley Hall was being held back by both heredity and environment, and that she would be strengthened if she were a separate entity. Inevitably one had to review the vigorous studies of 1934, 1954, and 1958 — the latter unequivocally recommending separate governing boards. After preliminary discussions with many individuals, including the Ohio Bishops, the Dean of Bexley, and the Standing Committee on Bexley Hall, I presented my recommendation to the Executive Committee of the Board of Trustees, and insisted that it was the prime responsibility of the Board of Trustees to make its own decision.

The Trustees, on recommendation of the Executive Committee, appointed an *ad hoc* committee to consider the future ties of the College and the Seminary. This group, with the Right Reverend Roger W. Blanchard as chairman, examined various courses of action for many, many months. From the outset there had been almost unanimous agreement on the principle of separation of the two institutions in order that both might have the opportunity of becoming stronger. The Committee saw no distinction between geographical or administrative separation, but it noted the trend away from small college-seminary alliances and advocated separation.

This *ad hoc* committee, in February, 1966, proposed that Bexley continue as a graduate school of the College until June 30, 1967; that provisions be made for equitable division of endowments and property, and of responsibility for the existing accumulated deficit. The proposal was conditioned on the presentation of a plan that would enable Bexley Hall to continue as a viable institution financially after such a separation. The Trustees adopted this recommendation, and in February, 1967, at the request of the Committee, agreed to an extension of the administrative association of the College and Bexley Hall until June, 1968. By then the joint action of the Kenyon Trustees and the Bexley committee of clergy and laity will have established independent governing bodies for both institutions, and the final decision concerning the location of the Seminary will be made jointly by the Board of Bexley Hall and the Trustees of Kenyon College.

There are some who have imagined that the Administration was taking advantage of the assets of the Seminary, but we have been concerned rather that Bexley should have all possible support and every opportunity for growth. Indeed, the committee of clergy and laity appointed to study the question has recognized that the Trustees have presented Bexley with a new freedom and a greater future: "An opportunity," in the words of Bishop Roger Blanchard, "to become a real force and catalyst for a new and more relevant institution for theological education in this day of change." To quote Bishop Nelson Burroughs, "As the days go on it becomes increasingly evident that Bexley's future can be a great one, something in scope and dimension beyond anything we could have foreseen."

Kenyon will remain a church-related college. Indeed, it clearly sees its responsibilities and has offered students a vital and effective program in religion, particularly since the introduction of a major in the Department of Religion. We believe the separation will ultimately be the means of strengthening both the College and the Seminary. We know that you who share our love for Kenyon and devotion to it, those who befriend it, and those who will come to know and love it will join in our firm pledge that this fine College will become an even greater force for enlightenment and benefit to our fellow man: that both Bexley Hall and Kenyon College will flourish and both may prosper.

When the Committee on Bexley Hall let it be known that there was a definite intention of moving the institution, several possibilities came up for consideration. The most promising of these was the proposal of the Colgate Rochester Divinity School in Rochester, N.Y. for a merger with Bexley Hall to form the Rochester Center for Theological Studies. At that time Bishop Fulton J. Sheen of Rochester declared Roman Catholic intention to cooperate in the new venture. He said the

217

new study center would have "much to give" St. Bernard's Seminary in Rochester "and we trust St. Bernard's in turn will have much to give" the merging Protestant schools.

The Board of Trustees approved the recommendations of the *ad hoc* Committee on the future of Kenyon College and Bexley Hall at its meeting of December 2, 1967. Under the heading *Provisions Concerning Securities in Endowment* Kenyon transferred a proportional share of the securities and principal cash in the general endowment fund. The fraction used as a multiplier to determine Bexley's share was .271976515.

In settling the tangible personal property: "Bexley would receive the entire library now located in Colburn Hall, all furniture and equipment located in Bexley, Colburn and Harcourt Halls, all chapel equipment (including without limitation the organ), furnishings and decorations in the chapel at Bexley Hall, the contents of the deanery to the extent owned by Kenyon and the automobile heretofore used by Dean Thorp."

Trustee Caples in giving the report spoke of an additional matter. From the minutes: "He (Caples) said that Colburn Library going *in toto* with Bexley would leave a gap in the Kenyon Library insofar as concerned classes in the undergraduate Department of Religion. There were, he said, three houses which had come as gifts for occupancy by Bexley faculty, and the Bexley alumni had requested their disposition to be in a religious sense. It was the recommendation of the *ad hoc* Committee that two of these houses be sold and sufficient moneys from these sales be used for purchase of books to ensure an adequate library for the undergraduate Department of Religion, with the balance to be added to endowment in support of the Kenyon Library. It was recommended that the third house — the Tucker House — be offered in exchange for the house presently serving as the Rectory of Harcourt Parish." (Actually, as it worked out, the College traded the Tucker House for the Parish House which stood at the northwest corner of Brooklyn and North Acland Streets; the Parish House was then razed to provide space for the building of Gund Commons.)

218

Three of the Bexley faculty did not make the move to Rochester: Professors Oscar J. F. Seitz and Alden G. Kelley decided to retire and remain in Gambier, and Librarian M. Edward Hunter returned to the Methodist Theological School of Ohio in Delaware.

During the summer of 1968 the big yellow vans of the Mayflower Moving Company rolled up to the rear doors of Bexley and the move to Rochester began. Thus ended Bexley Hall in Gambier.

Retirement of President Lund

President Lund announced at a special meeting of the Executive Committee of the Board of Trustees held on April 20, 1968 that he wished to retire on July 1, 1968. Although the unexpected announcement shocked the Kenyon community, those who had worked closely with Dr. Lund were not surprised at his decision. He revealed to the Committee that a year before he had expressed his opinion to Mr. McBride that the challenge for the next ten years really required a new leader. Mr. McBride had pointed out that the stage was not completely set for the next ten years — that the capital funds drive and the working out of an amicable separation for Bexley Hall must be accomplished.

During the school year 1967-1968 it apparently became evident to Dr. Lund that he did not feel that he had sufficient physical and mental stamina to carry through the very difficult years which he saw approaching. Addressing the Board of Trustees on April 27, 1968 he recalled that the chief charge to him at the time of his selection had been the rehabilitation of Bexley Hall. To quote the minutes: "He (Lund) observed that the separation of the seminary and the college had brought bitterness and discord and a palpable feeling of hostility in many places but especially apparent within some circles of the Church . . . He said there had been not only a guilt problem but a psychological tear within himself. . . . Dr. Lund said this frustration had in some manner driven him inward, with great distress, the result being apparent in his administration: apathy, lack of creativity, irresoluteness in decision — above all, lack of decision and will. He believed his closest colleagues had sensed even if they could not understand his inner division of the soul; and that the students, not comprehending, had openly derided what certainly produced an appearance of apathy and indifference."

In announcing his resignation to the faculty on May 22, 1968, President Lund said, "I am proud of the past decade. I have great hope at the present and for the future of the College. But for continued achievement, it is my conviction that a new, more aggressive and energetic leader is needed. My resignation is motivated equally to prepare for another decade in my own career — and to open the door for a fresh new leader at Kenyon."

Looking back on his eleven years at Kenyon, Dr. Lund said, "I did not choose to be a brick and mortar president, but such has been my lot." Indeed, his administration had sponsored the most rapid growth in all ways that Kenyon had ever known. During his tenure nearly $6,000,000 in new building and renovation took place on the campus. Other forward steps taken included the introduction of major programs of study and the expansion of the departments of art, music and religion; the establishment of the Public Affairs Conference Center; and the increase in enrollment from about 500 to 800. Another milestone of Dr. Lund's administration was the settlement of the separation of Bexley Hall from Kenyon and the completion of plans for Bexley's move to Rochester. A most important and far-reaching step was the planning for the coordinate college for women, which was part of the Program of Expansion announced in 1967.

On June 2, 1968, Kenyon granted Dr. Lund the honorary degree of Doctor of Laws. The degree was given *in absentia* because he had become ill while in New York. Dr. and Mrs. Lund spent a part of the next year in Cambridge, England, and in September 1969 Dr. Lund became head of the department of history and political science at Virginia Commonwealth University in Richmond, where he died May 29, 1973.

At a Memorial Service on October 27, 1973 President Caples read the Resolution of the Board of Trustees:

> Franze Edward Lund, an experienced teacher, administrator, and scholar, came to Kenyon College at a time of deep faculty concern for the intellectual integrity of the College, as well as a time of acute financial crisis. Endowed with a warm and humane understanding of

the problems of the students and the faculty, he led the College in the difficult and often divisive years of self-study, curriculum changes, and expansion; and the anxious years of financial strain brought on by the absolute need for new buildings, rising costs, and depletion of resources during the war years. Although plagued by bouts of ill health, he endeavored manfully to bring Kenyon College through the years of expansion from a small men's college to what is now a coeducational college three times the size it was in 1957 when he first came to the Hill. The New Kenyon College of 1969, when women were first admitted, owes a debt of gratitude to Franze Edward Lund for what he accomplished in every area of his presidential responsibilities.

CHAPTER VIII

Art, Music, and Drama

Although courses in art, music, and drama did not find their way into the Kenyon curriculum until well into the second century of the existence of the College, departments in these areas have flourished enthusiastically during the past ten years. Since their introduction as major subjects during the administration of President Lund, the number of course offerings in art, music, and drama has increased so rapidly that today almost 15% of the total enrollments are in these fields of study.

During most of Kenyon's history, art activities were confined to extra-curricular work such as the preparation of posters for plays, cartoons for the *Collegian*, and decorative illustrations for the *Reveille*. When the College was small the supply of artistic talent sometimes ran dry. In desperation the editors of the 1903 yearbook traveled to Columbus to enlist the aid of an Ohio State athlete against whom they had played baseball and basketball. They had heard that he could also draw, so turned to him for help since they could find no one at Kenyon who could illustrate their book. He was George Bellows, who was to become one of the most illustrious American artists. The drawings he did for the 1903 *Reveille* make it a collector's item. Strangely enough, by the next year the problem was solved; the 1904 Kenyon *Reveille* was illustrated by Clarence Coles Phillips (K1905), better known as Coles Phillips, who became a top magazine illustrator during the 1920's. Of him the *New York Times* said, "His brush was a rival of Florenz Ziegfeld in glorifying the American girl. His popularity was based on his illustrations for magazines and his depiction of girls in sheer hosiery and silken garments in advertisements." Mr. Phillips also designed the cover for the fine book, *Songs of Kenyon*, compiled by Alfred Kingsley Taylor (K1906), and published in 1908.

Founding of the Department of Art

A listing for the Department of Art first appeared in the Kenyon catalogue for 1937-38, showing as the instructors William Peters Reeves and Norris Walton Rahming. "Pete" Reeves was retired from the Department of English by that time, but was a competent amateur painter, with a good grasp of art history. Apparently he had been called upon to assist Mr. Rahming in launching the new department.

Norris Rahming was the real founder of the Department of Art. At the time he came to Kenyon he had a wealth of art experience behind him. He had studied at the Cleveland School of Art, and in New York at the Art Students League, the National Academy of Design, and the New York School of Art.

In 1924, after a distinguished career in advertising art, Mr. Rahming left the United States to spend six years painting and studying in France and Italy.

Many of Mr. Rahming's paintings are in private collections. Others are in the galleries of the Pennsylvania Academy and the Cleveland and Newark, N.J. museums. His work most familiar to Kenyonites is the mural in the Gambier Post Office which portrays Kenyon's founder, Bishop Chase, surveying the Hill on which Kenyon was established.

Mr. Rahming was also an expert photographer. Many of the beautiful photographs of the College which were used in promotional brochures were his work.

The Department of Art for many years offered two basic one-year courses. In the catalogue Mr. Rahming stated as the purpose of the Department: "to provide a foundation for the appreciation of the plastic arts and for graduate work in the field of Fine Arts. Students draw and paint in the studio, and read the theory and history of the subject."

The "studio" referred to was a room in the Chase Memorial Tower of Peirce Hall. Although the view from its windows was magnificent, its inaccessibility because of the narrow stairs and its lack of running water made it a very inconvenient classroom for art.

As the years went on Mr. Rahming was drawn into the field of administration and became Dean of Admissions. This cut into his teaching, and Kathryn Clark Rice (Mrs. Philip

Blair Rice) became a visiting instructor of art. Although her service was not entirely continuous, she taught art at Kenyon for many years between 1945 and 1961, attaining the rank of assistant professor. During this period David Lombard Strout was an instructor of art for three years. Mr. Rahming retired in 1953 and died six years later.

Expansion of the Department of Art

The expansion of Kenyon's Department of Art to a major subject department with over 400 students enrolled in about twenty-five courses dates from the arrival of Joseph Frank Slate in the middle of the school year 1961-62. After joining the faculty with the rank of instructor, he moved up the promotional ladder to full professorship in 1969.

The art faculty has expanded very rapidly. Faculty members who served during this period of expansion and who have left Kenyon include Trond Sandvik, Donald E. Boyd, Stefan S. Wolff, Mary Fifield, and Richard O. Swain.

The specialties of the present department members reflect a wide range of talents: Mr. Slate (painter); Daniel Fleckles (painter, also film maker); Richard F. Baronio (sculptor); Martin J. Garhart (print maker); Michael J. O'Brien (K1968) (photographer); and Eugene J. Dwyer (art historian).

Before finally coming to rest in Bexley Hall, the Department of Art occupied a series of buildings spread out all over Gambier. During one period it carried on activities in five different locations at once. The sculpture studio moved five times. From 1962 to 1966 Professor Slate's studio and classroom area was in the northeast corner of Rosse Hall basement. As the department expanded, the following buildings were utilized: Professor Boyd's sculpture studio behind 102 North Acland Street; the building at 105 Chase Avenue, formerly the old Commons, Post Office, and bookstore; the former Adams house at 100 Gaskin Street, now the Student Affairs Center; the residence at 101 Chase Avenue, now the College Relations Building; the former Harvey Matthews Garage on West Scott Lane; and the LaFever house at 107 Ward Street.

Art Department in Bexley Hall

After the theological seminary moved to Rochester, New

York during the summer of 1968, all of the business offices of the College moved into Bexley Hall. Then during the summer and early fall of 1972 Bexley was remodeled for the exclusive use of the Department of Art, and for the first time in many years the department was all under one roof.

Art activities in Bexley Hall.

The only exterior change made in Bexley was the hardly noticeable provision for ground floor entrances at the east and west ends. A former student returning to Bexley would notice very little shifting of walls in the interior, since many of the smaller rooms could be converted into studios. The chapel furnishings and the organ had been taken to Wade Park Manor, Cleveland when the seminary moved. At the present time the basement houses print making activities; faculty offices and photography occupy the first floor; and there are classrooms and studios on the second and third floors. The former library, Colburn Hall, is now Colburn Gallery, and the sculpture studio is located in its basement.

Art students are traditionally messy, and are prone to

make a quick sketch or try some paint on the nearest wall when the mood seizes them. But the Kenyon art students so far have taken great pride in their beloved building and have shown their appreciation of the splendid facilities by keeping Bexley in excellent condition.

Art Exhibition Space

One of the greatest handicaps under which the Department of Art labored during its early years was lack of suitable space for the exhibition of its own work and that of traveling shows. Exhibitions were hung in Philomathesian Hall, Nu Pi Kappa Hall, Rosse Hall, and the old Alumni Library, but poor lighting and lack of proper supervision made these locations quite unsatisfactory. In the building of Chalmers Library in 1962 provision was made for excellent exhibition space. The Robert Bowen Brown Gallery, located on the second floor of Chalmers, is a most attractive, well-lighted area. Comfortable chairs and couches were provided opposite the exhibition walls, and the Brown Gallery quickly became recognized as one of the most pleasant spots on the Hill.

When Art moved north to Bexley Hall, the adjacent Colburn Hall, the former library of the seminary, was converted into Colburn Gallery. Mr. Slate considers it to be one of the finest exhibition areas for its size he has seen. He admits, however, that it has the disadvantage of being remote from the center of gravity of the campus. Crowding in the Chalmers Library has made necessary the utilization of the Brown Gallery for study space.

Ryerson Fine Arts Prize

A bequest from the Ryerson Foundation provided funds for art lectures and an annual Fine Arts Prize for the purchase of paintings judged best in the annual competition. The winners for the past ten years are:

1965 Koichi (Wang) Ohara (K1966)
1966 R. Michael Bundgaard (K1966)
1967 Joel A. Fisher (K1969)
1968 Joel A. Fisher (K1969)
1969 Joel A. Fisher (K1969) & Gregory P. Spaid (K1969)
1970 Eric L. Bauer (K1972)
1971 J. Christopher Fahlman (K1972)
1972 Sophie Andorfer (Special) & Eric L. Bauer (K1972)
1973 Peter M. Bloomfield (K1973) & Stephen K. Pavlovic (K1973)
1974 Kathryn S. Halbower (K1974)

Art Department Aims

The Department of Art has come a long way since the first course in painting was given. The offerings now are divided into studio courses and art history courses. As stated in the latest catalogue: "It is the Art Department's conviction that a broad general preparation, an introduction to the major intellectual and aesthetic modes of apprehension, is essential to all educated men. Consequently, the Department's basic offerings are designed for the generalist. The studio problems are both analytical and creative, so that any student may learn to apprehend the formulation behind the craft, the craft behind the finished work. The art history courses concentrate, as well, on the development of form. How well a student learns to perceive form, how well this perception is organized into works of a permanent nature, and how well these works convey feeling is our concern."

Early Musical Efforts

Kenyon has always been a music-loving college. Philander Chase saw to it that the College had music right from the beginning by providing an English barrel organ which played hymns when someone pumped the bellows and turned the crank. It was later converted into a key organ and was used in Rosse Chapel for many years. Songbooks of Kenyon came out in 1859 and in 1866. A Kenyon orchestra was formed right after the Civil War. At the turn of the century glee clubs and mandolin clubs were very popular, and in 1908 Alfred K. Taylor (K1906) gathered together from every available source all the songs of the College which could be found, and published them in a handsome book, *Songs of Kenyon*.

President Peirce wrote in the foreword to this songbook: "The Kenyon Song Book should appeal strongly to the heart of every son and friend of the old college. Nowhere is there a more intense and earnest spirit of college loyalty, and nowhere is singing a more distinctive feature of academic life. Every Kenyon man knows what the Kenyon spirit is. He may find it difficult to express in words, but he feels its emotional thrill. And the Kenyon song is perhaps the best method of expression."

Before the introduction of music as an academic subject,

musical activities were confined mainly to three areas: the college Commons, the fraternities, and the Chapel.

A common dining hall for the entire College was established in 1912, and almost immediately the singing of Kenyon songs after meals became a pleasant tradition which was carried on until recent years. The songfest after the noon meal on Sundays was a special occasion; highpoints included the singing of "The Weaver's Song" and "That Oldtime Religion," with the names of the professors inserted.

Each of the fraternities managed to come up with one or two members who were willing to train the brothers in the singing of the fraternity songs. All of the fraternities had songbooks, generally furnished by the national organization, which contained arrangements of the songs, usually in four-part harmony. It was the responsibility of the song leaders to rehearse the men in their parts and to encourage those who sang off-key to keep their voices down. For a time a competition was held and prizes awarded for the best fraternity singing group.

Choir Activities

By the beginning of Kenyon's second century the College Choir had been a center of musical activities for many years. During all of its early history the Choir had student leaders and student organists; occasionally one student filled both positions. There was a period during World War II when the Choir was inactive, but in 1946 the Rev. Clement W. Welch, Chaplain of the College, revived the organization. When Dr. Paul Schwartz arrived in 1947 to become the first full-time faculty member in the Department of Music, he took over the directorship of the Choir. Professor Frank T. Lendrim became the choir director when he came to Kenyon in 1961, and is the director at the time of this writing.

The Coordinate College Choir was formed when women came as students in 1969. It is reputed to have been the first women's organization on the campus. This group and the Chapel (Men's) Choir formed in effect a single mixed group, but were technically separate organizations, each electing its own officers. The Coordinate College Choir became the Kenyon Women's Choir when the College became coeducational in

1972. Women's and Men's Choirs are still organized separately within the Kenyon College Choir, but this is done largely for rehearsal purposes; most of the performances are as a mixed group.

Professor Paul Schwartz (left) directing the 1947 College Choir.

The Advent Concert of the Choir has filled the Chapel to capacity every year. Recently the group has also performed in concert during Parents' Weekend. The Kenyon Choir regularly makes weekend trips to perform in churches and schools within a radius of two or three hundred miles, and during the spring vacation embarks on an eastern tour of four or five days covering six or seven stops. Highlights of these trips have been the presentation of programs at the National Cathedral in Washington and at Bruton Parish in Colonial Williamsburg, Virginia.

By far the most ambitious undertakings of the Choir have been the European tours during the summers of 1968 and 1972. Funds for the trips were raised by such activities as selling refreshments at the college movies, selling Christmas cards, and conducting auctions. Of the 1972 trip Dr. Lendrim said, "The students have raised over $10,000 over the last two years to make the trip possible. Even those who knew they could not make the trip helped out." Traveling by plane, bus, and boat on the three-week trips, the Choir made appearances in France, Switzerland, Germany, Belgium, The Netherlands, and Great Britain. One of the most notable visits in England was to the Welsh border district where they sang for Lord Kenyon at his estate and were entertained by him. 45 men went on the 1968 trip; the 40 members who went in 1972 were evenly divided between men and women.

The 1972 Choir which toured Europe.

The Chasers

The Chasers, a special singing group drawn from the Choir, was founded by Professor Lendrim in 1964. Originally consisting of ten men, they were noted for "their high spirited presentation of fraternity songs, barbershop numbers, spirituals, and 'fun' songs." The Chasers is now a coed organization, and the present membership includes six men and six women. Most of the Choir performances feature one or more numbers by this popular group.

The Kenyon Singers

A musical organization entirely separate from the Choir was the Kenyon Singers, the so-called glee club, founded by mathematics professor Charles T. Bumer about 1933 and continuing until 1970. Professor Schwartz was pleased with the name of the group when he came to Gambier; he did not like the name "glee club." Although both the Singers and the Chapel Choir were directed by Dr. Lendrim in recent years, they had separate membership and officers, sang their own music, and in no sense competed with each other. The Singers also went on tours, and many of their concerts were with choirs from women's colleges, such as Lake Erie, Western, Stephens (Missouri), and Notre Dame (Cleveland). Professor Lendrim succeeded in building up membership in the singing groups until at its high point the Singers numbered forty and the Chapel Choir had a membership of about fifty-five.

The Kokosingers

The Kokosingers, an independent singing group not sponsored by the College, was founded in 1965 by James S. Hecox (K1969), Pedro L. Arango (K1968), Thomas E. Ulrich (K1969), and Lee P. Van Voris (K1967). They assembled a group of undergraduates who felt the need for a small informal singing group on the campus. The Kokosingers started performing at college functions, informally at fraternity parties, and then moved on to sing at various women's colleges. For a time it became an annual affair for the Kokosingers to tour the Eastern States during the end of the Christmas vacation from college, performing at many high schools and colleges.

Although this organization always includes some of the old traditional Kenyon songs, their music can in no way be stereotyped. The selections range from madrigals such as "Come Again, Sweet Love," to the barbershop rendition of "Coney Island Baby;" from the traditional sound of "Kokosing Farewell," to the mock-operatic "Quartet from Rigoletto." Also included are modern arrangements of contemporary songs such as "Five Hundred Miles," "Feelin' Groovy," and "By the Time I Get to Phoenix." Many of the fine arrangements were made by Jim Hecox, the music director during the early days. Two recent music directors have been Jeffrey W. Shachmut

(K1973) and Douglas C. Bean (K1975). Phonograph records by the Kokosingers were made in 1967, 1969, 1972 and 1974.

Music Department Housing

The first quarters of the Department of Music were in a surplus army barracks located on the slope between Shaffer Pool and the Shaffer Speech Building. This was not a very satisfactory structure; Professor Schwartz recalls that the space heaters always seemed to produce temperatures which were either too high or too low, and after a heavy rainstorm the pebbles and sand washed through the doors had to be swept out. In 1954 Music moved to the basement of the Chapel. Still later the Department, with the exception of Dr. Lendrim, who retained an office in the Chapel basement, moved to Rosse Hall basement. Beginning in 1971 the first floor of the white frame house immediately west of Chalmers Library was taken over for practice rooms and designated the Music Annex. Then in 1972 extensive internal alterations were made on the former "Chaplain's House," just west of Cromwell Cottage, and the Department of Music moved in. Both floors of the Music Annex have been retained for rehearsal space. The Music Building now provides classrooms, faculty offices, practice rooms, and a music library with listening facilities for tapes and discs.

Kenyon has always been handicapped because of an inadequate hall for musical performances. Rosse Hall, the only building large enough to accommodate audiences of any size, has very undesirable acoustical properties. In desperation the Department has turned to other facilities: the Great Hall of Peirce, Philomathesian Hall, Dempsey Hall, Colburn Hall, Gund Commons, and the Chapel. One of the first improvements planned in the Sesquicentennial Program is adequate concert facilities at Kenyon.

Visiting Musical Performers

Because of its isolated character, the College has worked hard to bring musical artists to Gambier and to promote student performances. Concerts provided by Frank H. Ginn (K1890) featured the Cleveland String Quartet in a series of annual performances beginning in 1928 and lasting for about

232

ten years. More recently the George Gund Concerts, which began in 1962, have made welcome contributions to the cultural life of the community.

It would be impossible to list here the hundreds of artists who have performed at Kenyon, but there has been a definite effort to satisfy many tastes. Among the internationally known soloists and groups which have appeared in concert since the establishment of the Department of Music are: the Vienna Octet, the Netherlands Chamber Choir, Paul Doktor and Yaltah Menuhin, the Bartok Quartet, the Chigiano Sextet, the Warsaw Quintet, and the Early Music Consort of London.

Music Faculty

The founder of the Department of Music, Dr. Paul Schwartz, came to Kenyon in 1947. He was joined in 1960 by Charles S. Wilhite, who left the following year to pursue an advanced degree and was replaced in 1961 by Frank T. Lendrim. The Department was expanded still further when Kenneth L. Taylor arrived in 1966. The fourth member of the Department is Anita R. Burt who came to Kenyon in 1971. In addition to the full-time members, the Department of Music also includes several part-time Associates in Applied Music: Lois Brehm, Anthony Ginter, Joseph Lord, Leonard Rivenburg, and Janet Slack.

Music in the Community

The Department of Music has been instrumental in promoting community-wide musical efforts. Professor Schwartz conducted a performance of "The Messiah" on December 13, 1953, featuring the Beethoven Club Chorus, the Kenyon Singers, and "a chorus of Kenyon, Bexley, and Gambier ladies." The Knox County Symphony was organized by Dr. Schwartz in 1966; many of the members of this group are men and women of the Kenyon community.

Music Department Aims

Kenyon's Department of Music does not try to compete with a musical conservatory. From the catalogue: "The courses are designed to foster an understanding of music, past and present, both from the critical and the creative points of view." The wide variety of musical experiences offered to students is

233

revealed in the special interests of the members of the Department: Professor Schwartz — theory and composition; Professor Lendrim — choral work, introductory courses, and musical history of the 19th and 20th centuries; Professor Taylor — musicology and history of the Renaissance and baroque periods; Professor Burt — studio voice and introductory courses.

Music Prize

The David B. Perry Music Prize is awarded each year for outstanding musical research. The winners have been:
1970—John L. Schaeffer, Jr. (K1972)
1971—Stephen H. Huber (K1973) and Cathy Ann Werner (K1973
1972—Shelley L. Stillwell (K1973) and Hugh D. McElrath (K1973)
1973—Stephen F. Stettler (K1974)
1974—David Effron (K1976)

Early Theater

Several sources state that there has been recorded activity in the theater at Kenyon since 1848. However, Professor W. Ray Ashford, who delved extensively into the history of the theater on the Hill, states in some unpublished notes that "there is no extant evidence that plays were given by Kenyon students before 1885." According to Dr. Ashford, "In November of that year the students performed in *Tom Cobb or Fortune's Toy*, a Comedy in Three Acts." Probably the theatrical fare prior to that date included principally vaudevilles, minstrels, parodies, and topical performances under the literary societies.

The Puff and Powder Club

The activities of the Puff and Powder Club dominated drama production during the early part of the 20th century. Although the Club put on plays as early as 1904, it was the original musical comedies it produced beginning in the school year 1919-20 that brought fame to Kenyon and generated comparisons with the musical plays of such institutions as Princeton, Cornell, and the University of Michigan.

Louis Melayne Latta (K1923) wrote all of the music and

some of the lyrics for the productions: *Certainly Cynthia, Pretty Please, Marrying Marilyn, Patch O' Blue,* and *Naughty Nita.* Other students involved in the writing, producing, and directing included: Henry S. Downe (K1920), Philip T. Hummel (K1923), John G. Loofbourrow (K1923), Donald E. Reid (K1926), and James M. Wade (K1922).

Poster for *Patch O' Blue,* 1922-23.

The female parts were all played by Kenyon men; no doubt the success of these ventures was due in part to this intriguing idea and to the excellent costuming and acting of these characters. Some of the "beauties" who played the principal girls' parts were Edward C. Dudley (K1924), Philip T. Hummel (K1923), Charles B. Norton (K1922), Erwin J. Schmick (K1924), Gerald P. Van Arnam (K1923), and Charles C. Riker (K1927).

Each winter for four years the troupe went on tour through Ohio and Michigan, playing in as many as 17 cities. Typical of the arrangements were those described in the *Collegian* for January 23, 1923: "The night of December 18th, 46 students left Gambier in a Pullman equipped with a baggage car, after having given three performances on home ground. They did not return until Saturday, January 6th." The article went on to tell how the itinerary called for a break of three days between circuits for Christmas and one day off for New Years. Other articles attest to the splendid reception given the plays. One metropolitan newspaper said *Marrying Marilyn* "equaled if not surpassed any college show that has been seen this season," and Princeton, Michigan, and Ohio State had been there before.

Although the Club was a big factor in advertising the College, by the fall of 1923 the novelty of musical comedy production had worn off to the point where there was insufficient enthusiasm to warrant another such enterprise. During the tour of the 1922-23 play, *Patch O' Blue*, there had been lack of support by the sponsoring alumni, and there was talk of difficulties arising from the drinking habits of some members of the cast. The real reason, however, for giving up these productions was that Kenyon simply did not have the resources in money and time to put into them. Each year the production costs ran higher and higher; the cast rehearsed twice a day for eight weeks before going on a three-week tour. The College simply couldn't afford to continue with these plays.

After a lapse of three years, the Puff and Powder Club resumed its musical activities in the fall and winter of 1925-26 with a production of *Naughty Nita*. Again Melayne Latta, by now an independent producer, wrote and directed the show.

236

Chorus line for *Naughty Nita*. From left: George D. Hitler (K1929), Robert M. Weh (K1928), Marcus W. Pender (K1928), D. Morgan Smith (K1928), Edward H. Stanton (K1928), Robert E. Baxter (K1929), and Wayne M. Singer (K1929).

Although this edition compared favorably with its predecessors from a theatrical standpoint, it was a financial disaster. Engagements in Cincinnati and Detroit were cancelled on account of the unwillingness of alumni in these cities to support the production, and the audiences were sparse at several of the performances. The Puff and Powder Club never recovered from this setback and ceased to exist after 1926.

Senior Plays

So extensive were the musical shows of this era that they attracted all of the dramatic talent in the College, and there was none left for the production of pure drama. For several years after the death of the Puff and Powder Club there was no active dramatic club on the Hill. However, Kenyon was not without some dramatic activity during this time. In 1903, the Senior Class decided to put on a Commencement play. Under the guidance of Professor Reeves, they chose Beaumont and Fletcher's *The Knight of the Burning Pestle*. The play was so successful that the Class of 1904, in its turn, decided to present a Commencement play. From then on until 1930 each Senior Class, excepting the Class of 1916, presented a play at graduation time. Dr. Reeves was the moving spirit of these performances. He chose plays that were unusual for literary and historical interest, and he directed them well. When his health declined after 1930, the custom of giving a senior play died out. Professor Ashford provided the faculty impetus for theatrical ventures for a few years, and John Malcolm Haight (K1933) was a prominent figure in play production during the early Thirties.

Founding of the Department of Speech

In the fall of 1935 Dr. John Wilson Black came on the Gambier scene to become the founder of Kenyon's Department of Speech. Although Professor Black's primary concern was in the field of speech, he was greatly interested in the theater. He began the long and impressive series of productions by the Kenyon College Dramatic Club, the organization that is still the principal, though not the only, producer of plays on the Hill. Eric A. Hawke (K1939) taught speech for one year, and Thomas M. Sawyer (K1939) for four years during the pre-war and war periods. During World War II Professor Black was involved in military research for several periods of time and the teaching was carried on by his wife, Helen Harrington Black. Two other instructors who served during the post-war era were Donald B. Tescher and James Chadeayne Amo.

Shift Toward Drama

With the arrival in 1947 of James Elder Michael as Associate Professor of Speech, emphasis in the Department veered sharply toward dramatic studies. When Dr. Black left Kenyon in 1949 to become Director of the Speech and Hearing Science Areas at The Ohio State University, the name became the Department of Speech and Dramatics. In the 1956-57 catalogue it was first given its present name, the Department of Drama. However, the current catalogue still lists Mr. Michael as Professor of Speech and Drama.

Drama Faculty

Department members who are no longer at Kenyon include Clifford E. Hamar, Frederick W. Thon, Phyllis P. Bigelow, Thomas P. Cooke, Michael D. Birtwhistle, Clark Hobbie, Jr., and James A. Patterson.

In addition to Mr. Michael, the present full-time members of the Department are Daniel O. Parr, II, Harlene Marley, and Thomas S. Turgeon. In 1972 Professor Marley became the first woman department head in the history of Kenyon.

Theater Locations

Prior to the completion of the Shaffer Speech Building in 1941, most of the plays were given in Rosse Hall, but there are accounts of dramatic performances in Philomathesian Hall, Nu Pi Kappa Hall, Colburn Hall, and the Chapel. In a letter written in 1974 Professor Black recalls the play production experiences in Nu Pi Kappa: "Some of the good work was done there under pretty adverse circumstances. Mr. Shaffer attended a production there and got the idea of building the Speech Building as he witnessed a performance. During the performance a short in the wiring developed and there was a minor blaze that left a mark on the ceiling of the hall. It may still be there, around the only electrical receptacle in the ceiling."

Today the upsurge in the number of productions has made necessary the regular use of several locations in addition to the Speech Building. The theater in Shaffer Building is generally known as the Hill Theater; this dates from the 1953 production of *The Show-Off*, when the players began using that name. The Department of Drama also occupies the building immediately south of the Post Office under the name "Drama Annex."

Wide Variety of Plays

The Department has gone to great lengths to expose the drama students and the Kenyon community to a wide variety of theatrical experiences. These range from the far-out *(End Game, Serjeant Musgrave's Dance, The Hostage,* and *The Caretaker)*; to the classical (Shakespeare and Moliere); to Broadway farces and melodramas *(The Little Foxes, Room Service, Charley's Aunt,* and *The Fantasticks).*

Some popular plays have been given several times. For

example, there have been three Kenyon performances of *Charley's Aunt*. In 1907, the late Professor Raymond D. Cahall (K1908) played Lord Fancourt Babberly. When the Dramatic Club did it in the Speech Building theater in March 1949, Paul Newman (K1949) had the role. The third Kenyon performance of the play in 1967 featured Edward R. Hallowell (K1967) in the part.

Part of the cast of the 1947 production of *The Front Page*. Paul Newman, who played Hildy Johnson, is in the center, bottle in right hand.

The 1949 production took place less than a week after the Old Kenyon fire. It was remembered as being very funny and helping to dispel the gloom over the disastrous fire. Commenting "Exemplifying the old theatrical maxim of 'the show must go on,'" the *Collegian* for March 11, 1949 described the leading man's performance: "Paul Newman starred as Lord Fancourt Babberly, the impersonator of Charley Wyckeham's real aunt, Donna d'Alvadorez. Dressed in demure black, he looked and acted convincingly enough to convince almost all that he might be the real aunt. However, he could have been more careful when he was pouring tea." A few weeks later, in the May 4, 1949 *Collegian*, Mr. Newman wrote his farewell to Kenyon in a lengthy article entitled, " 'Good Night, Sweet Prince,' A Brief Autobiographical Encomium." In the last few lines he revealed that his dream had come true: "Finally in my senior year I became adjusted mentally. Professors tore out mit der hair. Why? 'Barrymore' made the Merit List — right between Moorman and Nugent."

Drama Awards

The Ashford Cup is given annually to the Kenyon student who has made the most notable contribution to the theater. Recent winners are:

1965—James C. Cowlin (K1966)
1966—Edward R. Hallowell (K1967)
1967—William N. Cumming (K1968)
1968—Gerald B. Ellsworth (K1969)
1969—Lyn Uttal (K1970)
1970—Lawrence A. Ropp (K1970)
1971—John G. Decker (K1971)
1972—Thomas E. Allen (K1973)
1973—Christopher M. Townsend (K1973)
1974—Stephen F. Stettler (K1974)

The Paul Newman Trophy and the Joanne Woodward Trophy, both given by Paul L. Newman (K1949), the latter in honor of his wife, are awarded annually to the actor and actress who have given the most skilled and successful performance in an acting role during the year. Recent winners are:

Newman Trophy	Woodward Trophy
1965 Edward G. Heimerdinger (K1966)	1971 Lisa A. Meyers (K1973)
1966 Edward R. Hallowell (K1967)	1972 Lisa A. Meyers (K1973)
1967 Eric E. Linder (K1968)	1973 Janice E. Paran (K1975)
1968 Michael C. Johnston (K1968)	1974 Charlotte M. Jones (K1975)
1969 Stephen G. Hannaford (K1970)	
1970 Murray L. Horwitz (K1970)	
1971 James C. Price (K1971)	
1972 David C. Wickenden (K1975)	
1973 Thomas E. Allen (K1973)	
1974 Robert M. Jaffe (K1975)	

Impact of the Women's College

Writing in the *Alumni Bulletin* for July-September 1969, Mr. Michael describes the end of one theatrical era and the beginning of a new one:

> The season that has just been completed in the Hill Theater is remarkable for a number of reasons. To begin with, the Dramatic Club produced both parts of Shakespeare's *Henry IV* (Part 1 in February, under the direction of James Patterson, and Part 2 in April, under the direction of James Michael, and then both parts in repertory), a pair of plays notable for their masculine tone and for the relatively slight demands they make on actresses, and thus signaled the end of the men's college and a theater which has tended, of necessity, to be oriented toward the male.
>
> That will all be changed this fall, and, as if to give special attention in the theater to the arrival of women on the campus, the Dramatic Club will offer, along with a varied bill of other entertainments, *Lysistrata*, Aristophanes' great comedy of women's opposition to the war, and what they do about it. What could be more appropriate.
>
> The fact that girls are about to join us as students and participants in the activities of the theater, with resulting far-reaching consequences — some of them suggested here — does not, of course, make us forgetful of the extent to which we have in the past been dependent for the success of our productions on the women and girls of the community, who have acted in them, worked to fit them out, most notably in the costume department, and have thus, quite literally, made them possible. What effect, if any, the arrival of the Coordinate College for Women will have on these arrangements, whether the theater will be more or less community oriented, it is still too early to say. It is pretty clear, however, that there will be changes, and certainly one sort of significant change is indicated by these play selections: *Henry IV* in 1968-69 and *Lysistrata* in 1969-70.

Actually the first performance in which Kenyon women students appeared was in *Iolanthe*, produced by John J.D. Sheehan (K1970) for the Kenyon Gilbert and Sullivan Society in the Memorial Theater in Mount Vernon on November 21, 1969. Two of the new women students cast in lead roles were Shelley Stillwell (K1973) and Mia Halton (K1973)

242

Informal Performances

Throughout the years there have been informal performances of groups and individuals. Typical of these groups was the Kenyon Impromptu Players, a popular troupe which gave spur-of-the-moment performances all over the Hill during the school years 1967-68 and 1968-69. The members of the Players were Gerald B. Ellsworth (K1969), Murray L. Horwitz (K1970), James C. Price (K1971), and C. Reed Woodhouse (K1970). Their offerings were mainly hilarious burlesques and improvisations, but the most popular bits were their devastating impersonations of members of the faculty.

Kenyon Playwrights

In his 1969 *Bulletin* article Mr. Michael went on to list some of the Kenyon-related authors whose works have been produced in play form on the Hill: Robert Frost, Robert Lowell (K1940), Irving Kreutz, Morton Segal (K1935), John J.D. Sheehan (K1970), Peter Taylor (K1940), and Harold Patterson Williams (K1953).

Majors in Speech and Drama

A major in speech was offered from the beginning of the Department. The major in dramatics was instituted under the new curriculum in 1964-65, with three juniors enrolled. Graduated as the first drama majors in 1966 were James S. Cowlin, William B. Gibson II, and Christopher F. Wilson. During the school year 1973-74 the number of drama majors had risen to 32, of which twelve were seniors.

Visiting Dramatic Performers

Although the lack of facilities at Kenyon has handicapped bringing in outside performers, some of the dramatic artists and groups who have appeared at the Memorial Theater in Mount Vernon under Kenyon auspices are: the National Theater of the Deaf; Judith Anderson in *Medea*; and the Cleveland Playhouse (twice). Visitors to the Hill Theater have included: the Barter Theater of Virginia; Le Theatre Du Passe-Temps of France; puppeteer Peter Arnott; and The Ohio State University Dance Groups.

Drama Department Aims

In the *Bulletin* article Professor Michael discussed the aims of the Department of Drama: "It is the conviction of the Department of Drama that some of man's most revealing and significant statements about himself have been made in his dramatic writing, and that a play is to be understood in relation to the theater and particularly to the theater for which it is written. And it is therefore with the pleasant task of understanding plays of all sorts, particularly the better sort, and their connection with the theater and with the theater's audience, that the Department is principally concerned."

CHAPTER IX

The Caples Years

The resignation of President Lund took place at the beginning of what proved to be the greatest period of activity and growth in the 150-year history of Kenyon College. The separation of Bexley Hall had just been effected. The Decade Plan of 1968 had laid out guidelines for the solution of the pressing financial problems. But looming ahead was the gigantic task of implementing the Plan, and building and getting into operation the women's college. It was obvious that the selection of a new president would have to be made as quickly as possible.

Election of President Caples

Not since the election of Charles P. McIlvaine as the second president of Kenyon College in 1831 did the designation of a new president proceed with such speed.

On April 11, 1968, William Goff Caples picked up his telephone in Chicago to hear Pierre B. McBride, Chairman of the Executive Committee of the Board of Trustees, ask him if he would consider becoming President of Kenyon College. After recovering from the sudden shock, and making sure that Mr. McBride was speaking seriously, Mr. Caples stated that he was not an academic person, and expressed doubts that the faculty would approve his selection. However, Mr. McBride assured him that the Faculty Council had been consulted and that they were very favorable to him. Mr. Caples said that he would confer with his wife, Jean, on the prospect of their coming to Gambier, and would await further word from Mr. McBride. The call came on April 13, and the news was that the entire faculty had been polled and unanimously approved the selection of Dr. Caples. Since he was at that time involved in labor negotiations for Inland Steel Company, of which he was a vice president, he felt obligated to consult with Inland officials before permitting his name to be presented to the Board of Trustees.

The minutes of a Special Meeting of the Board held on April 27, 1968 record that " . . . Bishop Blanchard advised that the Board of Trustees unanimously elected fellow trustee Mr. William G. Caples . . . as President of Kenyon College effective July 1, 1968, with the sincere hope that he would accept the position.

"Mr. Caples said that he would at this time give provisional acceptance of the presidency. He advised that he had arranged with Dr. Lund to go to Gambier May 3-5 to meet with the faculty and that it was his hope in the interim between the meeting this day and his trip to Gambier the following week he could work out matters to enable him to accept the position . . . and he asked that announcement of his election and acceptance be made simultaneously by the College and Inland Steel Company." The announcement was released to the newspapers for publication on May 6, 1968.

Since his graduation from Kenyon in 1930, Dr. Caples had maintained a strong connection with the College. He began his service on the Board of Trustees as an alumnus member in 1952, became a permanent trustee six years later, and in 1959 was elected to the Executive Committee. Minutes of the Board reveal his untiring efforts and his ability to penetrate quickly to the heart of matters. He also headed several successful fund drives for the College. Kenyon recognized his great help by awarding him the degree of Doctor of Laws in 1961.

After his undergraduate days at Kenyon, Dr. Caples spent three years at the Northwestern University Law School, where he received the degree of Doctor of Jurisprudence in 1933. His practice of law was interrupted by four years of service in the Engineer Corps of the U.S. Army during World War II. He was overseas for 30 months in Australia, New Guinea, and the Philippines; at the time of his discharge he held the rank of Lt. Colonel.

Immediately after the war's end, Dr. Caples joined Inland Steel as Manager — Industrial Relations, and at the time he came to Kenyon held the title of Vice President — Industrial and Public Relations.

During his residency in Chicago, Dr. Caples involved himself deeply in educational and civic affairs. He was a member

246

of the Chicago Board of Education for five years, and was its president in 1961-62. He served as President of United Charities of Chicago. It was during this period that he was also a member of commissions on housing, human relations, and equal job opportunities.

At the Federal level he was widely known in Washington through his participation on committees dealing with labor management, equal employment, manpower development and training, and civilian personnel management for the Army.

At the time of his election, Dr. Caples and his wife, the former Jean Dunbar, resided in Chicago with their son, William, and daughter, Cynthia. An older daughter, Mrs. Gilbert Wilkes, lived in Charleston, S.C.

Dr. Caples was the first lawyer and businessman ever to become president of the College, and the first Kenyon graduate to bear that title since the election of Lorin Andrews as president in 1854.

Commenting on his selection in the *Mount Vernon News* for May 6, 1968, the president-elect said, in part:

> As to my own skills, I make no claim to being an academic. I do claim to be a first-rate administrator. With an excellent faculty and provost, the academic tradition, I am sure, will continue. Funds will be necessary to make its continuance possible and I think I can help attract those funds by making donors — private and public — understand the value of and need for the small liberal arts college in our society. Its real strength is in furnishing to our society men and women trained in the fundamental disciplines, the principal background which gives hope of producing the enlightenment necessary to solve the problems of this complex and troubled society.
>
> . . . As an individual, I believe devoting the next six years of my life to this achievement of these objectives is of more value than the work I am now doing in industry — important, necessary and interesting as it is. In this belief, I have agreed to devote the next six years of my life to Kenyon.

Approval of the selection of Dr. Caples came immediately from the students. The *Collegian* for May 9, 1968 editorialized:

> The newly-elected president, William G. Caples, comes to Kenyon with fine credentials that indicate he will be able to get Kenyon moving again.
>
> He is an accomplished administrator with the ability to straighten out problems within the College. His 35 years of business experience

247

well-equip him for clear-cut decisions, sound administration, and fund-raising success.

Mr. Caples is coming to Kenyon at the sacrifice of a lucrative career at Inland Steel. An alumnus and a long-time trustee of Kenyon, he knows the College well and is devoted to solving its problems. In his meeting with students last Saturday, he demonstrated a dedication and a willingness to keep open channels of communication that are essential in the crucial years ahead. He exhibits a strong desire to do everything well. He is determined to perpetuate the liberal arts college and continue Kenyon's tradition of innovation with educational experimentation and the establishment of a coordinate women's college.

This summer he will begin to sort out and to attack the maze of problems facing Kenyon now and in the immediate future. These include re-allocating building space in College buildings as well as spurring on the women's admissions program, raising funds and contracting a builder for the women's dormitory and the dining complex.

Kenyon needs dynamic leadership to succeed in its new venture. It looks as if William Caples will be able to provide this leadership.

Professor James E. Michael told of the role of the faculty in the events leading up to the presidential selection in the *Kenyon Alumni Bulletin*, July-September, 1968:

> Almost as soon as it was known that the College would need a new president, it also became apparent that our well-known plans for the next decade would suffer a severe set-back if ranks were not closed quickly, if something were not done almost at once to effect a change of command without the loss of momentum that must inevitably accompany an interregnum. Something rather special was in the air because, almost at once, one began to hear expressions of hope that someone like Bill Caples — perhaps even Bill Caples himself — might be persuaded to take the helm. To those on the faculty who knew him well, the possibility of persuading him to accept the post seemed a slim one, but there was a feeling of expectancy, and here and there a look of "wild surmise."
>
> The faculty's sense of urgency and importance of the moment was shortly borne out when a small delegation from the trustees came to Gambier to meet with the Faculty Council and to discuss the choice of a new president. It was, one sensed, an important meeting, one which might have far-reaching consequences. And it was perhaps significant that it was a member of the Council who first raised the question of the candidacy of Mr. Caples at this meeting. Obviously, many of those who were party to the discussion had already given the subject some thought, and had come to the same conclusion. So it was no surprise to discover rather quickly that there was consensus. Mr. Caples would indeed be an ideal candidate for the post at this crucial moment in the

history of the College. There was less confidence that he would be available. In addition, some uncertainty was expressed by the trustees present as to the acceptability to the faculty of one from outside the academic world. It was also felt that Mr. Caples might be more inclined to give serious thought to the possibility of changing jobs if he were to receive some kind of assurance that the faculty was indeed prepared, or would be prepared, to accept his leadership.

Council was persuaded by its own convictions as well as by its understanding of sentiment in the faculty, that everything possible should be done to help bring Mr. Caples to Kenyon. It made plans, then and there, to take an official reading of faculty opinion on the subject. There were to be two questions: a general one, having to do with the acceptability of a candidate of the type represented by Mr. Caples, that is, a distinguished administrator from the world of affairs/or business, rather than from the academy; and a specific one, seeking a response to the particular nomination of Mr. Caples himself. It became my privileged chore to collect and tally the results of this survey, and to communicate them, on behalf of the Council and the faculty to the trustees. Most members of the faculty were ready with their answers and it was quickly done. Because of his close association with the College over many years — as a trustee, and alumnus, and in both roles as a frequent visitor to the campus — Mr. Caples' qualities were already well-known to many members of the faculty. Newcomers found it difficult to resist the general enthusiasm for the proposal. The two questions indicated above were put to each of seventy members of the faculty, and the response indicated an overwhelming approval of both. There was complete unanimity in favor of the Caples nomination, and nearly every member of the faculty accompanied his affirmative vote with an expression like "enthusiastically" or "emphatically." This was the faculty position before the event.

The labor negotiations in which Dr. Caples was involved ended somewhat sooner than the expected date of October 1, 1968, and the Caples family moved to Gambier during August. The Board of Trustees designated Samuel S. Lord, Vice President for Finance, Chief Executive Officer of the College for the summer interim period.

A Difficult First Year

President Caples' first year in office took place against the backdrop of the most violent student unrest in U.S. educational history. Starting soon after the assassination of President John F. Kennedy in 1963, students disrupted the University of California at Berkeley, and campus revolt spread rapidly across the country with Eastern universities such as Columbia, Cornell, and Harvard becoming prime targets for disruption. In April 1968 students at Columbia occupied the administrative offices and paralyzed all operations of the university for two weeks. It was during this period that black riots in major cities such as Newark, N.J. and Detroit killed dozens of people, injured thousands, and left more thousands homeless by rioting, burning, and looting. The assassinations of Dr. Martin Luther King, Jr. and Senator Robert F. Kennedy brought tensions in the nation to the breaking point.

Kenyon students in the fall of 1968 were greatly disturbed by the disruptions taking place throughout the nation. In Gambier there were no riots, no destruction of property, but there was much speaking out on national grievances: the treatment of blacks, the war in Vietnam, the military draft, and the alleged indifference of "The Establishment" to the needs of the people. Locally, they wanted a black studies program, abolition of restriction on visiting hours for women, and more of a voice in decision-making in administrative and academic affairs.

President Caples had scarcely moved into Cromwell Cottage before an event occurred which was of grave concern to the entire Kenyon community. During the weekend of October 11-13, 1968, there was brought to the Hill a quantity — believed to have been about 250 capsules — of a mescaline-based drug which came to be known as MDA. A number of normally non-drug-using people took the drug, which had the property of inducing bizarre behavior. Some students were punished by being asked to withdraw from college or by being placed on strict probation; there was arrogance among the students and threats of exposure to the press by students who thought the College would try to hush up matters. Obviously it was time for a clear-cut policy statement outlining how the administration proposed to handle the situation. The *Collegian* for October 18, 1968 reported:

> President William G. Caples addressed the College from the Rosse Hall steps yesterday in a statement of policy concerning liberty, license, and responsibility.
> Mr. Caples noted that society places definite restrictions on individual behavior, that these restrictions are necessary for protection and order.

He observed that "a few men mistaking liberty as license can destroy" an institution built over generations. He said, "No one has any *right* or *license* to conduct himself as to destroy the good work or name of others or the community . . . Yet, here people have assumed it . . . This kind of behavior has to be stopped."

He termed the use of MDA, "almost idiocy on the part of seemingly intelligent people who voluntarily put into their system a drug the content of which they do not know."

He said that the argument that such use is a "moral" right "is an idle and useless pastime so long as the act is illegal. Like it or not the law establishes the morality or immorality of any act."

President Caples said that the extent of violation of college rules was such that he could have declared a state of emergency and suspended the rules and the student government. But he "chose not to follow that course," and to adhere to the constitution of the campus government.

He said that if the "principles and rules of behavior" written in the student handbook were followed, "all of you would be proud of yourselves and the reputation of this college would be great."

He referred to the section on drug abuse, saying, "It is my intention to keep drugs, including marijuana, off this Hill, if possible . . . I will use every legal means at my disposal.

Although the firm action of the administration against drugs got overwhelming support from the students and the faculty, there were some who took exception to the tone of the President's statement. David W. Hoster (K1969), President of the Student Council, spoke of what he considered the President's "dangerously extreme statement." Addressing the Council on October 21 he said:

I regard as the key operative phrase in the President's extended comments the following: . . . "Like it or not the law establishes the morality or immorality of any act." Believe me, I don't like it, and I don't like that line of reasoning at all.

This is a community where thinking men can come together to question the order of things and hopefully in that process come to understand themselves and their relation to that society, whether they place themselves within it or outside of it. Like it or not, there are no standards anywhere, and that includes the law, that are so perfect that they are beyond question or exclude violation out of hand; and one who asserts that law is an absolute unto itself and in the same breath says there are no easy or final answers has involved himself in a massive contradiction. I believe it may be to the ultimate good of the society to violate demonstrably some laws, and a liberal arts experience at Kenyon should give us reasonable intellectual bases for action in this area.

> Having written the law, having established a necessary standard relating to drugs, we must now behave as an academic community. The law should be upheld, by legal action if necessary, but it must be questioned as well, or there is no college.

The phrase, "like it or not," quickly became a watchword on the Hill. "Like it or not" T-shirts appeared, and outside speakers who used the phrase must have been mystified by the sudden burst of laughter which followed its use.

The MDA weekend was a one-of-a-kind phenomenon. After that time the overt use of drugs at Kenyon ceased, and by 1971 it appeared that drug-taking was diminishing. Strangely enough, there are those who claim that the use of alcohol has increased — a clear case of the substitution of one drug for another.

All during the school year 1968-69 there was a testing of the new president. Although a *Collegian* editorial for February 6, 1969 took Dr. Caples to task for criticizing its news coverage, the same issue in reporting an open Student Council meeting with President Caples commented: " ... students in attendance were treated to an entertaining and historic moment. For the first time, many students saw Bill Caples in action. Some seemed to feel that Kenyon's new president was a little more energetic and forceful than what they had bargained for. It also seemed that Bill Caples was finding the student body more zealous and demanding than what he had bargained for.

"At the end of the meeting there was a spontaneous round of applause, which was the crowning amusement of the night, considering the heat of the discussion. Perhaps the students instinctively felt that the basic meeting of views was a good thing."

The *Collegian* for April 17, 1969 described the last event of a year of student unrest on Sunday evening, April 13. What started out as a spring frolic, with students throwing water bags and standing around on Middle Path, escalated into a march to the President's house by about 200 students. Dr. Caples was in Mount Vernon, but Mrs. Caples told the students they could wait for his return. Provost Haywood spoke briefly with some of the students, and Professors Gerrit H. Roelofs and Joseph F. Slate engaged in a discussion with students on the steps of the house. The main issue was the lack of progress in instituting a black studies program and in the abolition of visiting hours for women. The principal spokesmen for the students were Eugene Peterson (K1970) and Murray Horwitz (K1970).

President Caples returned home at about 8:30. He did not propose to settle the issue on his front steps, and said that differences should be discussed in his office. He said that he intended "to follow the rules you made before I came here. The only changes that have been made here have been made by the campus government. If you don't like the kind of government you have here there's a way to change it and this isn't it."

Murray Horwitz later described the event as "a mediocre riot with mediocre people at the front. The real student leaders were not involved."

Many students disapproved heartily of the march on Cromwell Cottage. In a letter in the *Collegian* for April 24, John Breithaupt (K1972) and Mark Lewis (K1972) wrote: "We assert that President Caples is neither an ogre nor a fascist, bent on the imposition of his 'life-style' upon Kenyon students, but an honest man trying to cope with a complex and difficult job. He deserves the respect of every student — even those who feel that the tempo of change at Kenyon could be increased."

Building Construction

Groundbreaking ceremonies on October 15, 1968 launched a period of building construction unparalleled in the history of Kenyon College. That date marked the official beginning of the building of Kenyon's new Coordinate College and the Biology Building which completed the Science Center. Although the major construction took place during the year 1968-69, it was not until the summer of 1972 that this phase of the expansion program was completed. The total building cost was over $9,000,000.

The ceremonies for the groundbreaking were preceded by an academic procession, which formed at the gates and marched northward along the Middle Path to the site of the new commons building at the northeast corner of Brooklyn and Gaskin Streets. Fred Barry, Jr. (K1942) read the resolution of the Board of Trustees authorizing the establishment of the Coordinate College, and President Caples responded, pledging the full cooperation and support of the Kenyon College family. The formal address was made by Dr. John D. Millett, Chancellor of the Ohio Board of Regents. The official launching was celebrated by breaking a bottle of champagne over a piece of construction equipment and by the traditional turning of earth by Chancellor Millett and President Caples.

Academic procession on Middle Path preceding the ceremonies for the ground-breaking for the Women's College.

With the exception of the Weaver House and the homes of Professors Michael and Roelofs, the entire area bounded by Gaskin Street, Brooklyn Street, and what was then Acland Street was cleared for the new women's college buildings. This required the demolition of two faculty homes and the Harcourt Parish House on Brooklyn Street, and the temporary building on Gaskin Street used for many years by the Student Health

Service. One of the faculty houses torn down was the beautiful "White Wing," built in 1833 for Professor Marcus Tullius Cicero Wing at the northeast corner of Brooklyn and Gaskin Streets. The passing of this architectural landmark was lamented by the entire community. The house formerly occupied by William H. Thomas, Jr. was moved a few hundred feet eastward on Acland Street, and became the residence of Miss Doris Crozier, Dean of the Coordinate College.

President Caples launching the Women's College by breaking a bottle of champagne over a piece of construction equipment. Chancellor Millett is at the left.

The new women students admitted in 1969 were mainly freshmen, and the full complement of women was not reached until 1972. The building of the dormitories was staggered as it was not necessary to build all of the housing units at the same time. However, the dining commons had to be built immediately, so construction on it started even before the opening of school in the fall of 1968.

The beautiful old Wing house had to be demolished to make way for the construction of the Women's College.

Dining Commons

The commons was constructed by the Albert M. Higley Company of Cleveland, according to plans drawn by The Perkins and Will Partnership of Chicago. The total building cost of $1,500,000 was financed through the Ohio Higher Educational Facility Commission. Working fast to take advantage of legislative action approving the Commission a few months earlier, Kenyon finance officers were able to push through applications which resulted in the new commons being the first building in the state to obtain financial backing from the Commission. The Commission issued tax-free bonds for the financing, holding title to the facility, and leasing it to Kenyon until the mortgage is retired in 30 years.

The new commons had coeducational dining from the day that it opened, but an article in the *Mount Vernon News* for September 9, 1968 gives the thinking of the planners at the time construction started: "The commons has been designed to be more informal and feminine in nature. Warm colors will be used throughout, along with local brick and aggregate, which will give color tones in the large areas of sand-blasted concrete to be used in the building. Accents will be provided by black anodized aluminum door and window frames."

The commons is laid out in three pods, entered through a central foyer or from outside doors. The dining area has a balcony-lounge around its perimeter. One of the other pods is set aside for a quiet study area, while the third is designated for informal recreation. All of the buildings built during this construction phase are air conditioned and carpeted.

Construction of Gund Commons.

Dormitories No. 1 and No. 2

At the same time as work on the commons was progressing, the Freeman Construction Company of Wooster began construction on Dormitories No. 1 and No. 2, located respectively west and north of the commons. Each planned to house 159 students and a resident adviser, the buildings were designed by Perkins and Will "to provide social units assembled in various ways to achieve a diversified architectural setting." They were constructed of brick, precast concrete, limestone trim, with black anodized aluminum door and window frames to match the commons. Again the news releases emphasized that "the architects have given the building a curved appearance to enhance the feminine and informal atmosphere they are creating in the Coordinate College."

The total cost was $2,683,000 for the two dormitories; part of the money came from a $1,855,000 loan from the Department of Housing and Urban Development, and the remainder from the Kenyon Program for Expansion Campaign.

A state-wide laborers strike June 2-18, 1969 made it touch-

and-go whether Dormitory No. 1 and the commons would be ready for the opening of school. Working from the top down, the contractor had the second and third floors of the dormitory ready, but some of the new women students slated for the first floor had to be housed for a few days in the Alumni House, Watson Hall, Bexley Hall, the College Infirmary, and in the homes of President Caples, Dean Crozier, Miss Katherine Allen, and other members of the community. However, delay in the installation of kitchen equipment put off the opening of the new commons until about October 1. In the meantime all the students ate in Peirce and Dempsey Halls.

Since the use of Dormitory No. 2 was not essential to the operation of the Coordinate College during the 1969-70 school year, finishing touches on this building were delayed temporarily and then completed in time for occupancy in the fall of 1970, when the second class of women students arrived.

Naming of the Buildings

At a ceremony on May 30, 1970, Dormitory No. 1 was dedicated as the Virginia Hyatt McBride Residence, and the commons became the Jessica Roesler Gund Commons. McBride Residence was named in honor of the wife of Pierre B. McBride (K1918), the long-time trustee and generous benefactor of Kenyon. Honored in the naming of the Commons was the wife of George Gund, holder of a Kenyon degree, a member of the Board of Trustees, and a liberal contributor to Kenyon for many years.

Not long after these dedications, Dormitory No. 2 became known as Madeleine A. Mather Residence, honoring the wife of Philip R. Mather, known also to all Kenyonites as a long-time trustee and benefactor.

Dormitory No. 3

The original plan for the third dormitory of the women's college called for a three story building similar to the first two, but a decision was made to build a high-rise dormitory of nine stories instead. One of the prime considerations for the change was the desire of the architects, Perkins and Will, to break up the institutional flat-top aspect of the first two dormitories. The initial shock of the local community over the prospect of a tall building in Gambier was greatly softened by the revelation that construction of a "high-rise" would save many of the beautiful trees.

The Kokosing Construction Company began work on Dormitory No. 3 during the summer of 1970, and by mid-May the nine-story structure had been "topped-out." A $1,500,000 loan from the Ohio Educational Facility Commission financed the project, under fiscal arrangements similar to those for Gund Commons. Students moved into the dormitory as school opened in September 1971.

The "high-rise" conformed well with the other buildings of the women's complex, and the surrounding tall trees have minimized its height. The *Mount Vernon News* for March 17, 1972 carried a striking full-page picture of the new facility and commented: "The new architecture of the 20th century can be blended with the peace and serenity of a town which dates back to the early 19th century as proven by the new dorm in Gambier. While it tends to stress the modern architecture of steel, glass, and concrete, it blends in well with the surrounding rural atmosphere of the tiny college community."

With a capacity of 146 residents, building costs per student were slightly higher than for the first two dormitories. But Kenyon could boast of having the tallest building in Knox County.

New Apartments

During the school year 1969-70, a committee representing students from both colleges, and headed by Professor Charles E. Rice, had studied the housing situation and recommended that a break was needed from the dorm-style of life provided at that time. The College decided to go along with this suggestion for the final phase of the housing expansion, and built an apartment complex on what had been a sloping meadow just north of Bexley Place. The Albert M. Higley Company contracted to design, build, and furnish ready for occupancy six buildings of typical apartment house construction. The total cost, including landscaping, parking lot, laundry building, and four tennis courts, was about $750,000. Financing was by a self-liquidating, 25-year loan from the Ohio Higher Educational Facility Commission. The buildings vary in size from two to eight apartments, and each apartment houses from four to six students. The total capacity is 152. Each apartment is a self-contained unit, with bedrooms, bathroom, and living room. The whole complex was completed in time for school opening in September 1972.

The Higley Company hired Joseph Baker and Associates of Newark, Ohio as the architects, and their designs provided informal living arrangements at low cost — about half of the cost per occupant as Dormitory No. 3.

Biology Building and the Renovation of Samuel Mather Hall

Simultaneously with the beginning of the Coordinate College construction in 1968, a start was made on two projects to bring to completion Kenyon's long-needed Science Center — the building of the Biology Building and the renovation of Samuel Mather Science Hall.

The cost of the work on the buildings plus that of furnishings and equipment was in excess of $2,500,000; roughly three-quarters of this amount was spent on the new Biology Building.

The entire project was designed by Perkins and Will, and the contractor was the R.G. Beer Corporation of Mansfield, Ohio. The construction was financed by a $650,000 Federal Title I grant under the Educational Facilities Act; a Title III 30-year loan of $850,000; a gift of $100,000 from Mrs. Ailsa Mellon Bruce; a $25,000 grant from the Kresge Foundation; and the remainder through funds of the Kenyon Program For Expansion.

To keep the Gambier community informed of the progress on the four major buildings going up, the Kenyon Department of Public Relations published and distributed a series of *Construction Flashes*. Typical of the reports given was that of January 27, 1969: "There is a certain amount of work going on, about which people are unaware. This is in Old Mather where students and faculty are (literally) gritting their teeth and showing good humor despite the inconvenience of renovation, which began during the Christmas vacation. The plaster dust, which during the operations caused zero visibility and covered the floor to a depth estimated at one inch, continues to filter down leaving a white haze over all surfaces."

Samuel Mather Hall was in use despite the handicaps all during the renovation. By December of 1969 the Biology Building began to be used, but it took most of the school year 1969-70 to complete the Science Center.

Professor Francis W. Yow, Chairman of the Department of Biology, who visited more than 50 new biology facilities across the nation when planning the Biology Building, termed it "the finest undergraduate facility in the country." Dr. Yow was on sabbatical leave during the school year 1969-70, so the tremendous task of moving the Department of Biology and getting settled in the new building fell on Professor Robert D. Burns, who was the chairman that year.

The completed Science Complex. From left: Philip Mather Hall, Samuel Mather Hall, and the Biology Building.

The new building was designed, basically, for laboratory work. Each of the eight laboratories to serve faculty has all the facilities for normal research. Flexibility in the use of the teaching laboratories was achieved by providing furniture which could be moved to fit various requirements. For the first time Kenyon had a greenhouse, divided into three sections, each with individual temperature and humidity controls. From the standpoint of the Kenyon community, the Biology Building's lecture center turned out to be a most useful addition. This small auditorium, seating about 200, has excellent acoustical properties, and is one of the most desirable locations for lectures.

The Biology Building was faced with Briar Hill sandstone with limestone trim to match Old and New Mather. Although the three science buildings are of different styles of architecture and were constructed over a period of almost fifty years, they are cohesive and harmonious in feeling. There is an attractive patio with plantings and benches in the center of the science area.

Parents' Organizations

In the fall of 1968, when student unrest and drug problems were plaguing campuses all over the country, the College decided that a closer relationship with the parents of Kenyon students might help to alleviate some of the difficulties in Gambier. The result was the Kenyon Parents' Association, organized by a group of parents who met on the Hill on November 2, 1968. All Kenyon parents are considered members of the Association. The Kenyon College Parents' Advisory Council is the working body of the organization. The Council consists of from seven to thirteen parents of students from each current Kenyon class, for a total of about 40. The members are appointed by the Kenyon College president, and are organized into five committees. According to news releases at the time of its formation the Advisory Council was formed "to provide parents with a formal means of communication with the college administration; an opportunity to select projects to which they can designate their gifts; and to promote a feeling of unity in the Kenyon family by means of a continuing communication between parents and faculty, alumni, administration, and students."

At the time of its formation, the Advisory Council was viewed with suspicion by some students. An editorial in the November 7, 1968 *Collegian* said: " . . . It is not quite clear what role this group of parents will play. It seems that it could do quite important work in raising funds and furthering interest in Kenyon . . . The forty members are by no means representative of all Kenyon parents on an elected basis, and it would be far from their realm, we believe, to make a policy statement for the parents of Kenyon students." However, as the years have gone by, the Advisory Council has become an increasingly vital and effective organization, especially with the coming of women to Kenyon.

Almost 200 parents of Kenyon students were in Gambier on April 12, 1969 for the first Parents' Day program, sponsored by the Advisory Council. So successful was the affair that in 1970 the program was extended for three days and renamed Parents' Weekend. The general format for the Weekend since that time has offered the parents such programs as symposia, athletic events, concerts, plays, films, faculty open houses, dances, and reports by the president and other members of the college staff.

The Kenyon Parents' Fund was revitalized by the Advisory Council. In September 1969, J.R. Killpack, chairman of the financial advisory committee of the Council, was able to announce: "Parents have contributed a record $48,747 to help the College in carrying forth worthwhile programs." Mr. Killpack set as the 1969-70 goal 30% participation of parents for a total of $35,000. This goal was achieved and the meeting of subsequent goals has assisted the College greatly to carry out programs for which funds would otherwise not be available.

Dean Doris Crozier

The College was interested in making an early selection of a new head for the women's college, and the *Collegian* for December 12, 1968 announced: "The newly-chosen Dean of Women is Miss Doris Crozier, a career educator, who currently is assistant to the president and assistant professor of anthropology at Chatham College. Miss Crozier has visited Kenyon twice this semester and she has said she will accept the post. President Caples was in Pittsburgh this week to determine if Miss Crozier would be able to spend next semester in residence."

(In order to avoid confusion, Miss Crozier was given the title, Dean, the Coordinate College, and Thomas J. Edwards was called Dean, Kenyon College. When Kenyon went coed in 1972, Mr. Edwards again became Dean of Students).

Miss Crozier came to Gambier with a wide background of teaching and educational administrative experience, both in the United States and abroad. She was selected from a list of 20 nominees representing all sections of the country. Of the candidates, six were brought to Gambier to be interviewed by the administration and the Faculty Council.

One of Dean Crozier's overriding concerns was that the Coordinate College, with its small numbers, would be overwhelmed and ignored by the men's college. She was constantly alert to any possibility that "her girls" were being regarded as second-class citizens in the college community. She resigned in the spring of 1972, just as Kenyon College became a coeducational institution, but Dean Crozier will always be identified as the guiding force in the short life of the Coordinate College.

Bishop Burt (right) congratulates President Caples at the inauguration.

Inauguration of President Caples

The formal inauguration of William Goff Caples as the fifteenth President of Kenyon College took place on the afternoon of April 15, 1969 in Wertheimer Field House.

The induction of the president was performed by the Right Reverend John H. Burt, Bishop of Ohio, and the inauguration address was delivered by J. Douglas Brown, Provost and Dean of the Faculty, Emeritus, Princeton University. President Caples was particularly pleased with Dr. Brown's giving the address "as an inaugural present," since the Princeton scholar had long been a staunch friend of Kenyon and an outspoken advocate of liberal arts education. Dr. Brown, an economist, was one of the architects of the original 1935 Social Security legislation, and was among the leaders who broadened its coverage and scope after its passage.

About 125 representatives of colleges and universities, and delegates from professional and learned societies from coast to coast marched in the academic procession. A luncheon at noon and a reception following the ceremonies provided entertainment for the distinguished visitors. The whole affair was efficiently and tastefully coordinated by John A. Fink (K1936).

Entirely separate from the formal celebration was a lavish Inauguration Ball given in honor of President Caples by the faculty and staff on the same evening in The Great Hall of Peirce.

Women Students Come To Kenyon

September 8, 1969 marked the official opening of the Coordinate College. The actual settling-in of the new women students started on September 4 and went fairly smoothly, considering that a small number of the newcomers had to be housed in temporary quarters for about a week. Kenyon men viewed the tradition-breaking event with a great variety of emotions. Some thought that it was great to have women on the campus. Others could not see how coordination — with separate governments, separate clubs and organizations, and different rules of conduct — could work. Still others, especially seniors, worried that an important tradition had been lost. The male freshmen wondered what all the fuss was about. One of the most vocal of the senior critics was seen helping a woman student carry her luggage to her room.

There were some dislocations. John K. Morrell (K1970)

wrote in an account preserved in the Archives: "In September 1969 the men returned to find their second floor men's room in the Library changed to a ladies' room. Some men (who don't read signs but rely totally on their instincts) did not notice the change and continued to use the new ladies' room as their old men's room. This resulted in a number of embarrassing situations for the new ladies as well as the old men."

Women students of the Class of 1973 when they arrived in September 1969.

Each fall for the next three years the female population increased, while each fall the number of male students who had attended an all-men's college dropped, until, with the graduation of the Class of 1972, there were none left who had known the all-male Kenyon.

Kent State

Student unrest throughout the United States reached the boiling point on May 4, 1970 with the killing of four Kent State University students by members of the Ohio National Guard, which had been called out to quell many days of rioting on the Kent, Ohio campus. Violent disturbances erupted in colleges and universities throughout the land. In some sections of the country virtually every institution of higher learning canceled classes and examinations, and closed its doors. Some did not reopen until the following fall.

It so happened that Robert Novak, a nationally-known news analyst, whose daily column was bought by more than 160 U.S. newspapers, was in Gambier as a guest scholar at the time of the Kent State shootings. He devoted one whole issue of his column to the reaction of the Kenyon students, faculty, and administration. The headline was "Notable Victory Scored at Kenyon For Cause of Academic Freedom." The column as printed in the *Washington Post* for May 15, 1970 follows:

Tense and dramatic days last week on the normally pastoral campus of Kenyon College revealed the extent of the crisis for liberal education in America under even the best of conditions.

What happened at Kenyon was a signal triumph by administration, faculty and students against politicizing the campus despite the volatile atmosphere. While some 450 colleges were shutting down, Kenyon not only remained open but displayed some unfashionable virtues: civility, an appreciation of academic freedom, and mutual respect between faculty and student body.

Yet, even at Kenyon with less than 1,000 students and physically isolated in rural Ohio, worried professors amid student leaders warily approach the future — fearing the barbarians are at the gates. They wonder how long sanity can survive here while student fury, often abetted by faculty, engulfs Harvard, Michigan, and Berkeley. "How long can we stay quiet when all hell is breaking loose around us?" asks one Kenyon professor.

Every campus has its own peculiarity, and Kenyon's conspicuous success is no prescription for restoring liberal education nationwide or even a surefire formula for saving it here. What the Kenyon story underlines is that a firm stand by the faculty in the interest of intellectual civility is the one essential for survival of the American university.

Following the pattern of every campus today, students and faculty at Kenyon are emotionally opposed to the Vietnam war. Nor were they immune from the campus frenzy over the Cambodian operation and the killing of four Kent State University students. When Kenyon's students watched fellow students elsewhere man the barricades via the evening television news, they started planning their own student strike.

Where Kenyon differed from most other campuses was the reaction of administration and faculty. Instead of submitting to students' demands, Kenyon's professors persuasively argued with the students that closing down the campus would accomplish nothing and that a planned student march on the State Capitol might only lead to more tragedy.

The appeal to reason succeeded. After a long meeting last Thursday night, the students voted not to participate in the Columbus march and to recommend that the college stay open. But they also recommended cancelling final examinations. Instead, they wanted "symposiums, open forums, and teach-ins" on the Indo-china war, on violence and dissent, and on the use of force on the campus.

At most campuses, the administration would have eagerly gobbled up this seeming panacea. Indeed, a proposal for teach-ins, passé to student radicals, departs from the present collegiate principle that important matters should be settled by conscience instead of intellect.

Remarkably, however, the Kenyon faculty did not accept that easy way out. Realizing that the cancellation of final examinations would open the door to disruption of education whenever external political developments intrude, the faculty voted to hold examinations as scheduled but to arrange three days of "convocations and seminars" on transcendent political events.

Even more remarkably, the students overwhelmingly endorsed that decision at a meeting Saturday night. There was no hissing or booing. When a student referred to the faculty as "honest men and good men," there was sustained standing applause. This was only possible because the Kenyon faculty has consistently opposed politicization of the campus and had implanted that principle with a significant number of students.

Moreover, when a few students at Saturday night's meeting proposed a student voice in determining curriculum and faculty selection, they were politely but firmly rebuffed. President William Caples, a non-academician who retired as a vice president of Inland Steel to run his alma mater, will not permit any such trampling on academic freedom. The fact that speakers will actually be permitted to defend the Cambodian operation during the Kenyon seminars proves that devotion to academic freedom is no mere slogan here.

. . . The tenuous nature of academic freedom was apparent at Saturday night's meeting. When some students started probing the loopholes in the faculty's decision, Provost Bruce Haywood urged them not to pressure individual professors to cancel examinations. As Haywood put it: "Academic freedom is a very delicate flower."

(By Evans and Novak, Courtesy of Publishers-Hall Syndicate)

The Novak column sparked editorials in newspapers all over the U.S. lauding Kenyon's handling of the situation. Many of them referred to Dr. Haywood's final phrase.

On the day following the Kent State killings, an all-college assembly, chaired by Clark J. Dougan (K1971), President of the Student Council, took place from 10:00 a.m. to after 2:00 p.m. The next day there was another all-college assembly from 4:00 to 9:00 p.m. Rosse Hall was jammed with college and town residents. The march on Columbus was given up as not appropriate. President Caples agreed to invite other Ohio college presidents to request an interview with Governor Rhodes. (Twenty-three ultimately joined, but the Governor never agreed to meet.)

On May 7 another all-college assembly was held. The students formulated a series of recommendations to the College: that examinations be canceled (formal classes were scheduled to end on May 9); a series of forums and teach-ins be substituted along with daily assemblies; daily quiet prayer in the Chapel; invitations to Mount Vernon residents to join in the assemblies and symposia. A meeting of the faculty was called for the following morning.

The faculty passed a compromise motion which delayed examinations till the 20th through the 27th and excused seniors from course examinations. Particularly overwrought students were to be permitted to take incomplete grades. A supplemental program of convocations and seminars was approved.

Altogether 26 seminar groups were organized and met on May 13, 14, and 15. A sampling of the topics includes: "Responsible Dissent," "Violence in the Arts and Media," "History, Morals, and Politics," and "Science and Society."

The students made a great effort to involve the surrounding community in their concern. On Sunday, May 10, Kenyon students appeared at 22 churches in Mount Vernon and elsewhere in Knox County to give five-minute statements about their concerns and reactions. Booths were set up on Mount Vernon's Main Street to discuss issues with those who would listen and participate. Students passed out thousands of postcards, addressed to Congressmen and Senators, and asked that persons write, whatever their opinions. Huge advertisements were run in the Cleveland and Columbus papers condemning the violence at Kent State. Those who signed the published statement paid for the cost of the advertisements: over $1,000.

The local reaction to the behavior of the Kenyon students was highly laudatory. The *Mount Vernon News* printed daily accounts of the events in Gambier, and on May 12 carried an editorial headed, "Kenyon Chooses A Course" which ended: "Kenyon is one of the Ohio colleges still open and in session. Its faculty, students, and administration showed that they have the ability to meet crises and try to overcome problems sanely and without violence and destruction. If Kenyon can continue on this path, its students will have demonstrated to the collegiate world that it is possible for people to sit down and talk their way to acceptable decisions. Perhaps it is this quality which has long kept Kenyon in the top rank of American colleges."

Section of the half-page advertisement in the *Cleveland Plain Dealer*.

From May 20 revised procedures went on: examinations were held and Commencement took place on the 31st. Kenyon emerged from this crisis with a new feeling of cohesion on the Hill and a greatly enhanced public image in American educational circles.

Olof Palme Returns To Kenyon

The *Collegian* for January 22, 1970 announced:

Kenyon College will be the scene of a major address by Olof Palme, Swedish Prime Minister, early this year. President Caples received confirmation that the 1948 alumnus of Kenyon desires to speak here within the first five months of 1970.

The Prime Minister's office noted that they had received literally hundreds of such invitations elsewhere in the country but that Mr. Palme desired to make one major speech in the U.S. — at Kenyon.

It is expected that Prime Minister Palme's address will deal with the nature of freedom. While at Kenyon Palme was a dual major in political science and economics.

However distinguished Palme may be, he is exciting a rash of mail to Caples' office — preponderantly against his visit. U.S.-Swedish relations have gone adrift in recent years due to their stand on Vietnam. Their condemnation of United States intervention has been compounded by their financial support of the North Vietnamese government.

Only recently has the United States resumed diplomatic relations with Sweden. A campaign spearheaded by Ohio Senator Stephen Young (K1911) has recently persuaded the Nixon administration to re-fill our Ambassador's seat in Stockholm.

President Caples refuses to be influenced by mail regarding him and other college presidents as "Reds." The comments have been coming from alumni, newspaper editorials, and readers who regard Kenyon's welcome of Palme — not to speak of the intention to grant him an honorary doctoral degree — as un-American, foolhardy, and Communistic. Caples . . . said in a *Collegian* interview, "If we are truly an institution of inquiry, we should welcome this type of forum for discussion."

There were comments in newspapers, large and small, all over the country. A typical vitriolic dissent came in an editorial in *The Mexico Daily Ledger*, Mexico, Missouri, which read, in part:

Make a note of Kenyon College as a place not to send your son, your daughter, or your donations to further education in America.

Instead of standing up for our allies, our friends, Kenyon College has announced that it is going to give an honorary degree this year to the Prime Minister of Sweden. What a shame Ho Chi Minh is not alive so that he could get one, too.

However, Kenyon does have a special reason in that the Prime Minister once attended Kenyon. Many colleges have graduates of which they are proud, and of which they are ashamed.

Kenyon proves to be the kind of college that is proud of a former

271

student now leading one of the world's most anti-American countries.

It makes us wonder if Kenyon taught him anti-Americanism or if he learned it on his own in Sweden.

The Swedish Prime Minister gave his major U.S. address, "On the Freedom of Men and Freedom of Nations," on June 6, 1970, in front of Samuel Mather Hall to an audience of about 1,000. The only jarring note was the presence of two bus-loads of members of the International Longshoremen's Association who came to protest Sweden's criticisms of the United States policies in Vietnam. Although this group had agreed to sit quietly in the audience after a protest parade, they fanned out to the edges of the crowd, and booed and shouted when Palme began to speak. Eventually many of them succumbed to the charms of an idyllic Gambier June day, and lay down on the grass for a snooze.

Backed by a Kenyon banner, Olof Palme holds a press conference.

Mr. Palme refused to be shouted down by the hecklers, and at one point departed from his prepared text when he said to the audience that academic freedom "also includes the right to be heard." The demonstrators kept up their interruptions until Mr. Palme finished speaking. Then they boarded their buses and left, just as President Caples was presenting the Prime Minister with an honorary degree of Doctor of Humane Letters. Dr. Caples said, "I apologize publicly for those who were not invited. It's tragic that those who needed to hear your words the most refused to listen."

Despite the tight security enforced by at least 50 uniformed and plain-clothes law enforcement officers, Mr. Palme and his charming wife, Lisbet, mingled freely with other alumni assembled for the Alumni Reunion Weekend, held press conferences, and talked with groups of students who had remained in Gambier for the occasion.

Gambier Experimental College

Scott Hauser (K1976) in the *Kenyon College Bulletin* for April 1973 wrote an article on the Gambier Experimental College. In it he quoted from the first brochure of the GEC:

> The Gambier Experimental College is an educational laboratory. Courses have no grades, tests, fees, or requirements other than a genuine interest in learning. Within this educational laboratory experiments in education take the form of seminars, workshops, and small interaction groups. Each is aimed at learning through personal initiative and involvement rather than grading and testing. We offer no rewards; though we think that they are there, for the trying. The success of a GEC course is not guaranteed; it depends entirely on the continued participation and energies of the students and townspeople who choose to enroll . . . We can promise nothing except an opportunity to become involved with the concept of education in ways not traditionally provided for in college curriculums.

Founded in 1969 as a project of the Experimental Foundation at Kenyon, the GEC aimed to offer short-term courses in an enjoyable atmosphere, and to develop more interaction between the College and the surrounding communities. Instructors and students came from the College, the village, and from Knox County. The GEC has seen professors sitting in the classes of their students. Classes began in the school year 1969-70, coordinated by Saul Benjamin (K1970) and John Flanzer (K1970). Under the directorship of Harold M. Real (K1974), interest in the courses boomed during 1972-73 and this momentum carried through 1973-74, when the coordinator was Christopher M. Reidy (K1974).

The organization of the Experimental College was kept as simple as possible. The registration fee was low (typically $1.00), and courses met at times and places convenient to the instructors. The course offerings ranged from the serious: Elementary Japanese, and The History of Kenyon College and Gambier; to the utilitarian: Bagel Making, The Brewing of Malt Wine, and Furniture Refinishing and Minor Repair; to the recreational: Basic Ragtime Guitar, and Israeli Folk Dancing; to the supernatural: The Mysteries of Life.

Changing Scholastic Patterns

The Self-Study Program of the early 1960's resulted in a curriculum which broke many of the proscriptive bonds. Several small changes in curriculum took place in the years which followed, and then in 1972 a new format was introduced which Provost Haywood described as "pleasingly simple, honest, and — not unimportantly — eminently saleable."

The program called for a student to earn a unit of credit in at least five departments and in at least three divisions; the student had to enroll in at least two departments at a time; and the student took no more than seven credits of the sixteen required for graduation in one department. The student also completed the senior exercise and passed the comprehensive examination.

During the 1960's emphasis on science and technological education boomed with the ascendancy of Sputnik and the fear of being overtaken in scientific developments by the Russians. But Dr. Haywood noted in 1970 that the academic trend at Kenyon had swung away from the sciences and social sciences toward the humanities and fine arts. He reported that four departments — English, Political Science, Biology, and History — accounted for two-thirds of the majors in the College.

Faculty Retirements

During the period covered by this chapter three long-time members of the faculty retired: Professors Samuel B. Cummings, Paul M. Titus, and H. Landon Warner.

Professor Cummings left active teaching December 31, 1971. The Spencer and Wolfe Professor of Psychology, he was educated at Amherst, Columbia, and Princeton, where he took his Ph.D. degree in 1938. That same year he joined the Kenyon faculty, and, except for three years in the Navy, he was at Kenyon for the remainder of his teaching career.

The degree of Doctor of Humane Letters was presented to Professor Cummings at Commencement in 1972. Part of his citation read: "Humane psychologist, gourmet, art collector, *bon vivant*, the Phineas Fogg of Gambier who circumnavigated the world in less than half of his eighty days: You early chose to teach at Kenyon College despite the seductive singing of such institutions as Dartmouth, Princeton, and Syracuse . . . Eight happy student generations of Kenyon men and three-quarters of a generation of co-ords-now-coeds salute you for your fairness, faithfulness to Kenyon and the tradition of the Liberal Arts, and your urbane banter about 'mice and men.' "

Only one semester later Dr. Titus retired, ending an active teaching career at Kenyon of 39 years. He came to Gambier in 1933 immediately after receiving his Ph.D. from Princeton and became the Edwin M. Stanton Professor of Economics. Except for several temporary leaves of absence, his teaching career at Kenyon was continuous until his retirement in June 1972. During the school year 1962-63, he served in Amman, Jordan as a consultant for the Economic Development Board of the Kingdom of Jordan. His appointment was under the auspices of the Ford Foundation Overseas Program. He served as an associate and consultant in a number of governmental, industrial, and academic conferences and twice was President of the Association of Ohio Economists and Political Scientists. He was director of Kenyon's Self-Study program during its first year.

Professor Titus was also honored with the degree of Doctor of Humane Letters at Commencement 1972 as he retired from active teaching. Some parts of his citation were: "You have enlightened ten student generations of Kenyon men in the often dark mysteries of your discipline, and in so doing, civilized the barbarous cupidity of those who think only in terms of material gain. You have taught and counseled wisely strong but self-willed young men who because of your example became public spirited, unselfish civil servants in state and federal government and leaders in industry ... Your colleagues know that you guard and care for Kenyon and for all its splendid traditions, many of which you helped to shape. You truly exemplify all the gifts and ornaments of the liberally educated man."

Professor Warner came to Kenyon immediately after service in the U.S. Navy during World War II; he stayed for 27 years, retiring in June 1973. He took his A.B., A.M., and Ph.D. in history all at Harvard. Among the many scholarly works he contributed while teaching on the Hill were his studies of progressivism in Ohio and his biography of Mr. Justice Clark. A former President of the Ohio Academy of History, he won several awards given by the Academy, including the "1973 Distinguished Service Award."

Kenyon College honored him with the degree of Doctor of Humane Letters in May 1973. In giving Professor Warner's citation, President Caples said, in part: "With sparkle and devotion you have helped seven generations of Kenyon men and one of Kenyon women to come to terms with the nation's past. With sanity and charity you have led, guided, and soothed your often ruffled and confused colleagues. You have shown that civility is a part of wisdom, and modesty a part of justness. You once described yourself as 'not very good at trying to be popular.' This judgement was one of the few errors you ever spoke."

Mr. Caples Goes To Washington

On October 11, 1971 the news was released that President Nixon had asked Dr. Caples to serve as a public member of the Pay Board established as part of Phase II of the program aimed at the control of inflation in the United States.

President Caples' acceptance involved many considerations. One concern was his health; the preceding year he had suffered a stroke, and he felt that he should get a clearance from his doctor. He also did not feel that he could answer President Nixon's request until he had consulted with the Trustees, his colleagues, and his family. After receiving assurances from all of these people, he accepted the invitation to serve on the Pay Board. He was absent from Gambier from the middle of October until Thanksgiving, and thereafter went to

Washington for two or three days a month. His service with the Pay Board formally ended when he and the other members resigned on February 28, 1973.

At the time of his appointment Dr. Caples commented: "I am willing to accept the assignment because I believe a citizen, regardless of party, when asked to assist in a Presidential program, should do so if he believes his efforts can aid in the solution of a problem which affects all citizens."

First Women Graduates

Although the first complete class of women was not graduated until 1973, transfer women students received degrees at the Commencement of 1971. At that time Belinda Bremner, Judith Goodhand (wife of Professor Robert Goodhand), and Patricia B. Sellew became the first women to earn degrees from Kenyon College, and Miss Sellew became the first woman undergraduate to be elected to Phi Beta Kappa. Other firsts for women students — first woman Danforth Scholar: Jean Dunbar (K1973); first woman Watson Fellow: Flora N. Katz (K1972); first woman Student Council officer: Ann E. Wiester (K1973). Winner of both a Watson and a Danforth, M. Kristina Peterson (K1973) earned two bachelor's degrees from Kenyon, in 1973 and in 1974. The distinction of being the first woman to become an active member of a Kenyon fraternity went to Kim Stapleton (K1974), who was initiated into Psi Upsilon on January 24, 1974.

From Coordinate College to Coeducational College

At the time of the establishment of the Coordinate College, there were persuasive arguments for the coordinate format. When the College changed to coeducation, President Caples reviewed the original plan in a March 1972 newsletter to alumni and parents: "Our thinking in establishing the Coordinate College was ruled by two main considerations: first, to ensure that women's opportunity to decide about the forms and styles of their life here not be crushed by the weight of the male majority or by the mass of tradition; and second, to provide that the academic life of the whole community be disrupted as little as possible in a time of expansion."

Coordination did not turn out in the way expected. Reviewing the changeover in the *Kenyon College Bulletin* for November 1972, William R. Chadeayne (K1950), Secretary of the Board of Trustees, wrote: " . . . even during the first year when women came to Gambier, it became apparent that the women themselves preferred coeducation to coordinate education, or, in other words, that they preferred to participate in and share Kenyon traditions rather than create their own. This manifested itself in various ways as for example being excluded from the matriculation oath and not sharing fully in student government. In short, it developed that the concept of coordinate education was being a divisive influence on campus rather than a unifying one with the result that polarization began to emerge."

Dr. Bruce Haywood, Provost of the College, presented a strong case for the change to coeducation in a report to the Trustees dated October 25, 1971 which read, in part:

> I would remind you that it was never our intention that there should come into being here something called The Coordinate College for Women. We had expected that, before the first women arrived, the place would have a name. We had thought of a Harcourt College (or a Jones College, a Gund, a Watson) which together with Kenyon College would be part of the larger Kenyon, even as Radcliffe and Harvard are part of the larger Harvard. I cannot tell you just how much — and how negatively — that lack of a name has worked against us. Instead of considering what arrangements and adaptations make the best sense for our students, people argue fruitlessly over what "coordination" demands. Women, having been recruited for Kenyon as they see it, reel confused before the claim that they are not part of Kenyon. Told that they may not sing "Philander Chase," that they have less claim on the faculty than men, that they give up their integrity by working with men on committees, the women wonder to what foolish idea their interests are being sacrificed. They all come eventually to feel that they have no sense of identity with something called "The Coordinate College for Women," which bespeaks the anonymous, the newly arrived, the unwanted — as they see it.
>
> By the second semester of last year it was plain to me that the women were becoming bitter and frustrated. I was ready by the end of the last year to urge the Board to give a name, any name, to the place. But I have come to see now that that would have been a mistake. In the meantime something else has become clear to me: that the women have been working to create, step by step, little by little, their own Kenyon identity. Last week, in yet another discussion with women, I asked

what their reaction would be, if the Board now put a name on their college. One junior, after a pause, said: "I should have to leave. That would be proof to me that women are never going to be part of Kenyon." The others agreed.

We should now acknowledge that a form which has worked beautifully to accomplish our larger aims is now working against the best interests of individual women. We can proudly say that women have a permanent place in this community. We can be certain that their numbers will be what we wanted them to be. We have provided them with splendid residences and a lovely campus. Yet all this will be as naught, if the form that made these possible becomes a source of women's alienation.

We decided long ago that women would earn a Kenyon A.B., that they should be Kenyon graduates. They want only to be Kenyon undergraduates too. The answer seems to me plain. We must let them have Kenyon's name from their very first day here.

The March 9, 1972 *Collegian* announced: "At its meeting on February 19th, the Board of Trustees of Kenyon College at long last voted that, effective on July 1, Kenyon will become a coeducational institution. As one local paper rather insanely but correctly stated, 'Kenyon will admit its first class of women in September 1972.'"

Coeducational Housing

By the action of the Board of Trustees on June 3, 1972, coeducational housing arrangements came to Kenyon: "Resolved that the action of the Executive Committee at its meeting of May 13, 1972 in approving the recommendations of the *ad hoc* committee on coeducation that several forms of housing that bring men and women into closer proximity be tried experimentally during the 1972-73 academic year along the general guidelines suggested in the committee's report, be and it is hereby approved, confirmed, and ratified by the Board of Trustees."

The buildings selected for the experiment in coeducational housing were Farr Hall, Dormitory No. 3, the Bexley Apartments, and the newly-built apartments north of Bexley Place. In Farr Hall suites of two rooms and connecting baths were assigned to groups of all men or all women, Dormitory No. 3 had separate floors for men and women, and the apartments were assigned to groups of all men or all women. At this time women moved down to the south end of the campus when Bushnell Hall became an all-women dormitory.

The success of the first year of coeducational housing encouraged the administration to extend the idea to freshmen housing during 1973-74. McBride Residence became a coed freshmen dormitory, with separate wings for men and women. At the same time Gund Hall became a freshmen women's dormitory.

Parents were informed of all these changes, and the Student Housing Agreements which parents must sign contained statements of the occupancy policy of each housing area and the visitation arrangements. There are many students who do not wish coeducational housing, and the College has provided as options dormitories exclusively for men or for women.

New Department of Anthropology and Sociology

The first new department of instruction to be established by the College for many years was launched during the school year 1972-73. At its meeting on January 11, 1971 the faculty approved the creation of a Department of Sociology and Anthropology. Provost Haywood communicated the faculty action to the Trustees on February 13, 1971, noting that: "The faculty were persuaded that the introduction of the new department was warranted on three counts: the modes of apprehension represented by these disciplines, particularly their quantitative approach to problems of societies, are inadequately represented in the College; there is need for a new department for those students who wish to concern themselves directly with questions pertaining to man in society; there is a demonstrably large amount of student interest in these disciplines which the College cannot ignore."

The new department had some difficulty getting off the ground. Dr. Edwin S. Harwood came to Gambier in September 1972 as Associate Professor and Chairman of the Department of Sociology and Anthropology. Only sociology courses were given that year. Professor Harwood left after one year and Assistant Professors of Anthropology J. Kenneth Smail and Marie K. Freddolino joined the faculty in September 1973. In the 1973-74 catalogue anthropology courses only were listed, and the name designation was the Department of Anthropology and Sociology, with Professor Smail as chairman. Plans for 1974-75 call for the addition of two more department members: Assistant Professor of Anthropology Edward C. Furtek, Jr. and Assistant Professor of Sociology Lilah J. Pengra.

Reorganization of the Work of the Board of Trustees

A move to streamline the work of the Board of Trustees was formulated by President Caples in 1971, adopted by the Trustees on February 19, 1972, and implemented by an amendment to the Constitution on June 3, 1972.

By this plan the number of full Board meetings was cut from three to two per year, the number of committees reduced from ten to seven, and the Executive Committee had no set meeting dates. The arrangement called for more frequent meetings of the committees, with the staff work for each committee assigned to a department of the college administration. The president hoped "to organize work so that we may minimize the time required away from home to discharge responsibilities fully; best utilize skills; and have a maximum of contact of nonresident trustees with that part of the community in Gambier."

It was during this period that the Trustees invited students to be auditors on many of their committees.

Administrative Reorganization

In April 1973 President Caples announced that John R.O. McKean had been selected from over 200 applicants to become the first Vice President for the College. Dr. McKean came to Gambier from Geneva, N.Y., where he had been Dean of Hobart College.

Also announced for the school year 1973-74 were the appointments of Lewis F. Treleaven as Vice President for Development, and Susan Tuttle (Mrs. Douglas L.) Givens as Dean of the Residential College.

By these appointments the president completed a realignment which put the responsibility for the administration of the College under four heads. As of August 1973 the areas covered by each of these officers were: *Provost* (Bruce Haywood) — instruction, registrar, admissions, library, Kenyon Public Affairs Forum, computer service, off-campus study, and scholarships and student aid; *Vice President For Finance* (Samuel S. Lord) — accounting, security, bookshop, buildings and grounds, Alumni House, and purchasing; *Vice President of the College* (John R.O. McKean) — athletics, counseling, health services, student housing, Chaplain, Dean of Students, and Dean of the Residential College; *Vice President For Development* (Lewis F. Treleaven) — development, alumni affairs, and public relations.

Financial Solvency

The pathway to financial salvation had been charted by the Decade plan of 1968. Fiscal officers of the College and their advisers tried to take into consideration every conceivable aspect of the financial operations for the next ten years: increasing enrollment, periodic increases in tuition and other charges, salary increases for all employees, increase in the cost of materials, increasing utility costs . . . the list was endless. The plan projected an elimination of the accumulated deficit in six or seven years. It was supposed to work, and — miracle of miracles — it did.

Built into the plan was a huge increase in accumulated deficit for two years, reflecting the building and start-up costs of the women's college, and the expansion of the faculty and staff. The cumulative deficit rose from $271,000 in 1968 to $903,000 in 1970, then dropped sharply until in 1973 there was a slender surplus of $22,000. The Decade Plan had to be revised slightly as time went on, but the administration's insistence on rigid adherence to the basic scheme plus a strict economy program put the finances in the black.

There were some crises. Like all businesses it was customary for Kenyon College to borrow money for operating expenses during certain periods of the year. In the summer of 1969 money was very tight, and the College found itself with payrolls to meet and banks reluctant to lend. It took some fast work on the part of President Caples to arrange loans to carry Kenyon through the summer.

One of the most difficult problems in this period was that of estimating enrollment. Time and time again the number of students called for in the budget did not materialize. An enrollment discrepancy of even 20 students translated into a budgetary deficit of $50,000 to $80,000 — a severe blow to a small college.

Route 229 By-Pass

No sooner had the disruption caused by the construction of the new women's buildings and the Biology Building died down, than the din and dust of the relocation of Ohio Highway 229 began. For some years Route 229 had gone through Gambier as "Temporary 229." There had always been a condition hazardous to pedestrians at the junction of the old road with the Middle Path, and with the increased enrollment this danger was heightened. All of the Kenyon community approved the relocation which got under way in the spring of 1972.

The new route followed closely County Highway 7, which went around the base of the hill close to the Kokosing River. The exact route of the old road could not be used, however, since it was so low that it was subject to flooding, and was considered to have too soft a base to support the new highway. So a new roadbed twenty or more feet higher than Route 7 and farther from the river was cut into the hillside. The College was asked to deed about nine acres of land for the construction. Although the community was concerned over the loss of some trees, the State Highway Department did a good job of landscaping the edges of the road and on Middle Path Day in April 1973 volunteers under the direction of Gambier Mayor Richard A. Baer planted ivy and honeysuckle. The relocation cost about a half-million dollars, but it eliminated a hazard for pedestrians and a bottleneck for motorists.

Sculpture for the Campus

A sculpture, "created as a permanent and lasting tribute to the beauty and excitement of liberal arts education at Kenyon College" by the noted artist Charles Eugene Gagnon, was unveiled on June 2, 1973 during Alumni Reunion Weekend.

The bronze work, entitled *Renaissance Man and Woman*, was commissioned as a gift by an alumnus who wished to remain anonymous. It was presented "on behalf of all the graduates of Kenyon."

The sculpture was created in three stages of expansion, and the final size was cast by the "lost wax" method in bronze by a New York foundry.

Sculptor Gagnon working on the final model for *Renaissance Man and Woman*. At the left is the middle-sized model.

College officials selected a site for the sculpture near the Path in front of Chalmers Library. There was the usual criticism from the art experts among the students and faculty, but in general the sculpture has been accepted and enjoyed by the community.

Student Community Involvement

One of the most notable changes during this half century at Kenyon has been the increase — especially during the last ten years — in student involvement in community affairs. A steadily growing number of Kenyonites have served as volunteers in various social work agencies, such as the Head Start Program, and in the education work of the Mount Vernon State Institute. *LOOK* magazine for June 16, 1970 devoted several pages to a picture story of Kenyon volunteers tutoring children in the Gambier schools. Featured were M. Gay Garth (K1973), Stephen D. Hughes (K1973), and W. Theodore Wedig (K1973).

The Gambier-College Township Volunteer Fire Department has for some time been considered one of the best-equipped and best-trained volunteer organizations in Ohio. It exemplifies the highest possible cooperation between College people — faculty, students, and administrative staff — and other citizens of the Gambier community. Chief Hobart Brown has said: "We've had help and cooperation from everyone in the village and at the college in our projects. The voters have backed us all the time, and the college has donated equipment and given us all the assistance we could ask for." When the fire siren sounds it is a common sight to see students, professors, and other staff members come tearing out of buildings and rush to the center of the village to swing onto the rear step of a piece of equipment. One of the most important contributions of the organization is its ambulance service, provided to the community without charge. The firefighters all take first aid and rescue courses as certified by the state. The majority of calls made to the Department for help have been for ambulance service.

During the early 1970's the concern for ecology which had been developing nationwide for several years began to command the attention of many students. Ecological projects in the Department of Biology blossomed. The removal of any trees in Gambier was viewed with suspicion and questioned. Students responded with frowns rather than indifference at the sight of beer cans on the lawns. A spontaneous outgrowth of this concern was the annual Middle Path Day, first held on April 3, 1971. Sponsoring this first clean-up day was a subcommittee of the Student Council consisting of Stephen F. Christy, Jr. (K1971), Hal R. Griffith (K1971), Craig E. Johnson (K1972), Thomas C.J. Storck (1973), and Alan J. Rapoport (K1971), with the assistance of Professor and Mrs. William F. Klein and Richard Ralston, Superintendent of Buildings and Grounds. Middle Path Day proved to be a real community effort — one of those unifying projects which have served to break down the old barriers between town and gown. The *Collegian* for April 9, 1971 reported: "Last Saturday, an estimated 600 students, faculty, administrators, and villagers participated in the first Middle Path Day." The article went on to describe some of the work done: the raking of gravel back onto the Path and lining up its borders; planting of 500 seedling trees and several larger trees; and installation of a stone patio in front of Farr Hall. Small children supervised by students or other adults went trooping through the streets and vacant lots picking up cans, bottles, and other trash.

Middle Path Day 1972. From left: Steve Christy, Craig Johnson, Judith E. Ross (K1973), and James L. Donenwirth (K1974).

After his graduation in 1971, Steve Christy worked as a landscape planner for the College for over a year, making a notable contribution to the appearance of the Village when he laid out crosswalks and plantings on the Middle Path from Wiggin to Brooklyn Streets during the summer of 1972.

A Changing Social Pattern

Up until the late 1960's and early 1970's the fraternities were the major influence on the social pattern at Kenyon. At the height of fraternity membership about 90% of the men belonged to an organization. The fraternity divisions took on the responsibility for most of the social functions. They were generally of assistance to the Dean in helping to solve discipline problems, and housing difficulties were usually ironed out within the division.

The establishment of the Coordinate College, followed by coeducation, certainly contributed to the decline of interest in fraternity membership, but there were other powerful factors. The student revolt of the late 1960's and early 1970's — brought on by the Indochina conflict, the military draft with its scholastic evaluation program, the distrust of The Establishment, and the concern for the minorities — helped to foster a feeling of independence which did not lend itself to fraternity affiliation.

It was during this time that the local fraternities began to have membership difficulties, and some of the old, established national chapters began to wonder if national affiliation was in their best interests. In 1970 the Lambda Chapter of Sigma Pi disaffiliated from the national organization and became a local fraternity known as The Peeps, and in 1972 Alpha Sigma Chi, a local organization, went out of existence.

Dress and grooming styles underwent an abrupt change. Suddenly the chino pants, shirts, cashmere sweaters and crew-cut hair were replaced by blue jeans, long hair, and beards. All sorts of bizarre costumes and outlandish accouterments cropped up. Except for the beards, the uniformity of the costumes made it difficult at times to tell the sex of the students. By 1974 the blue jean phase appeared to be passing.

Another interesting social trend was noted: the students no longer seemed to prefer attending dances and other entertainments in large groups. Student leaders found that the large concerts planned did not draw a crowd; more spontaneous entertainment in smaller groups became the "in" thing.

In an attempt to bring into each division the responsibility for setting the rules and regulations of behavior, an idea known as divisional autonomy was tried for about two and one-half years, and ended when Kenyon became a coeducational institution. The real issue in divisional autonomy was visiting hours for women. Each fraternity or social group wrote up a proposal for rules of conduct based on those set forth in the Student Handbook. This had to be passed by the Senate, then went to the President for his approval.

As Kenyon's third half century draws to its close, a new social pattern has come into being and is heading toward implementation in the fall of 1974. Known as the House Plan, this scheme calls for each upperclass residence hall to be organized as a house, which will be funded so that it can sponsor academic and social activities. House members will have the option of returning to the same residence hall year after year. Elected officers will be the governing body of each house.

Fraternities at first were in opposition to the Plan, arguing that they already had their own organization, but recently there has been a growing trend of support by the fraternities.

Presidential Search

The *New York Times* for Sunday, June 2, 1974, carried an advertisement in the section for teacher openings: "PRESIDENT — Kenyon College, Gambier, Ohio. The Board of Trustees of Kenyon College invites nominations and applications for the position of President, to assume office on or before June 1, 1975."

A Presidential Search Committee was organized in the fall of 1973 to coordinate a search for a successor to President Caples, who had indicated that he wished to step down by June 1975. The committee was made up of six trustees: D. Bruce Mansfield (K1930), the Right Reverend John H. Burt, David W. Kendall, Richard L. Thomas (K1953), Edgar G. Davis (K1953), and John G. Smale; an alumni representative: William S. Reed (K1960); two faculty members: Professors Daniel T. Finkbeiner and Galbraith M. Crump; and two student representatives: Cornelia S. Ireland (K1976) and Kim M. Straus (K1976). By the time of their meeting on April 15, 1974, the committee had received over 200 names of possible candidates and had engaged the coordinating services of Paul Barringer of Educational Career Service, Princeton, N.J. The committee planned to submit its nominations to the Board of Trustees by October or November, so that by January 1975 Kenyon would have selected its next president.

INDEX

Music, Department of, 227-234.
Myers, Christopher A., 148, 150.
Myers, James W., 149.

Nasser, Eugene, 207.
National Leadership Conference, 214.
National Theater of the Deaf, 243.
Navin, William, 146.
Neff, Douglas, 163, 164.
Neff, John C., 52.
Nelson, James A., 94.
Nemer-Kaiser, Edward, Jr., 149.
Netherlands Chamber Choir, 233.
New Apartments, 259-260.
Newhouse, Stephen E., 155.
Newman, Paul L., 112, 240-241.
Newman Trophy, 241.
Newsweek, 118.
Nichols, C. D., 43.
Nichols, Douglas, 71.
Nichols, Red, 62.
North Central Association, 212.
Norton, Bayes M., 69, 126, 127, 184, 201-202.
Norton, Charles B., 236.
Norton, David Z., 130.
Norton Hall, 130.
Norton, Laurence H., 105, 130, 135.
Norton, Robert, 130.
Novak, Robert, 207, 267-268.
Nu Pi Kappa Hall, 18.
Nu Pi Kappa Society, 30.
Nystrom, Karin V., 175.

O'Brien, Frank X., 133.
O'Brien, Michael J., 224.
O'Connor and Kilham, 186.
Ohara, Koichi, 226.
Ohio Athletic Conference, 33, 61.
Ohio Higher Educational Facility Commission, 256, 259.
Ohio State University Dance Groups, 243.
Ohio University, 122.
Old Kenyon, 10.
Old Kenyon Fire, 119-122.
Old Kenyon Restoration Fund, 95, 122.
Omahon, Donald J., *vi.*
Opdyke, Charles C., 171.
Opie, Redvers, 108.

Paine, Lewis, 85.
Palme, Lisbet, 273.
Palme, Olof, 112, 169, 170, 271-273.
Palmer, Fred H., Jr., 88, 92, 94.
Pan-Hellenic Council, 22.
Panzer, Eric F., 159.

Paolozzi, Gabriel J., 146.
Pappenhagen, James M., 127, 128, 190.
Paran, Janice E., 241.
Paraska, William F., 133.
Parents' Advisory Council, 262-263.
Parents' Association, 262-263.
Parents' Day, 263.
Parents' Fund, 263.
Park Cottage, 10.
Parker, Elizabeth K., 175.
Parker, Harold, *vi.*
Parker, John E., 159.
Parmalee, Robert, 152, 162.
Parmalee, Terrence E., 150, 157.
Parr, Daniel O., II, 239.
Parson, Roland D., 115.
Partisan Review, 105.
Pasini, Humbert F., 114, 146, 150, 155.
Pasternak, Boris, 104.
Patterson, James A., 239, 242.
Patterson, James K., 48.
Pavlovic, Stephen K., 226.
Pavlovich, Joseph P., 150, 171.
Payton, Philip, 163.
Peck, Marc S., 125.
Peck, Stewart F., 171.
Peeps, 287.
Peirce Cup, 93.
Peirce Hall, 18-20, 99.
Peirce, William F., election as president, 4, 13; early life, 13-14; vitality, 14; relations with students, 14-15; groundbreaking for Mather Hall, 17; acting dean of Bexley Hall, 37; resignation, 63; divorce, 64; remarriage, 64; death, 64-65; preface, *Songs of Kenyon*, 227.
Pengra, Lilah J., 281.
Penny Sunday, 51-52.
Peoples Bank, 11, 58.
Peppers, Donald, 171.
Percy, Charles, 207.
Perkins and Will Partnership, 256, 257, 258, 260.
Perrin, Herbert T., 92, 136.
Perry Music Prize, 234.
Peters, Harold H., 145, 154.
Peterson, Eugene, 253.
Peterson, M. Kristina, 277.
Pflieger, Richard, 148, 168.
Phi Beta Kappa, 59.
Philander Chase (the song), 2.
Philander Chase Tower, 19.
Philip Mather Hall, 189-190.
Phillips, C. Coles, 222.
Philomathesian Hall, 18.
Philomathesian Society, 30-31.

Kenyon College In 1974

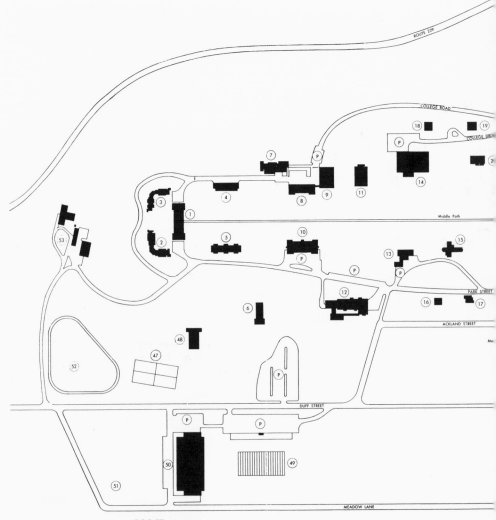

1. Old Kenyon
2. Bushnell Hall
3. Manning Hall
4. Hanna Hall
5. Leonard Hall
6. Shaffer Speech Building and Hill Theater
7. Biology Building
8. Samuel Mather Hall
9. Philip Mather Hall
10. Ascension Hall
11. Rosse Hall
12. Peirce and Dempsey Halls
13. Ransom Hall
14. Chalmers Library

15. Church of the Holy Spirit
16. Anthropology-Sociology Building
17. Public Affairs Conference Center
18. Music Annex
19. Music Building
20. Cromwell Cottage (President's Home)
21. Alumni House
22. College Relations Center
23. Drama Annex
24. Student Center
25. Student Affairs Center